Introduction to
Data Communications
and Computer Networks

£14.95

1987/86

£7.45

ELECTRONIC SYSTEMS ENGINEERING SERIES

Consulting Editor   **E L Dagless**
University of Bristol

Introduction to Data Communications and Computer Networks

Fred Halsall

ADDISON-WESLEY PUBLISHING COMPANY INC.

Wokingham, England · Reading, Massachusetts · Menlo Park, California
Don Mills, Ontario · Amsterdam · Sydney · Singapore · Tokyo · Mexico City · Bogota
Santiago · San Juan

Cover design by Sampson/Tyrell Limited.
Photoset direct from the author's text by Quorum Technical Services Ltd.
Printed in Great Britain by R. J. Acford.

British Library Cataloguing in Publication Data
Introduction to data communications and computer networks. – (Electronic systems engineering.)
1. Computer networks   2. Data transmission systems
I. Halsall, Fred   II. Series
001.64′404   TK5105.5

ISBN 0-201-14547-2
ISBN 0-201-14540-5 pbk

Library of Congress Cataloging in Publication Data
Halsall, Fred.
Introduction to data communications and computer networks.
Bibliography: p.
Includes index.
1. Data transmission systems.   2. Computer networks.
3. Local area networks (Computer networks).
4. Computer network protocols.   I. Title.
TK5105.H35   1985   001.64′404   85-5974
ISBN 0-201-14547-2
ISBN 0-201-14540-5 (pbk.)

CDEF 8987

Contents

Preface

The subject of data communications was, until recently, a relatively specialised area of electronic engineering. The dramatic advances in computer technology over the past few years, however, have resulted in an increasing number of information processing systems now being implemented as a linked set of computer-based equipment. The latter include not only computers per se but also a wide range of other types of equipment which incorporate some local intelligence: computer-based visual display terminals, advanced workstations as used in an automated office, intelligent instrumentation equipment as used in industrial process plants, point-of-sale terminals as used in large department stores, and so on. This means that an essential consideration in the design of most forms of computing equipment installed today is the type of data communications facility which is to be used to allow the equipment to communicate with other similar devices. In many instances this necessitates a knowledge not only of the alternative types of data transmission circuits that may be used but also an understanding of the interface requirements to the many different types of computer communication networks which are emerging for this purpose. Data communications and the allied subject of computer networks have thus become essential topics in all modern courses on computer systems design. This book has been written as an introductory text to both these subjects.

Although there are currently a number of text books on the market which cover some of the topics addressed in this book, the majority have been written primarily as reference texts and hence are best suited to practising engineers. Also, much of the material in this field is currently only in the form of standards documents which are intended primarily for system implementors. One of the primary aims of this book, therefore, is to assemble and convert much of this information into a form which is suitable for use by a student or a practising engineer who wishes to gain a general understanding of the different types of data communication networks and the associated devices and techniques which are used for connecting equipment to these networks.

The book is based on a course of lectures given by the author to both electronics engineering and computer science students and hence care has been taken to avoid any significant prerequisite knowledge in either subject. The amount of material covered in the book is sufficient for a course of lectures which runs over a full academic year but it has been structured so that it is possible for a lecturer to select just a number of chapters and still present a coherent set of lectures. Although the book has been written primarily as an undergraduate text, the avoidance of any significant prerequisite material means that it is also suitable for students on diploma and higher technician courses.

Because of the diverse range of applications of information processing systems, it is perhaps not surprising that there is also a wide range of data communications equipment and networks which are in use to link the various equipments together. For clarity, therefore, the different types of data communications facility and the associated hardware and software which are required for use with them are treated separately in different chapters. Whenever possible, however, the common underlying principles of the different types of system are emphasised.

In Chapter 1, a brief account of the historical evolution of information processing systems is presented. This is then followed in Chapters 2 and 3 with a description of the basic devices and techniques which are used for the reliable (error free and without replication) transmission of data between two pieces of equipment connected by a point-to-point data link. These three chapters, therefore, are considered to be essential reading and hence should be included in any course of lectures on this subject. Each of the following chapters is then reasonably self contained and it is possible to include or omit topics to suit the type of course being offered.

Chapter 4 is concerned with the properties of the electrical interface between the interconnected items of equipment and the different types of physical transmission media. The various internationally agreed standards which have been defined for this purpose are presented and, although care has been taken to avoid any specific previous knowledge of electronics, this topic has been deliberately covered in a separate chapter so that, if required, it can readily be omitted without any loss of continuity.

Chapter 5 is concerned with the different types of communications equipment which is in use in terminal-oriented distributed computing systems. Descriptions are presented of both the function and mode of operation of these types of equipment and also the alternative communications protocols which are in use in such systems.

Chapter 6 is concerned with descriptions of the various communication protocols which have been defined to enable computers from different manufacturers to freely exchange information. It is specifically concerned with the four highest protocol layers in the International Standards Organisation (ISO) Reference Model for open systems interconnection. It thus includes descriptions of the function and operation of the Application Layer, the Presentation Layer, the Session Layer, and the Transport Layer protocols. The descriptions presented do not strictly adhere to the standards – indeed some of the protocols are not yet finalised – but rather, are intended to give the reader a general understanding of the role of the various protocol layers in the Reference Model.

The lowest three protocol layers in the ISO Reference Model for open systems interconnection vary according to the type of data communications network which is being used to connect the various computers together. Thus Chapter 7 describes the function of the three lowest protocol layers which are used to interface a computer to a public data network and Chapter 8 with those required to interface a computer to a local area data network. Although there are currently a large number of different types of local area network in existence, only those which are currently in the various standards documents are described. Also, in addition to the protocols used in these networks, both chapters describe the function and operation of the various items of additional hardware and software which are required to interface a computer to each type of network.

I would like to take this opportunity to express my sincere thanks, firstly to Dr. Keith Bennett at the University of Keele for reviewing the draft manuscript and for his many helpful suggestions; secondly, to Christine Thornton-Clough for typing the manuscript and making numerous corrections and alterations without any word of criticism; and finally to my wife Rhiannon and children Lisa and Richard for their patience and understanding whilst I was writing the book.

Fred Halsall,
University of Sussex

Chapter 1 **Distributed System Architectures**

Objectives:
When you have completed studying the material in this chapter you should be able to:

- describe the historical development of the different types of distributed computing system;

- draw schematic diagrams to illustrate the architecture of the different types of distributed system;

- appreciate that irrespective of the application of the system, there is only a limited number of different types of data network that may be used to provide the underlying data communication services;

- understand that there is a degree of commonality to the structure and function of the communications software used within the various interconnected equipments which make up the system, which is independent of both the application of the system and the type of data communications network being used.

1.1 INTRODUCTION

Distributed computing systems are concerned with the processing and the communication of information between distributed communities of electronic digital equipment. In general, the various types of equipment are referred to as *data terminal equipments* or simply *DTEs*. These include not only computers but also a wide range of other devices: visual display terminals, for example, computer-based office workstations, intelligent instrumentation equipment for industrial process control, point-of-sale terminals as used in large department stores, microprocessor-based domestic electricity meters designed for remote reading, and many others.

This wide range of devices means that there are many different types of distributed systems. For example, a system may be made up of a large community of visual display terminals physically distributed over a wide geographical area and communicating with a large centralised computing complex. Alternatively, a system may comprise a number of computer-based office workstations physically distributed around a single block of offices providing, for example, word processing functions and access to various shared resources – printers, copiers, file systems etc.

Although the overall processing functions performed in the different types of distributed system may vary considerably from one application to another, there is only a limited number of types of data network that may be used to provide the underlying data communication services for the exchange of information between the various equipments. Moreover, the advent of international standards for both the structure and function of much of the communications software, which is needed within each piece of equipment to achieve the reliable exchange of information over these networks, means that there is a degree of commonality to the communications software within each equipment which is independent of the particular application of the overall system. When designing the data communications facilities to be used with any form of distributed system, therefore, it is necessary to have a working knowledge firstly of the different types of data communication networks which are available and their corresponding modes of operation and application areas, and, secondly, an understanding of the various international standards which have now been established to aid the use of these networks. This book is specifically concerned with these aspects of distributed computing systems.

1.2 HISTORICAL EVOLUTION

The evolution of distributed computing systems can perhaps best be traced by following the development of the computing resources used within any large organisation. The earliest commercially available computers that were used were characterised by expensive hardware and relatively primitive software. Typically, an organisation would purchase a single computer system which would then be centrally located in a large, air-conditioned room. It would consist of a central processing unit (CPU) with a limited quantity of primary (RAM) memory, some secondary (tape or drum) storage, a printer, a punched-card reader and an operator console. Users normally prepared their programs and data *off-line* on a card punch located in a different room and the operator would then load and run the prepared programs sequentially. This type of early computer system is shown in diagrammatic form in Fig. 1.1.

As computer technology and its operating software advanced, fast secondary storage – large magnetic drums and later discs – and multiprogramming operating systems were developed making it possible to *time-share* the central processing unit between a number of active programs (processes) thereby allowing multiple users to use the computer simultaneously. Each user was allocated a separate terminal which then allowed multiple users to access simultaneously stored information and run programs *interactively* at the terminals. The latter were normally electromechanical teletypewriters (TTYs) similar to those which were already in use in the international telex networks. They were designed, therefore, to transmit and receive data over long distances and operated in a *serial mode*.

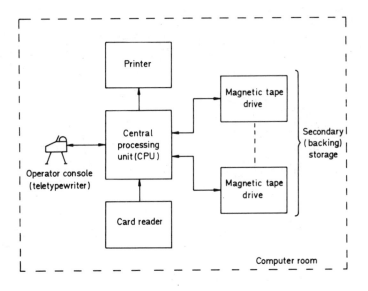

Fig. 1.1 Typical early computer system

To exploit these developments, the computers used within organisations were upgraded to support, say, five or more such terminals. The computers then became known as *multi-access* systems providing *on-line* access to stored data. Initially the terminals were all located close to the main computer complex but, because of their basic mode of operation, it soon became common practice to distribute the terminals around the organisation, firstly locally in different offices and later, with the aid of the ubiquitous switched telephone network and *modems*, nationally over wide geographical areas. A typical computer system in operation at that time, therefore, is as shown in Fig. 1.2.

The use of the switched telephone network as the basic data communications medium meant that communication line costs were not insignificant and indeed soon became a substantial proportion of the system operating costs. In order to minimise these costs, therefore, devices such as *terminal multiplexers* and *cluster controllers* were introduced. Essentially, these allow a single communication line – often permanently leased from the public telecommunications authorities – to be shared between a number of simultaneous users all located, for example, at the same remote site. In addition, the increasing level of usage of the computer within the organisation soon gave rise to systems containing many hundreds of terminals with the effect that the central computer could no longer cope with the processing overheads associated with servicing the various communication lines on top of its normal processing functions. This in turn gave rise to the *front-end processor (FEP)* which essentially off-loaded the processing overheads associated with the various communication lines from the central machine. This effectively signalled the beginning of distributed computing sytems and a

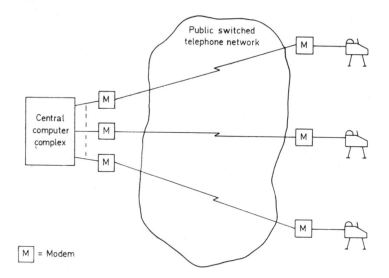

Fig. 1.2 Early terminal-oriented distributed system

large but typical system in use at this time is as shown in Fig. 1.3. This type of distributed system is still in widespread use today and aspects of this type of system are described in Chapter 5.

1.3 PRIVATE COMPUTER COMMUNICATION NETWORKS

The structure shown in Fig. 1.3 was particularly prevalent in large organisations such as the major clearing banks and airlines which normally held large quantities of information at a single central site. The distributed community of users then accessed and updated this information using the communication facilities outlined. In many organisations, however, it was not necessary to hold all information centrally and hence it soon became common place for an organisation to have a number of autonomous computer systems located at different sites around the country. Typically, these provided a local computing function but there was often a requirement for them to communicate with each other both to share resources – hardware and software – and also to exchange information. The requirements for the communications facility to meet this type of interconnection, however, are in many ways more demanding than a terminal-based system since instead of all communications being directed to a single known destination as before, a more flexible, effectively switched, communications facility is required.

The limited data capacity of a communications link established using the switched telephone network and modems meant that a conceptually different approach to providing the necessary data communications services was

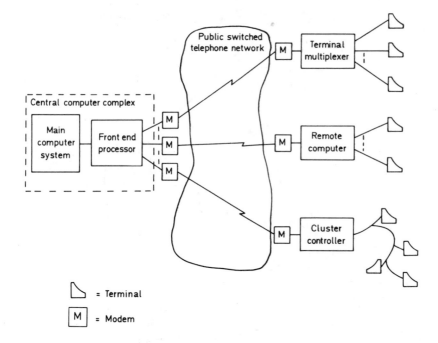

Fig. 1.3 Large terminal-oriented distributed system

required and it was at this point that it became economically more attractive to provide a separate autonomous *data communications subnetwork* to provide the required data communication services. The requirements for such networks were in many ways similar to those provided by the normal telex network. The latter operates in a *message store-and-forward* mode which, as will be expanded in later chapters, is also ideally suited to the sporadic nature of communications between computers and other computer-related equipment.

With the telex network the internal message units used may be long with the effect that the response time of such networks, that is the time delay between a message entering the network and subsequently leaving the network, can be degraded whilst a number of long messages are in transit. In order to overcome this limitation, therefore, communication subnetworks intended for carrying computer data normally operate using a smaller maximum message unit known as a *packet*. The resulting communications subnetwork is then said to operate using *packet-switching* or in a *packet store-and-forward mode*. This type of distributed system is shown diagrammatically in Fig. 1.4 and, because the interconnected computers are normally physically distributed over a wide geographical area, it is also known as a *wide area computer communication network* or *WAN*.

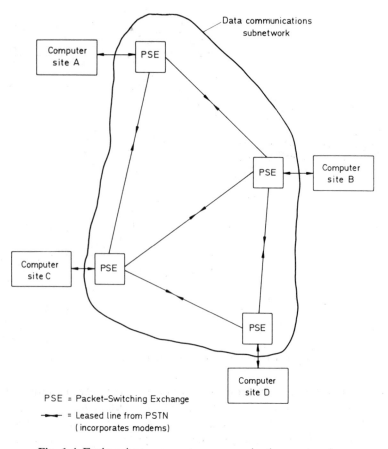

PSE = Packet-Switching Exchange

 = Leased line from PSTN
(incorporates modems)

Fig. 1.4 Early private computer communications network

1.4 PUBLIC SWITCHED DATA NETWORKS

Initially, organisations implemented their own private nationwide data communication subnetworks using communication lines leased from the public telephone authorities and their own proprietory switching equipment. The larger computer manufacturers then produced suitable communications software packages to enable their computers to communicate and exchange data using these networks. With time, however, as the impact of computer technology on the operation of organisations grew, the need arose for a computer in one organisation – and hence from one manufacturer – to communicate with a possibly different computer in another organisation; for example, to transfer funds from one bank computer to another.

It was at this point that the *public telecommunications authorities* in a number of countries – generally referred to as *PTTs* for Post, Telephone and Telecommunications – accepted that a *public switched data network (PSDN)* analogous to the normal *public switched telephone network (PSTN)* was justified. Moreover, since it was intended that this should be used to provide a communications facility for the interconnection of a possibly large number of different computers from a range of manufacturers, the definition of agreed interface standards became all important.

After much discussion in various standards committees, firstly at national and later at international level, a set of internationally agreed standard protocols was defined, firstly for interfacing and controlling the flow of information between the various data terminal equipments – computers and terminals – and the PSDN, and later to control the exchange of information between the two communicating items of equipment. An increasing number of public networks have now been implemented which support these standards. This type of distributed system is shown diagrammatically in Fig. 1.5 and some of the different types of PSDN are described in Chapter 7 of the book. Also, the so-called higher level protocol standards which have been

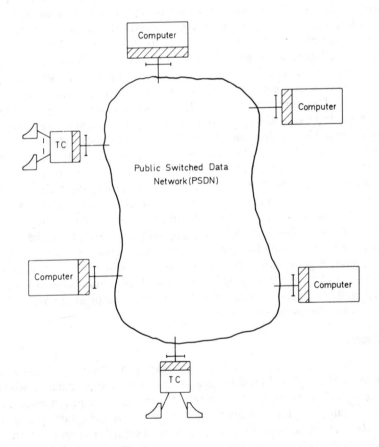

TC   = Terminal Controller

⊢——⊣ = Interface standards

▨ = Communication subsystem (hardware and software)

Fig. 1.5 PSDN-based distributed system

defined to control the exchange of information between two pieces of equipment using such networks are discussed in Chapter 6.

1.5 LOCAL AREA NETWORKS

Although the computing resources in an organisation steadily increased with developing technology, the advent of the microprocessor and the associated advances in integrated circuit technology meant that in addition to the systems just outlined, it soon became common to find a multiplicity of different computer-based devices physically located within the same building or block of offices; for example, a community of intelligent computer-based workstations performing word processing and other related functions. Although the availability of processing power within each of these systems means that many computing tasks can be carried out locally, in many situations there is often a requirement for these systems to communicate with each other; for example, to exchange (electronic) mail or to access an expensive shared resource such as a letter-quality printer or file system.

Since the linked computing devices in this type of network are physically located close to one another, the communication facility provided is referred to as a *local area data network* or simply a *LAN*. Although the different types of distributed system outlined in the earlier sections are now relatively widespread and established, this type of distributed system is relatively new. It is perhaps not surprising, therefore, that many of the current (1985) designs of LAN show significant differences from one another, both in terms of their topology and their mode of operation. In order to avoid a plethora of different network protocols being adopted, therefore, the standards bodies have responded swiftly and indeed a range of internationally agreed standards have now been defined for use with this type of network. Moreover, the structure of these standards is in keeping with the structure of the standards which have been defined for use with wide area networks, and it is intended that the same higher-level protocols will be used with both types of network. An example of a small but typical LAN-based distributed system is shown in Fig. 1.6 and the different types of LAN and their associated communication protocols are discussed in Chapter 8.

1.6 SUMMARY

It can be concluded from the above paragraphs that there is a wide range of different types of distributed system in operation today, each of which has been designed to meet a different set of application requirements. Indeed, when designing any form of distributed system, it is important to analyse the particular set of application requirements before deciding on the most suitable form of data communication system to be used. It is for this reason that the book has been organised into a number of distinct sections each devoted to a particular type of distributed system. It is felt that in this way the reader can more readily appreciate the reasons for the use of the specific types of network and protocols adopted.

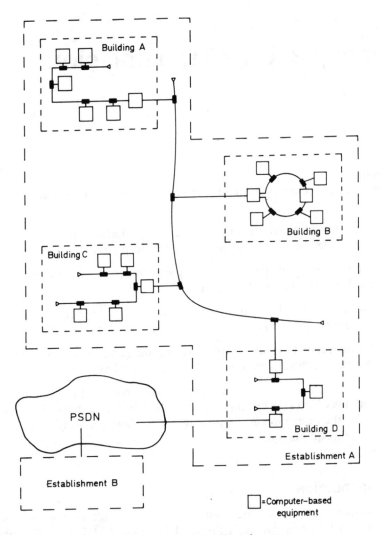

Fig. 1.6 LAN-based distributed system

As has been indicated, the need for data communications has evolved almost from the earliest days of computing. However, although the reader of this book is likely to be aware of the basic terminology and devices associated with computers themselves – bits and bytes, gates and highways, BASIC and Pascal, etc. – equally, there is a fundamental set of techniques and terminology associated with data communications and these are often less well understood. Before commencing with descriptions of the different types of distributed system and network types, therefore, the first two chapters of the book are devoted to a review of the fundamentals and terminology of data communications on which all forms of distributed system are based.

Chapter 2 **Data Transmission**

Objectives:

When you have completed studying the material in this chapter you should be able to:

- appreciate the function of the different steps that are necessary to achieve the reliable transfer of data across a point-to-point data link;

- describe the detail operation of a typical Universal Asynchronous Receiver Transmitter (UART) circuit;

- describe the detail operation of a typical Universal Synchronous Receiver Transmitter (USRT) circuit;

- explain some of the alternative data encoding and clock synchronisation schemes which are used on a synchronous data link;

- understand the operation and limitations of some of the alternative methods which may be employed to detect bit errors that may occur during the transmission of data across a data link connecting two data terminal equipments.

2.1 INTRODUCTION

Data communication is concerned with the exchange of digitally-encoded information between two data terminal equipments (DTEs). The physical separation of the two equipments may vary from a few tens of metres – for example between a computer and a locally connected terminal – to several hundreds of kilometres if the two devices are connected using a national data network, for example.

Within the data communications community the term data is normally reserved for describing a set or block of one or more digitally encoded alphabetic and numerical characters which are being exchanged between two devices. Typically, these represent a string of numbers or perhaps the contents of a computer file containing a stored document. When using a data communications facility to transfer this type of data, however, it is also necessary for the two communicating parties (DTEs) to exchange some additional control information (messages) in order, for example, to overcome the effect of transmission errors within the communications facility.

Throughout this book, therefore, the more general term *information* will also be used to describe any meaningful item – both data and control – being exchanged across the data communications facility.

In any form of digital system the loss or corruption of a single bit of information (binary digit) can of course be critical. It is thus essential when designing a communications facility for a distributed system to ensure that adequate precautions are taken to detect and, if necessary, correct for any possible loss or corruption of information whilst it is being transferred. Data communication is concerned, therefore, not only with the way data are transmitted over the physical transmission medium but also with the techniques which may be adopted to detect and, if necessary, correct for transmission errors; with the control of the transfer rate of the data; with the format of the data being transferred; and other related issues.

This and the next chapter of the book are concerned with the fundamental concepts associated with data communication and, in particular, the techniques which are available to achieve the reliable (error free and no losses or *duplicates*) transfer of information across a data link connecting two DTEs. This chapter is concerned with the basic techniques and circuits which may be used for the transmission of data between the two DTEs and this is followed in the next chapter by a description of the basic techniques which may be employed for the control of data transfer between the two communicating parties. It should be stressed that, irrespective of the type of error detection (and correction) scheme adopted, it is not possible to detect all possible combinations of transmission errors which may occur with 100 percent certainty. In practice, therefore, the various error detection and correction techniques which are utilised aim at making the probability of any undetected errors being present in a received message acceptably low.

2.2 DATA TRANSMISSION BASICS

All electronic digital equipment – computers, terminals etc. – operate using a fixed number of binary digits to represent a single element of data. Within a computer, for example, this may be 8, 16 or 32 bits and data requiring more than this precision are represented by multiple such elements. Because of this range of different numbers of bits to represent each element, it is usual when communicating data between two equipments to use multiple fixed-length elements each of 8 bits. In some applications the 8 bits may represent a binary-encoded alphabetic or numerical (*alphanumeric*) character whilst in others it may represent an 8-bit component of a larger value. In the latter case it is often referred to as an 8-bit *byte* but in general, within the communications facility each 8-bit element is simply referred to as an *octet*.

2.2.1 Bit serial transmission

Within a piece of equipment, the distance and hence lengths of wire used to connect each subunit together – printed circuit board, for example – is short and hence it is normal practice to transfer elements between subunits by using a separate piece of wire to carry each bit of the element. This means there are multiple wires used to connect each subunit together and elements are said to be exchanged using a *parallel transfer mode*.

Although this mode of operation results in minimal delays to transfer each element, when transferring information between two physically separate pieces of equipment, especially if the separation is more than several metres, for reasons of cost and varying transmission delays in the individual wires, it is more usual to use just a single line and transmit each element a single bit at a time using a fixed time interval for each bit. This is then known as *bit serial transmission* and is used extensively for transmitting data between two data terminal equipments. The two alternative modes of operation are shown in diagrammatic form in Fig. 2.1. A binary digit is normally represented within a piece of digital electronic equipment as a specific voltage or current level

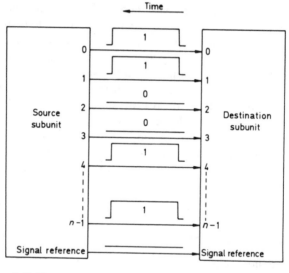

(a)

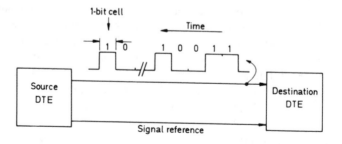

(b)

Fig. 2.1 Transmission modes: (a) parallel: (b) serial

relative to a reference level. Thus in the figure, a high signal relative to the reference is being used to indicate when a binary 1 is being transmitted and a low signal level – equal to the reference – when a binary 0 is being transmitted.

2.2.2 Communication modes

When a person is giving a lecture or speech, information is primarily conveyed in one direction only. During a conversation between two people, however, it is usual to exchange spoken messages (information) in both directions. The messages are normally exchanged alternatively but can, of course, also be exchanged simultaneously! Similarly, when data are being transmitted between two pieces of equipment, there are three analogous modes of operation which may be used:

simplex   this is used when data are to be transmitted in one direction only, for example in a data logging system in which a monitoring device returns a reading at regular intervals to the data gathering facility;

half duplex   this is used when the two interconnected devices wish to exchange information (data) alternately, for example if one of the devices only returns some data in response to a request from the other; clearly it is then necessary for the two devices to be able to switch between send and receive modes after each transmission;

duplex   this is also referred to as full duplex and is used when data are to be exchanged between the two connected devices in both directions simultaneously, for example if for throughput reasons data can flow in each direction independently.

The alternative communication modes are important since in many distributed systems the circuits (lines) used to provide the necessary communication facilities are often leased from the public telecommunication authorities and hence it is clearly less expensive to lease a single circuit – a pair of wires – if only simplex operation is required rather than two circuits.

2.2.3 Transmission modes

As has been mentioned, data are normally transmitted between two data terminal equipments in multiples of a fixed length unit typically of 8 bits. For example, when a terminal is communicating with a computer each typed (keyed) character is normally encoded into an 8-bit binary value and a complete message is then made up of a string (block) of similarly encoded characters. Hence, since each character is transmitted bit serially, the receiving DTE will simply receive one of two signal levels which is varying according to the bit pattern (and hence character string) making up the message. In order for the receiving device to decode and interpret this bit pattern correctly, therefore, it is necessary for it to know firstly the bit rate being used (that is, the time duration of each bit cell), secondly the start and end of each element (character or byte) and thirdly the start and end of each complete message block or frame. These are known as *bit* or *clock synchronism*, *byte* or *character synchronism*, and *block* or *frame synchronism* respectively.

In general, synchronisation is accomplished in one of two ways which are determined by whether the transmitter and receiver clocks are independent (asynchronous) or synchronised (synchronous). If the data to be transmitted are made up of a string of characters with random (possibly long) time intervals between each character, then each character is normally transmitted independently and the receiver resynchronises at the start of each new character received. For this type of communication *asynchronous transmission* is normally used. If, however, the data to be transmitted is made up of complete blocks of data each containing, say, multiple bytes or characters, the transmitter and receiver clocks must be in synchronism over long intervals and hence *synchronous transmission* is then normally used. Each will be considered separately.

2.2.3.1 Asynchronous transmission

This is primarily used when the data to be transmitted are generated at random intervals – for example, a user at a visual display terminal communicating with a computer. Clearly, with this type of communication the user at the terminal keys in each character at an indeterminate rate with possibly long random time intervals between each successive typed character. This means that the signal on the transmission line will be in the idle (off) state for long time intervals. With this type of communication, therefore, it is necessary for the receiver to be able to resynchronise at the start of each new character received. To accomplish this, with asynchronous transmission each transmitted character or, more generally, item of user data is encapsulated or framed between an additional start bit and one or more stop bits as shown in Fig. 2.2.

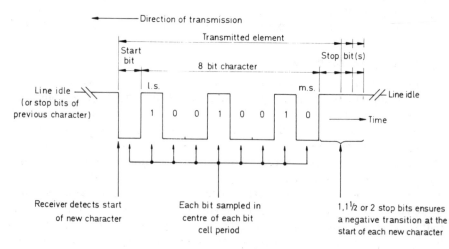

Fig. 2.2 Asynchronous transmission

As can be seen from the figure, the polarity of the start and stop bits are different. This ensures that there is always a minimum of one transition (1–0–1) between each successive character, irrespective of the bit sequences in the characters being transmitted. The first 1–0 transition after an idle period is then used by the receiving device to determine the start of each new character and, by utilising a clock whose frequency is N times higher than the transmitted bit-rate frequency (N equals 16 is typical) the receiving device can reliably determine the state of each transmitted bit in the character by sampling the received signal approximately at the centre of each bit cell period. This is shown diagrammatically in the figure and will be expanded upon in the next section.

It can be deduced from the above that in order to transmit each item of user data, ten (one start bit and one stop bit) or possibly eleven (one start bit and two stop bits) bits are utilised. Thus assuming a single start bit and two stop bits per 8-bit item and a data transmission rate of, say, 1200 bits per second (bps), the data rate is 1200/11 or approximately 110 bytes per second. The useful data rate is in fact less than this for reasons which will be described later.

When defining the transmission rate of a line, the term *baud* is often used by communications engineers. When correctly used, however, the term baud indicates the number of line signal transitions per second. Thus if each transmitted signal can be in one of two states, the term baud and bps are equivalent; but, as will be described in Chapter 4, in some instances the line signal can take on more than two states and hence each transmitted cell can be used to convey more than a single binary digit of information. To avoid confusion, therefore, the term signalling rate is used to define the number of line signal transitions per second (in baud) and data or information transfer rate the number of information bits per second (in bps). For example, a signalling rate of 300 baud with 4 bits per signalling element would yield an information rate of 1200 bps. The most common information rates in use on asynchronous lines are 110, 300, 1200, 2400, 4800, 9600 and 19 200 bps.

2.2.3.2 Synchronous transmission

Asynchronous transmission is normally used when the rate at which characters are generated is indeterminate and hence the transmission line can be idle for long periods in between each transmitted character. The use of additional bits per character for framing purposes is therefore not important. In many applications, however, for example for computer-to-computer communication, there is often a need to transmit large blocks of data – the contents of a disc file for example – which have already been preassembled ready for transmission. Clearly, the use of additional framing bits per character then becomes wasteful. Also, because of the clock synchronisation mechanism used with an asynchronous scheme, asynchronous transmission can only be used reliably at up to 19 200 bps. An alternative and indeed a more efficient approach for the transmission of complete blocks of data is to transmit each complete block – often referred to as a frame – as a single entity and to use synchronous transmission.

Using synchronous transmission, the complete block or frame of data – a string of characters for example – is transmitted as a single bit stream with no delay between each 8-bit element. Then, to enable the receiving device to achieve the various levels of synchronisation, firstly the transmitted bit stream is suitably encoded so that the receiver can be kept in bit synchronism and secondly each frame is encapsulated between a pair of specially reserved bytes or characters. This ensures that the receiver, on receipt of the first of these after an idle period (the opening byte or character), can determine that a new frame is being transmitted and, on receipt of the second (the closing byte or character), that this signals the end of the frame. During the period between the transmission of successive frames either idle (sync) characters are continuously transmitted to allow the receiver to retain bit and byte synchronism or each frame is preceded by a special synchronising bit sequence to allow the receiver to regain synchronism. This is shown diagrammatically in Fig. 2.3.

The alternative bit-encoding methods which may be employed to achieve bit synchronism will be described in Section 2.4. Also, with synchronous transmission, it is necessary to ensure that the special synchronising bytes or characters are unique and not present in the contents of the frame being transmitted. Clearly, if the frame contains, say, the contents of a binary code file, this cannot be guaranteed and hence additional steps have to be taken to allow for this possibility. These aspects will also be discussed in more detail in later sections.

2.2.4 Transmission error control

During the transmission of a serial bit stream between two devices (DTEs), it is very common – especially when the physical separation is large and, say, the switched telephone network is being used – for the transmitted information to become corrupted; that is, the signal level corresponding to a binary 0 is modified and, in the limit, is interpreted by the receiver as a binary 1 and vice versa. It is normal when data are being transmitted between two devices, therefore, to provide a means for detecting possible transmission errors and, should they arise, a means for correcting for such errors.

There are a number of alternative schemes which may be utilised and the one selected is normally determined by the type of transmission method being used. When asynchronous transmission is being used, for example, since each character is treated as a separate entity, it is normal to embed within each transmitted character an additional binary digit to enable the receiver to determine if any errors have occurred during the transmission of that character. The additional digit used is known as a *parity bit* and its function will be described in a later section.

When synchronous transmission is being used, the basic unit of transmission is a frame and hence it is more usual to determine possible transmission errors on the complete frame. Moreover, since the contents of a

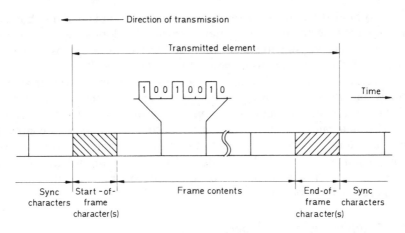

Fig. 2.3 Synchronous transmission

frame may be large, the probability of more than one bit being corrupted increases and hence a more sophisticated error check sequence must be used. Again, this may take a number of different forms but, in general, the transmitting device computes a sequence of error check digits which are based on the contents of the frame being transmitted and appends these to the tail of the frame before the character or pattern signalling the end of the frame. Hence the receiver, whilst the frame is being received, can recompute a new set of error check digits based on the received contents and, on receipt of the end-of-frame character or pattern, compare this with the transmitted check digits. If these are not equal a transmission error is then assumed.

Both of the above schemes only allow the receiver to detect if any transmission errors have occurred and consequently, in addition, it is also necessary to adopt a scheme to enable the receiver to obtain another copy of the transmitted information when errors are detected. Again a number of schemes are possible: for example, if the two communicating devices are a terminal and a computer and asynchronous transmission is being used, as the user keys in each character at the keyboard of the terminal, the encoded character is normally transmitted to the computer as outlined above and the character corresponding to the received bit stream is then 'echoed' back by the computer and displayed on the screen of the user terminal. Then, if the displayed character is different from the selected keyed character, the user may send a special (delete) character to inform the computer to ignore the last (erroneous) character received. This in general is referred to as error control and some of the more common error control methods are discussed in the next chapter.

2.2.5 Flow control

If the amount of data to be transmitted between two devices is small, it is possible for the sending device to transmit all the data immediately in the knowledge that the receiving device will have sufficient resources (storage space) to hold the data. In many data communication situations, however, this is not the case and hence it is often necessary to adopt a method to control the flow of data transfer to ensure that the receiver does not lose any of the transmitted data due to insufficient storage facilities. This is particularly important, for example, when the two devices are communicating through an intermediary data communications network. Very often the data network will only buffer a limited amount of data and hence, if the two devices operate at different data rates for example, it often becomes necessary to control the mean output rate of the faster device to prevent the communications network from becoming congested. The control of the flow of information between two DTEs is known as *flow control* and some of the alternative methods which are used will be introduced in the next chapter.

2.2.6 Communication protocols

Error and flow control are two essential components of the more general topic of communication protocols. Essentially, a communication protocol is a set of conventions or rules which must be adhered to by both communicating parties to ensure that information being exchanged between the two parties is received and interpreted correctly. Thus, in addition to error and flow control, a communication protocol also defines such things as the format of the data being exchanged – the number of bits per element and the type of encoding scheme being used – and also the type and order of messages which are to be exchanged in order to achieve a reliable (error free and no duplicates) information transfer between the two communicating parties. For example, it is normal before any data are transferred from one party to another first to set up a connection between the two parties to ensure that the receiving party is free and ready to receive the data. This is often accomplished by the sending device transmitting a specific command message – a call or connect request for example – and the receiver returning a defined response message – a call connected or reject for example. A number of different communication protocols are discussed in subsequent chapters of the book.

2.3 TRANSMISSION CONTROL CIRCUITS

As has been outlined, data are normally transmitted between two DTEs bit serially in multiple 8-bit elements using either asynchronous or synchronous transmission. Within the DTEs, however, each element is normally manipulated and stored in a parallel form. Consequently, the transmission control circuits within each DTE which form the interface between the device and the serial data link must perform the following functions:

1. parallel-to-serial conversion of each element in preparation for transmission of the element on the data link;
2. serial-to-parallel conversion of each received element in preparation for storage and processing of the element in the device;

3. a means for the receiver to achieve bit, character and, for synchronous transmission, frame synchronisation;

4. the generation of suitable error check digits for error detection purposes.

To satisfy these requirements, special integrated circuits are now readily available which perform all of these functions and a schematic diagram showing a simple point-to-point connection of two DTEs using these circuits is as shown in Fig. 2.4. Although different circuits can be used to control asynchronous and synchronous data links, circuits are also available which support both types of link. The latter are often referred to as *universal communication interface circuits* but, since the two halves of such circuits – asynchronous and synchronous – function independently, each will be considered separately.

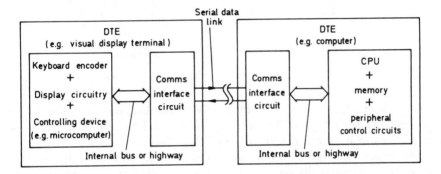

Fig. 2.4 Simple point-to-point link

2.3.1 Asynchronous transmission

The interface circuit used when asynchronous transmission is being used is known as a Universal Asynchronous Receiver and Transmitter or simply a *UART*. It is termed universal since it is normally a programmable device and the user can, by simply loading a predefined control word (bit pattern) into the device, specify the required operating characteristics to be supported. A schematic diagram of a typical UART is shown in Fig. 2.5.

To use such a device, the *Mode (Control) Register* is first loaded with the required bit pattern to define the required operating characteristics prior to data being transmitted or received from the data link – at power-on reset for example. Typically, the user may select 5, 6, 7 or 8 bits per character, odd, even or zero parity, one or more stop bits and a range of transmit and receive bit rates. The latter are selected from a standard range from 50 bps to 19.2 kbps by connecting a clock source of the appropriate frequency to the transmit and receive clock pins of the UART and defining in the control word the ratio of this clock to the required bit rate ($\times 1$, $\times 16$, $\times 32$ or $\times 64$). The use of the latter will be expanded upon later.

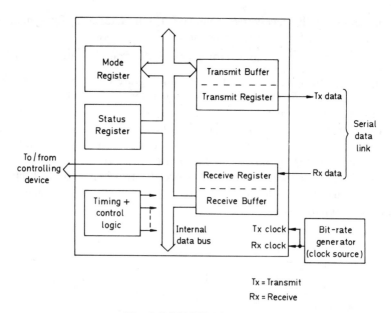

Tx = Transmit
Rx = Receive

Fig. 2.5 UART schematic

As an example, part (a) of Fig. 2.6 illustrates the meaning of the various control bits in a typical device – the Intel 8251/Signetics 2657. Hence, assuming the bit pattern 01001101 (4D hexadecimal) was loaded into the mode register at start up, the device would operate with seven data bits per character, an even parity bit, one stop bit and an external clock source of 16 × the bit rate.

The controlling device within the DTE (a microprocessor for example) determines the current state of the UART – ready to transmit a character, character just received, etc. – by reading the contents of the *Status Register* and testing specific bits within it. These are often referred to as *flag bits*. Their use varies for different circuit types but a typical status register composition is as shown in part (b) of Fig. 2.6. To use this circuit, when the controlling device wishes to transmit a new character, and assuming the UART has been initialised, it first reads the status byte to determine the state of the *Transmit Buffer Empty (TxBE)* bit. Then, assuming this is logical 1, this signals that the previous character has been transferred from the *Transmit Buffer* to the *Transmit Register* – from where it is shifted bit serially onto the data link – and hence a new character can be loaded into the buffer. The controlling device thus loads the character and, in turn, the control logic within the UART transfers it to the Transmit Register as soon as the final stop bit for the previous character has been transmitted. Each time a new character is loaded into the Transmit Buffer, the Transmit Buffer Empty (TxBE) bit is reset to logical 0. Similarly, when the internal control logic transfers a character from the Transmit Buffer to the Transmit Register, the TxBE bit is set thus allowing the control logic to load a new character if one is available. In addition, when each character is loaded into the Transmit Buffer, the control logic automatically determines the appropriate parity bit if this has been selected. Then, when the complete character – data plus parity – is transferred to the Transmit Register, a start bit and the specified number of stop bits are inserted and the complete envelope is transmitted bit serially onto the line at a bit rate determined by the externally supplied clock and the ratio setting.

For reception, the receiving UART must be programmed to operate with the same characteristics as the transmitting UART. Then, when the control

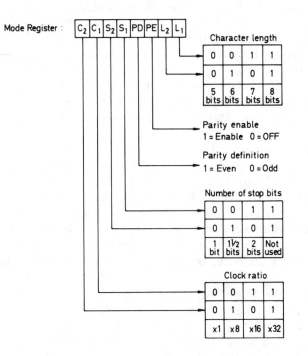

(a)

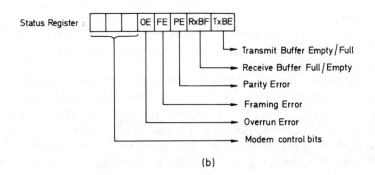

(b)

Fig. 2.6 Typical UART mode and status bit definitions: (a) Mode Register; (b) Status Register

logic detects the first transition on the receive data line after an idle period (1–0), because of the possibly random intervals between successive characters, the receiver timing logic must be resynchronised. This is accomplished by the control logic, on detecting the first transition, presetting the contents of a counter – the *Bit Rate Counter* – to one half of the clock rate ratio setting. Thus if the UART has been programmed to operate with a 16 × external clock rate, a modulo 16 counter would be used and preset initially to 8 on receipt of the first transition. The timing logic then decrements the contents of the counter after each cycle of the external clock and, since there are 16 clock cycles to each bit cell (16 × bit rate), the counter will reach zero approximately at the centre of the start bit and subsequently at the centre of each bit cell period. Each time the counter reaches zero, this triggers the control circuitry to determine the current state – logical 1 or 0 – of the receive data line and the appropriate bit is then shifted into the *Receive Register*. This is shown diagrammatically in Fig. 2.7 and, as can be deduced from the figure, the higher the clock rate ratio the nearer the midpoint the sampling instant becomes.

This process continues until the defined number of data and parity bits have been shifted into the Receive Register and the complete character is then parallel loaded into the *Receive Buffer*. The receive parity bit is then compared with the parity bit recomputed from the received data bits and, if these are different, the *Parity Error* (*PE*) flag bit is set in the Status Register at the same time as the *Receive Buffer Full* (*RxBF*) flag is set. The controlling device can thus determine from these bits firstly when a new character has been received and secondly, whether any transmission errors have been detected.

In addition, the Status Register contains two further error flags: the Framing and Overrun flags. The *Framing Error* (*FE*) flag is set if the control logic determines that a logical 0 – that is, a valid stop bit – is not present on the receive data line when the last stop bit is expected at the end of the received character. Similarly, the *Overrun Error* (*OE*) flag is set if the controlling device has not read the previously received character from the Receive Buffer before the next character is received and transferred to the Buffer. Normally, the setting of these flags does not inhibit the operation of the UART but rather signals to the controlling device that an error condition has occurred. It is then up to the latter to initiate any corrective action should it deem this to be necessary.

As can. be seen in Fig. 2.5, a UART contains both a transmit and a receive section both of which operate in an independent way. It is possible with a single UART, therefore, to control a full-duplex data link. Also, most UARTs normally have additional control lines to allow them to be interfaced with a modem rather than a data link directly. The use of these lines, however, will be considered in a later chapter when modems are discussed.

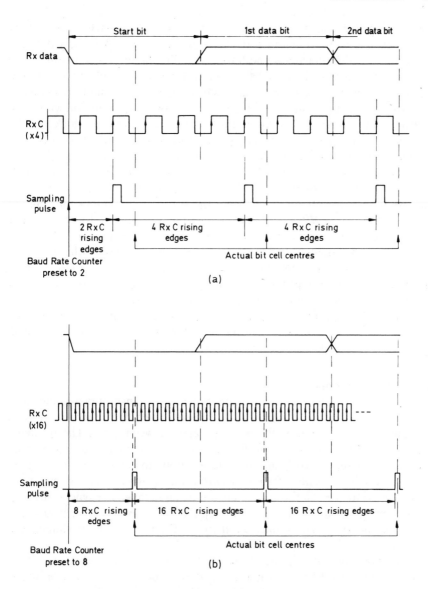

Fig. 2.7 Receiver timing waveforms: (a) × 4 Receiver Clock (R×C);
(b) × 16 Receiver Clock (R×C)

2.3.2 Synchronous transmission

Although the type of framing – character or block – is often used to discriminate between asynchronous and synchronous transmission, the fundamental difference between the two methods is that with asynchronous transmission the transmitter and receiver clocks are unsynchronised whilst with synchronous transmission both clocks are synchronised. Clearly this may be accomplished by having an additional line linking the two equipments to carry the transmit clock so that the receiving device can reliably determine when each new bit is being sent. In practice, however, it is more common to use a single data line, and embed the clocking (timing) information within the transmitted waveform. With this method, the receiver sampling clock must be extracted from the incoming data stream using a suitable *clock extraction circuit*. The different methods used to achieve this will be discussed later.

There are two alternative ways of organising a synchronous data link: character (or byte) oriented and bit oriented, the essential difference being the way the start and end of a frame – the string of contiguous information bits – is determined. With a bit oriented system it is possible for the receiver to detect the end of a frame at any bit instant and not just on an 8-bit (byte) boundary. This implies that a frame may be N bits in length where N is an arbitrary number but in practice, since the majority of applications tend to use frames which are multiples of 8-bit bytes, this feature is not often used. Nevertheless, a bit oriented system offers the potential of up to a two times increase in throughput over a character oriented system and hence is now the preferred mode of operation. Since character oriented systems are still in widespread use, however, both will be described.

2.3.2.1 Character oriented

With a character oriented scheme each frame to be transmitted is made up of a variable number of 7 or 8-bit characters which are transmitted as a contiguous string of binary bits with no delay between them. The receiving device, therefore, must be able firstly to detect the start and end of each character – character synchronism – and secondly, to detect the start and end of each complete frame – frame synchronism. A number of schemes have been devised to achieve this, the main aim being to make the synchronisation process independent of the actual contents of a frame. The synchronisation scheme is then said to be *transparent* to the frame contents or simply *data transparent*.

The most common character oriented scheme is that used in the binary synchronous control protocol known as *Basic Mode*. Basic Mode protocols will be discussed in more detail in Chapter 5 since they are used primarily for the transfer of alphanumeric characters between communities of intelligent terminals and a computer. A number of alternative forms of this protocol are in use but an example of the frame format used in one of these is shown in Fig. 2.8. The format selected is the one normally used to achieve transparency of the transmitted data.

When using Basic Mode, character synchronism is achieved by the transmitting device sending a minimum number of special synchronising characters (known as SYN), immediately preceding each transmitted frame. The receiver, at startup or after an idle period, then scans (hunts) the received bit stream a single bit at a time until it detects the known pattern of

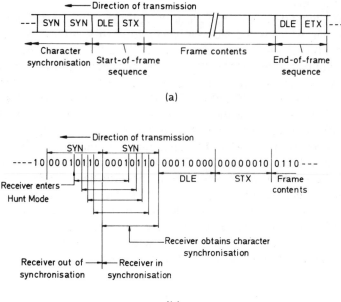

Fig. 2.8 Character oriented link: (a) frame format; (b) character synchronisation

the SYN character. It is then in character synchronism and the subsequent string of binary bits is then treated as a contiguous sequence of 7 or 8-bit elements as defined at setup time. This is illustrated in part (b) of the figure.

With the Basic Mode protocol, the SYN character – 00010110 – is one of the reserved characters from the International Standards Organisation (ISO) defined set of character codes. Similarly, the characters used to signal the start and end of each frame are from this set. Thus in the example, a Data Link Escape (DLE) character followed by a Start-of-Text (STX) character is used to signal the start of a frame and a DLE character followed by an End-of-Text (ETX) character is used to signal the end of a frame. A pair of characters is necessary to achieve data transparency: to avoid the abnormal termination of a frame due to the frame contents containing the end-of-frame character sequence, the transmitter inserts a second DLE character into the transmitted data stream whenever it detects a DLE character in the contents of the frame. This is often referred to as *character* (or *byte*) *stuffing*. The receiver can thus detect the end of a frame by the unique DLE/ETX sequence and, whenever it receives a DLE character followed by a second DLE, it discards the second character. As has been mentioned, with a frame oriented scheme, transmission errors are normally detected by the use of additional error detection digits computed from the contents of the frame and transmitted at the end of the frame. To maintain transparency, therefore, the error check characters are transmitted after the closing frame sequence. The different error detection methods will be expanded on in a later section.

2.3.2.2 Bit oriented

With a bit oriented scheme, each transmitted frame may contain an arbitrary number of bits which is not necessarily a multiple of 8. A typical frame format used with a bit oriented scheme is shown in Fig. 2.9. The opening and closing flag fields are the same – 01111110 – and hence to achieve data transparency it is necessary to ensure that the flag sequence is not present in the frame contents. This is accomplished by the use of a technique known as *zero bit insertion* or *bit stuffing*. As the frame contents are being transmitted to line, the transmitter detects whenever there is a sequence of 5 contiguous binary 1s and automatically inserts an additional binary 0. In this way the flag sequence 01111110 can never be transmitted between the opening and closing flags. Similarly the receiver, after detecting the opening flag of a frame, monitors the incoming bit stream and, whenever it detects a binary 0 after five consecutive binary 1s, it removes (deletes) it from the frame contents. As with a byte oriented scheme, each frame will normally contain additional error detection digits at the end of the frame but the inserted and deleted 0s are not included in the error detection processing.

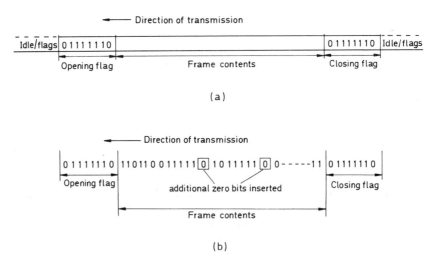

Fig. 2.9 Bit-oriented link: (a) frame format; (b) zero bit insertion

2.3.3 The USRT

Special integrated circuits are available for the control of both byte oriented and bit oriented synchronous transmission lines. The circuits available for the control of a bit oriented line, however, normally contain many additional features to those just described and hence this type of circuit will be introduced in a later chapter when bit oriented protocols are discussed in more detail.

The interface circuit used for the control of a byte oriented synchronous transmission line is known as a *Universal Synchronous Receiver and Transmitter* or *USRT*. Again the term universal is used since the device is

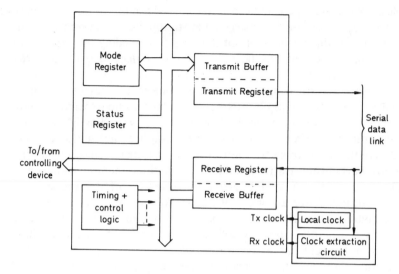

Fig. 2.10 USRT schematic

programmable and its detail operational characteristics can be changed under the control of the user. A schematic diagram of a typical USRT is shown in Fig. 2.10.

As with a UART, to use such a device the *Mode (Control) Register* is first loaded to define the required operating characteristics and, as an example, part (a) of Fig. 2.11 illustrates the meaning of some of the bits used in a typical device – the Intel 8251/Signetics 2657. The *Length* and *Parity* bits have the same effect and meaning as with a UART. The *Sync Character Select (SCS)* bit is provided to allow the user to operate the device, and hence data link, with either a single or

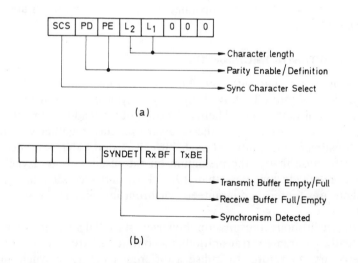

Fig. 2.11 Typical USRT mode and status bit definitions: (a) Mode Register;
(b) Status Register

double SYN character preceding each transmitted frame. (In fact the actual sync character used can normally be selected at startup also.) The controlling device then determines the current state of the USRT by reading the contents of the *Status Register* and testing specific bits – *Transmit Buffer Empty* (*TxBE*), *Receive Buffer Full* (*RxBF*) etc.

At the start of transmission, the controlling device initiates the transmission of several SYN characters to allow the receiving device to achieve character synchronism. This is achieved by loading SYN characters into the Transmit Buffer each time the TxBE bit becomes set (logical 1). The contents of the frame to be transmitted are then transferred by the controlling device to the Transmit Buffer a single byte at a time, the rate again controlled by the state of the TxBE bit. After the last byte of the frame has been transmitted, the USRT automatically starts to transmit SYN characters until the controlling device is ready to transmit a new frame. These are referred to as *interframe time-fill characters* and allow the receiver to maintain character synchronism between successive frames.

At the destination, the controlling device first sets the receiving USRT into the hunt mode, which causes the control logic to compare the contents of the Receive Buffer with the SYN character after each new bit is received. When a match is found the *Sync Detect* (*SYNDET*) *bit* is set in the status register to indicate to the controlling device that byte synchronism has been obtained. The latter then waits for the start-of-frame character sequence – DLE/STX for example – to indicate a frame is being transmitted. Each byte of the frame is then received by the controlling device – each determined by the setting of the Receive Buffer Full bit – until the end-of-frame character sequence – DLE/ETX for example – is detected. In the synchronous mode, all data are transmitted and received at a rate determined by the transmit and receive clocks respectively. The latter, as will be described in the next section, is normally derived from the incoming bit stream using a suitable *clock-extraction circuit*.

2.4 CLOCK (BIT) SYNCHRONISATION

It has been shown that with asynchronous transmission, at the receiver a separate clock is utilised whose frequency is typically several times higher than the transmitted bit rate. Then, on receipt of the leading edge of the start bit of each character envelope, the receiver uses this, together with its local clock, to estimate the centre of each bit cell period. This is an acceptable approach because firstly, the maximum bit rate used with an asynchronous scheme is relatively low (less than 19.2 kbps) and secondly, the encoding method ensures there is a guaranteed synchronising edge at the start of each character.

With synchronous transmission, however, start and stop bits are not used and instead each frame is transmitted as a continuous stream of binary digits. It is necessary, therefore, to utilise a different clock (bit) synchronisation method. One approach, of course, is to have two pairs of lines between the transmitter and receiver: one to carry the transmitted bit stream and the other to carry the associated clock (timing) signal. The receiver could then utilise the latter to clock the incoming bit stream into, say, the receiver shift register within the USRT. In practice, however, this is very rarely possible since if the switched telephone network is being used, for example, only a single pair of lines is normally available.

Two alternative methods are used to overcome this: either the clocking information (signal) is embedded into the transmitted bit stream and subsequently extracted by the receiver, or the information to be transmitted is encoded in such a way that there are sufficient guaranteed transitions in the transmitted bit stream to synchronise a separate clock held at the receiver. Both approaches will be considered.

2.4.1 Clock encoding and extraction

Two alternative methods of embedding clocking information into a transmitted bit stream are shown in Fig. 2.12. In (a) the bit stream to be transmitted is encoded so that a binary 1 is represented by a positive pulse and

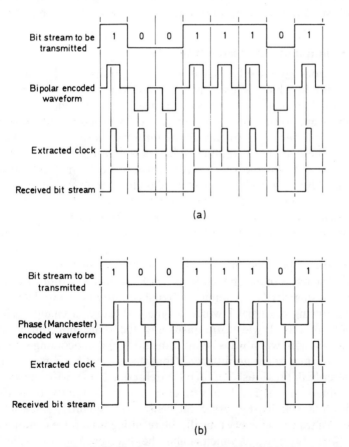

Fig. 2.12 Clock encoding methods: (a) bipolar encoding;
(b) phase (Manchester) encoding

a binary 0 as a negative pulse. Clearly therefore each bit cell contains clocking information and, by means of a simple rectifier and delay circuit, the clock can readily be extracted from the received waveform.

Since with this method the waveform returns to zero after each encoded bit (positive or negative), the encoded signal is referred to as a *return-to-zero* or simply *RZ* waveform. This method is known as *bipolar encoding*. It can be deduced from the figure that with an RZ waveform three distinct amplitude levels are required to represent the transmitted bit stream whilst in the scheme illustrated in part (b) only two levels are necessary. The waveform illustrated in (b) is referred to as a *non-return-to-zero* or *NRZ* waveform. It is an example of a *phase* or *Manchester encoded* (*PE*) bit pattern and, although the associated clock extraction circuitry required for use with this method is a little more complicated than with bipolar encoding, the presence of a positive or negative transition at the centre of each bit-cell period means that the extraction of the clock can be readily accomplished. It can be seen from the figure that with bipolar encoding the extracted clock is used to sample (clock) the incoming bit stream at the centre of each bit cell whilst with phase encoding the bit stream is sampled during the second half of each bit cell.

2.4.2 Data encoding and clock synchronisation

An alternative approach to encoding the clock into the transmitted bit stream is to utilise a stable clock source at the receiver (cf. asynchronous transmissions) which is kept in time synchronism with the incoming bit stream. Since there are no start and stop bits with a synchronous transmission scheme, however, it is necessary to encode the information to be transmitted in such a way that there are always sufficient bit transitions (1–0 or 0–1) in the transmitted waveform to enable the receiver clock to be resynchronised at frequent intervals. One approach is to pass the data to be transmitted through a *scrambler* which has the effect of randomising the transmitted bit stream and hence removing contiguous strings of 1s or 0s. Alternatively, the data may be encoded in such a way that suitable transitions are always naturally present.

The bit pattern to be transmitted is first encoded as in Fig. 2.13. The resulting encoded signal is then referred to as a *non-return-to-zero-inverted* or *NRZI* waveform. Using NRZI encoding the signal condition (1 or 0) does not change for transmitting a binary 1 whilst a binary 0 causes a change. This means that with an NRZI waveform providing there are no continuous streams of binary 1s there will always be bit transitions in the incoming signal. On the surface, this may seem no different from the normal NRZ waveform but, as was described previously, if a bit oriented scheme with zero bit insertion is adopted, an active line will always have a binary 0 in the transmitted bit stream at least every 5 bit cells. Consequently, since long strings of 0s cause a transition every bit cell, the resulting waveform contains a guaranteed number of transitions which enable the receiver to adjust its clock to ensure it is in synchronism with the incoming bit stream.

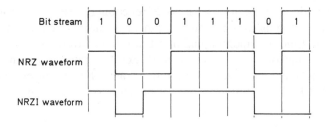

Fig. 2.13 NRZI encoding

The circuit used to maintain bit synchronism is known as a *digital phase locked loop* or *DPLL*. To utilise a DPLL, a *crystal controlled oscillator* (clock source) is connected to it which can hold its frequency sufficiently constant to require only very small adjustments at irregular intervals. The frequency of the clock is normally 32 times the bit rate being used on the data link and this in turn is used by the DPLL to derive the timing interval between successive samples of the received bit stream. Hence, assuming the incoming bit stream and the local clock are in synchronism, the state (1 or 0) of the incoming signal on the line will be sampled (clocked) at the centre of each bit cell with exactly 32 clock periods between each sample. This is shown in part (a) of Fig. 2.14.

Now assume that the incoming bit stream and local clock drift out of synchronism. The adjustment of the sampling instant is carried out in discrete increments as shown in part (b) of the figure. If there are no transitions on the line the DPLL simply generates a sampling pulse every 32 clock periods after the previous one. Whenever a transition (1–0 or 0–1) is detected, however, the time interval between the previously generated sampling pulse and the next is determined according to the position of the transition relative to where the DPLL thought it should occur. To achieve this, each bit period is divided into four quadrants which are shown as A, B, C and D in the figure. Each quadrant is equal to 8 clock periods and if for example a transition occurs during quadrant A, this indicates that the last sampling pulse was in fact too close and hence late. The time period to the next pulse is therefore shortened to 30 clock periods. Similarly, if a transition occurs in quadrant D this indicates the prevous sampling pulse was too early. The time period to the next pulse is therefore lengthened to 34 clock periods. Transitions in quadrants B and C are clearly nearer to the assumed transition and hence the relative adjustments are less (−1 and +1 respectively).

In this way successive adjustments keep the generated sampling pulses close to the normal centre of each bit cell. It can readily be deduced that in the worst case the DPLL will require 12 bit transitions to converge to the nominal bit centre of a waveform – 4 bit periods of coarse adjustments (+ or −2) and 8 bit periods of fine adjustments (+ or −1). Hence when using a DPLL it is usual before transmitting the first frame on a line or following an idle period between frames to transmit a number of characters to provide a minimum of 12 bit transitions. Two characters each composed of all 0s, for example, will provide l6 transitions with NRZI encoding. This then ensures that the DPLL will be generating sampling pulses at the nominal centre of each bit cell by the time the opening flag of a frame is received. It should be stressed, however, that once in synchronism (lock) only minor adjustments will normally take place during the reception of a frame. Further information relating to the DPLL can be found in the list of references at the end of the book.

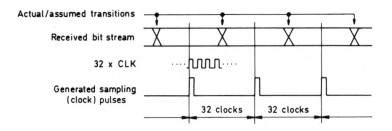

(a)

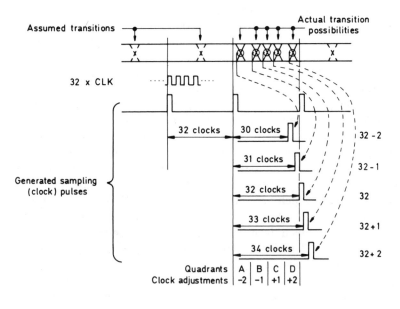

(b)

Fig. 2.14 DPLL operation: (a) in phase; (b) clock adjustment rules

2.5 ERROR DETECTION METHODS

When data are being transmitted between two DTEs it is very common, especially if the transmission lines are in an electrically noisy environment such as the switched telephone network, for the electrical signals representing the transmitted bit stream to be changed by electromagnetic interference induced in the lines by neighbouring electrical devices. This means that the signals representing a binary 1 may be interpreted by the receiver as a binary 0 signal and vice versa. In order to ensure that information received by a destination device has a high probability of being the same as that transmitted by a sending device, therefore, there must be some means for the receiver to deduce – to a high probability – when received information contains errors and, should errors be detected, a mechanism for obtaining a copy of the (hopefully) correct information.

There are two approaches to achieving this: either each transmitted character or frame contains additional (redundant) information so that the receiver can not only detect when errors are present but also infer from the received bit stream what it thinks the correct information should be – *forward error control* – or to include only sufficient additional information in each character or frame to enable the receiver to detect when errors are present and then to employ a retransmission scheme to request another, hopefully correct, copy of the erroneous information to be sent. This is known as *feedback error control*. In practice, the number of additional bits required to achieve reliable forward error control increases rapidly as the number of information bits increases and hence feedback error control is the predominant method used in the types of distributed system to be discussed in this book. Nevertheless, a brief introduction to the subject of forward error control is given in Appendix A.

As has been indicated, feedback error control can be divided into two parts: firstly, the techniques which may be used to achieve reliable error detection and secondly, the control algorithms which are available to perform the associated retransmission schemes. This section is concerned with the most common error detection techniques which are currently in use, and some of the alternative retransmission control algorithms are discussed in the next chapter.

2.5.1 Parity

The most common method used for detecting errors when the number of information bits is small and the probability of an error being present is low is by the use of a single additional parity bit per transmitted element. This method is particularly suitable with asynchronous transmission, for example, since, as will be seen in Chapter 5, using the standard coding methods each transmitted character contains either 7 or 8 data bits plus the parity bit itself.

Using the parity method, the data bits in each character are inspected prior to transmission and an extra bit – *the parity bit* – is then computed and added so that the total number of binary 1s in the complete envelope – including the parity bit itself – is either odd or even according to whether *odd* or *even parity* is being used. The receiver can then recompute the parity for the received character and determine whether any transmission errors have occurred. The format of a transmitted envelope is then as shown in part (a) of Fig. 2.15.

The ability of a particular type of error detection scheme to reveal errors depends strongly on the types of error that can arise on the data links being used. For example, it can readily be deduced that the inclusion of a single parity bit with each character will only reliably safeguard against single bits being in error – any odd number of digit corruptions in theory – since if two bits are corrupted the transmitted parity bit will not indicate the error. In

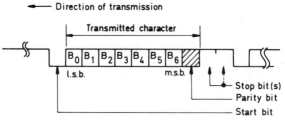

(a)

(b)

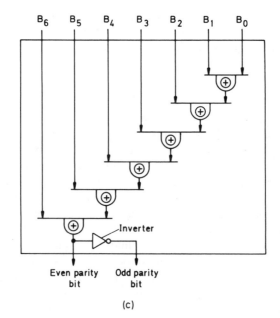

(c)

Fig. 2.15 Parity generation and checking: (a) character envelope; (b) XOR truth table; (c) circuit

practice, however, if two or more (even) errors do occur – and hence remain undetected by the line transmission control circuitry – the retransmission control schemes used with character oriented transmission provide a means for detecting this.

Since parity is used with asynchronous transmission control schemes and also with character oriented synchronous transmission schemes, both UARTs and USRTs – collectively referred to as USARTs – also contain facilities to compute and insert the appropriate parity bit into each transmitted character automatically prior to transmission and, on reception, to recompute the parity for each received character and to signal when an error is detected. The circuitry integrated into the USARTs to perform these functions, however, is relatively simple. It comprises a string of *exclusive-OR (XOR)* gates connected as shown in part (c) of Fig. 2.15. A *truth table* for an XOR gate is shown in part (b) of the figure and, since the output of the exclusive-OR operation between two binary digits is the same as the addition of the two digits without a carry bit, the XOR gate is also known as a *modulo 2 adder*. The least significant pair of bits are first XORed together and the output of this gate is then XORed with the next (more significant) bit and so on. The output of the final gate is then the required parity bit and this is loaded into the Transmit Register of the USART prior to transmission of the character. Similarly on receipt, the recomputed parity bit is compared with the expected parity bit – odd or even as agreed by the two communicating parties and hence set into the Mode Control Register at startup – and, if different, the Parity Error bit in the USART status register is set, thus indicating to the controlling device that a transmission error has been detected.

2.5.2 Block sum check

With a block (frame) oriented transmission scheme, an extension to the error detecting capabilities obtained with the use of a single parity bit per character can be obtained by the use of an additional set of parity bits computed from the complete string of characters in the frame. With this method, each character in the frame is assigned a parity bit as before by the USRT but, in addition, an extra parity bit is generated by the controlling device for each bit position (column) in the complete frame. The resulting set of parity bits for each column is then referred to as the *block sum check* and an example is illustrated in Fig. 2.16.

To discriminate between the parity bits generated for each character by the USART and the additional set of parity bits generated for each column by the controlling device, the former are known as the *row* or *transverse parity bits* and the latter as *column* or *longitudinal parity bits*. Since the final set of column parity bits computed by the controlling device are each computed by summing (modulo 2) the bits in each column, the final character in the block is known as the block sum check.

The example illustrated uses odd parity for the row and even parity for the column parity bits and it can readily be seen that although two-bit errors in a character may escape the row parity check, they will be detected by the

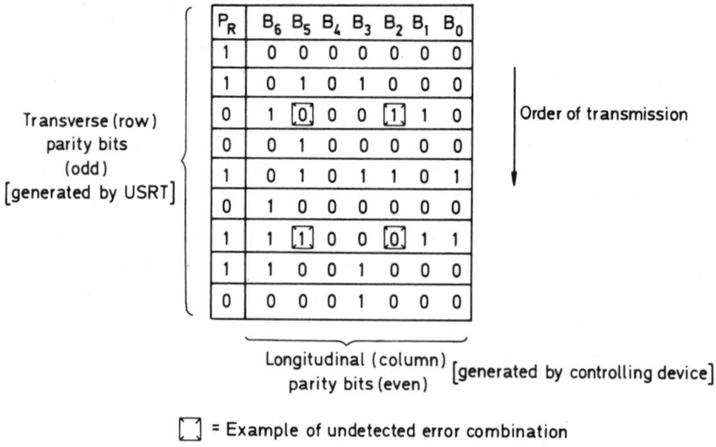

P_R	B_6	B_5	B_4	B_3	B_2	B_1	B_0
1	0	0	0	0	0	0	0
1	0	1	0	1	0	0	0
0	1	[0]	0	0	[1]	1	0
0	0	1	0	0	0	0	0
1	0	1	0	1	1	0	1
0	1	0	0	0	0	0	0
1	1	[1]	0	0	[0]	1	1
1	1	0	0	1	0	0	0
0	0	0	0	1	0	0	0

Transverse (row) parity bits (odd) [generated by USRT]

Order of transmission

Longitudinal (column) parity bits (even) [generated by controlling device]

[ ] = Example of undetected error combination

Fig. 2.16 Block sum check example

column parity check bits. This is true, of course, only if no two-bit errors occur in the same column at the same time. The probability of this occurring, however, is not insignificant on some types of line and hence this method is used only when a frame transmission scheme is being used on transmission lines which have only a low error probability rate. For more error-prone (noisy) lines the more rigorous polynomial type of error detection method is more common.

2.5.3 Polynomial codes

The most common type of error which arises when data are being transmitted over lines from the switched telephone network are those caused by a burst of electrical interference due, for example, to noise impulses caused by the switching elements within the exchanges. These, in turn, can cause a string or burst of consecutive bits in a frame to be corrupted and hence this type of error is known as an *error burst*. An error burst begins and ends with an erroneous bit but the bits in between may or may not be corrupted. It is thus defined as the number of bits between two successive erroneous bits including the two bits in error. Also, when determining the length of an error burst, the last erroneous bit in a burst and the first erroneous bit in the following burst must be separated by *B* or more correct bits where *B* is the length of the error burst. An example showing two different error burst lengths is shown in Fig. 2.17. Notice that the first and third bit errors could not be used to define a single 11-bit error burst since an error occurs within the next 11 bits.

Parity, or its derivative block sum check, does not provide a reliable detection scheme against error bursts and the most common alternative is based on the use of *polynomial codes*. Polynomial codes are used with frame transmission schemes: a single set of check digits are generated (computed) for each frame transmitted. These are based on the actual contents of the frame and are then appended by the transmitter at the tail of the frame. The receiver then performs a similar computation on the complete frame – data plus check digits – and, if no errors have been induced, a known result should always be obtained, a different answer from this indicating an error.

The number of check digits per frame varies to suit the worst-case type of transmission errors anticipated although 16 and 32 bits are the most common. The computed check digits are referred to as the *frame check sequence* (*FCS*) or the *cyclic redundancy check* (*CRC*). The precise computation process varies slightly from one implementation to another but Fig. 2.18 illustrates the principle of operation by considering the generation of a 4-bit FCS. Part (a) shows how the FCS is generated at the transmitter and part (b) how the receiver checks the incoming bit stream for errors.

The underlying mathematical theory of polynomial codes is beyond the scope of this book, but essentially the complete frame contents together with an appended set of zeros equal in number to the number of FCS digits to be generated – four in the example – are divided modulo 2 by a second polynomial – the *generator polynomial* – containing one more digit than the FCS. The division operation is equivalent to performing the exclusive-OR operation bit-by-bit in parallel as each bit in the frame is processed. The resulting remainder is then the FCS and is transmitted at the tail of the information digits. Similarly, on receipt, the received bit stream including the FCS digits is again divided by the same generator polynomial and, if no errors are present, the resulting remainder is all zeros. If an error is present, however, the remainder is non-zero.

The choice of generator polynomial is important since it determines the types of error which are detected. For example, an error pattern that is identical, or has a factor identical, to the generator polynomial will generate the same check bits as the correct transmission and hence be undetectable. A polynomial which is prime, in the modulo 2 sense, is therefore normally chosen.

An important characteristic of this method is that all bursts of errors with fewer terms than the generator polynomial will be detected. As an example, the generator polynomial defined by the CCITT for use on the switched telephone network is

$$x^{16} + x^{12} + x^5 + x^0$$

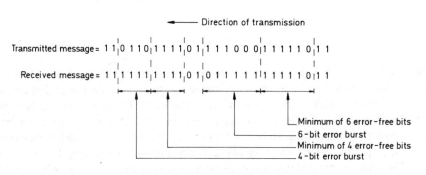

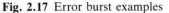

Fig. 2.17 Error burst examples

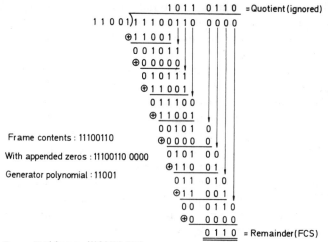

Frame contents : 11100110

With appended zeros : 11100110 0000

Generator polynomial : 11001

Transmitted frame : 11100110 0110

(a)

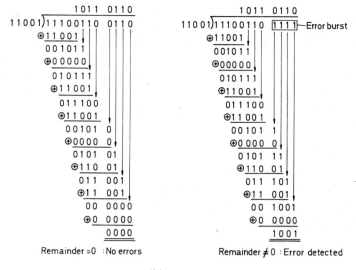

(b)

Fig. 2.18 FCS coding and decoding example: (a) coding; (b) decoding

In binary form this is equivalent to 10001000000100001, the power in x being represented as a 1 or 0. In this case sixteen zeros would be appended to the frame contents prior to the generation of the FCS. The latter would then be the 16-bit remainder. The generator polynomial selected will detect any one error burst not exceeding 16 bits in length and in addition, all odd numbers of errors, any 2-bit errors and any two error bursts not exceeding 2 bits.

This type of error detection method is now very prevalent, especially with the more recent bit oriented transmission control scheme and hence all of the integrated circuits available for use with this scheme support this type of error detection method. Although the requirement to perform multiple division operations to compute the FCS digits may seem difficult to implement at a fast transmitter bit rate – cf. computer arithmetic – in practice, since the arithmetic is all performed modulo 2, it is possible to implement an FCS generator-checker very readily in hardware using just a combination of shift registers and exclusive-OR gates (modulo 2 adders). A typical arrangement for the example shown earlier in Fig. 2.18 is as shown in Fig. 2.19.

In the example, since four FCS digits are to be generated, just a 4-bit shift register is sufficient to represent bits x^3, x^2, x^1 and x^0 in the generator polynomial. These are often referred to as the *active bits* of the generator. Thus with an active generator polynomial of $x^3 + x^0 - 1001$ binary – the two XOR gates between the intermediate shift register elements x^1 and x^2 simply

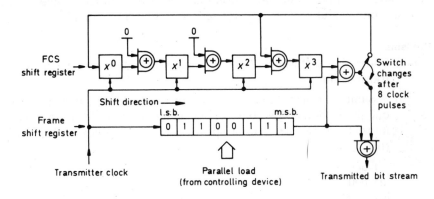

Transmitter clock (shift) pulses	Frame shift register contents l.s.b							m.s.b	FCS S-R contents x0	x1	x2	x3
0	0	1	1	0	0	1	1	1	0	0	0	0
1	0	0	1	1	0	0	1	1	1	0	0	1
2	0	0	0	1	1	0	0	1	0	1	0	0
3	0	0	0	0	1	1	0	0	1	0	1	1
4	0	0	0	0	0	1	1	0	1	1	0	0
5		0	0	0	0	0	1	1	0	1	1	0
6			0	0	0	0	0	1	1	0	1	0
7				0	0	0	0	0	1	1	0	0
8					0	0	0	0	0	1	1	0
9						0	0	0		0	1	1
10							0	0			0	1
11								0				0

Fig. 2.19 FCS generator-checker hardware

pass on the existing contents of x^0 and x^1 respectively unmodified whilst the new states of x^0 and x^3 are determined by the intermediate XOR gate connections.

The frame contents to be transmitted are shifted out from the frame shift register unmodified to the transmission line – most significant bit first at a rate determined by the required transmitter bit frequency – and simultaneously to the FCS shift register. An additional bit counter (not shown) is used to determine when all the frame contents bits have been transmitted – 8 in the example – and at this point switches the output to be the output of element x^3 of the FCS shift register. In the figure for clarity the frame shift register is shown to contain the same number of bits as there are bits in the frame. In practice, however, only a, say, 4-bit shift register would need to be used with the example selected and this would be (parallel) loaded with successive 4-bit groups after each preceding 4-bit group had been transmitted to line. Thus the first group would be 1110 and the second 0110 in this example.

Problems

2.1 a) State the difference between asynchronous and synchronous transmission.

   b) Assuming asynchronous transmission, one start bit, two stop bits, one parity bit and two bits per signalling element, derive the useful information transfer rate in bps for each of the following signalling (baud) rates:

      i) 300
      ii) 600
      iii) 1200
      iv) 4800

2.2 a) With the aid of a diagram, explain the clock (bit) and character synchronisation methods used with an asynchronous transmission control scheme.

   b) Draw a schematic diagram showing the various registers used in a UART and outline the operation of the device and the use of the various bits in the Mode and Status Registers.

2.3 Assuming a synchronous transmission control scheme, explain how character and frame synchronisation are achieved:

      i) with a character oriented link,
      ij) with a bit oriented link.

2.4 a) Explain what is meant by data transparency and how it may be achieved using:

      i) character stuffing,
      ii) zero bit insertion.

b) Draw a schematic diagram showing the arrangement of the various registers used in a USRT and outline the operation of the device and the use of the various bits in the Mode and Status Registers.

2.5 a) With the aid of diagrams, explain how clock synchronisation may be achieved using:

   i) bipolar encoding,
   ii) phase (Manchester) encoding.

b) Explain under what circumstances data encoding and a digital phase lock loop (DPLL) circuit may be used to achieve clock synchronisation and, with the aid of a diagram, explain the operation of the DPLL circuit.

c) Assuming the receiver is initially out of synchronism, derive the minimum number of bit transitions which are required for a DPLL circuit to converge to the nominal bit centre of a transmitted waveform. How may this be achieved in practice?

2.6 a) What are the two basic methods of error control used on a data transmission link? What is the most prevalent method and why?

b) Explain the operation and application areas of the following error detection methods:

   i) parity,
   ii) block sum check,
   iii) polynomial codes.

Give examples showing how each check sequence is derived.

2.7 a) With the aid of an example, illustrate the type of transmission errors which are not detected with a block sum check. Clearly identify the row and column parity bits used assuming an odd and even parity respectively.

b) Sketch a schematic circuit diagram showing how the frame check sequence bits for a transmitted block of information may be generated using a generator polynomial of $x^4 + x^3 + 1$.

c) Use an example to show how an error pattern equal to the generator polynomial used in part (b) will not be detected. List other error patterns that would not be detected with this polynomial.

Chapter 3 **Link-Level Protocols**

Objectives:
When you have completed studying the material in this chapter you should be able to:

- appreciate that a communications protocol is made up of a number of functional components which include error control, flow control, and connection management;

- understand the meaning and application areas of echo checking and the X-ON/X-OFF flow control mechanism;

- draw and explain typical frame sequences for both Idle RQ and Continuous RQ frame oriented error control schemes;

- understand the differences between Selective Retransmission and Go-Back-N control strategies and draw typical frame sequences to illustrate their operation;

- explain the reason for having a timeout mechanism associated with a protocol and draw typical frame sequences to illustrate its operation;

- describe the operation of a window flow control mechanism and its effect on the range of sequence numbers required;

- understand the various phases associated with the overall management of a data transfer across a logical data link.

3.1 INTRODUCTION

The previous chapter described the circuits and techniques which may be employed to transmit a character or frame of information between two data terminal equipments across a point-to-point data link. In addition, the various error detection schemes described allow the receiving DTE to determine, to a known probability, the presence of any errors in the transmitted bit stream. Alternatively, if forward error correction is being used, this allows the receiver to deduce from the received bit stream, again to a known probability, the actual information being transmitted even when errors are present. In general, however, the techniques described provide only the basic mechanism for transmitting information between two DTEs and in addition, therefore, it is necessary to define a set of rules or control procedures which must be adopted by both communicating parties to ensure the reliable (that is, to a high probability free of errors and duplicates) exchange of meaningful messages between the two parties.

For example, the various error detection schemes described in the previous chapter allow the receiver only to detect when errors have been induced into the transmitted bit stream; they do not provide a means for correcting the erroneous character or frame. Normally this is accomplished by the controlling device at the destination informing the source that an error has been detected and hence another copy of the affected character or frame should be sent. The combined error detection/correction cycle is known as *error control* and it can be implied that this necessitates the two controlling devices at each end of a link exchanging an agreed set of defined characters or frames to achieve the reliable transfer of each element. In addition, however, as will be described in later sections of this chapter, there are often other control mechanisms which must be observed by the two communicating parties and collectively these constitute the *communications protocol* for that link. Some of the basic components of a communications protocol are now considered.

3.2 ERROR CONTROL

There are two basic strategies which are in common use to enable a sending DTE to determine whether the receiving DTE has correctly received a transmitted element: *echo checking* and *automatic repeat request* or *ARQ*. Each is applicable to a different set of application requirements and hence will be considered separately.

3.2.1 Echo checking

Echo checking is primarily used with character oriented asynchronous transmission between, for example, a terminal communicating with a remote computer. Normally, terminals have a facility to allow them to be used in either *local* or *remote mode*. In local mode, when a key is depressed on the terminal keyboard the resulting character is transmitted to the remote computer and simultaneously printed or displayed on the terminal screen. In remote mode, however, when the key is selected the resulting character is transmitted to the remote computer but is not displayed on the terminal screen. Instead, the character received by the computer is retransmitted or *echoed* back to the terminal and it is at this point that it is displayed on the terminal screen. Then, if the displayed character does not match the character selected on the keyboard, the user assumes a transmission error has occurred and, as a result, transmits an agreed control character – a DELete for example – to inform the computer to ignore the previously transmitted (and hence echoed) character. On receipt of this character, the computer performs the necessary deletion and again echoes the character back to the terminal and hence the user can confirm the previous character has been ignored. In fact, the transmission error may have corrupted the echoed character rather than the originally transmitted character but the control scheme outlined allows for this possibility.

It can be deduced from the foregoing that echo checking is relatively inefficient in its use of transmission bandwidth since each character is transmitted at least twice. The overhead associated with retransmitting each character is quite low, however, since a computer normally processes each character as it is received from a terminal in order to determine if further processing is necessary as a result of the character just received – a command to an editor utility, for example, or to the computer operating system. This aproach, therefore, is in widespread use for this type of application environment.

3.2.2 Automatic repeat request

Clearly, the above scheme relies on the intelligence of the user for its correct operation. In many data communication situations, however, a user is not involved and the requirement is to transmit information between two equipments automatically with no user intervention. Consequently, although it is possible to program one of the equipments to function as a terminal as in the above example and to use echo checking as before, in practice there are a number of more efficient alternatives that may be considered, especially with a frame oriented transmission scheme. In general, these necessitate the return of only a small control message or frame to acknowledge correct receipt (or otherwise) of each transmitted frame rather than retransmitting a complete copy of each frame transmitted. This is particularly significant when frame transmission is being used since each transmitted element may then contain a substantial number of bytes or characters. The use of an acknowledgment scheme in this way is known as *automatic repeat request* or *ARQ*. A number of derivatives of the basic scheme are possible, the choice of which is determined by the relative importance assigned to the use of buffer storage compared with the efficiency of utilisation of the available transmission capacity. The two most common alternatives are Idle RQ (Send-and-Wait) and Continuous RQ, the latter employing either a Selective Retransmission strategy or a Go-Back-N mechanism. Each will be considered separately.

3.2.2.1 Idle RQ

This is the simplest ARQ scheme; it requires a minimum of buffer storage for its implementation but, as can be deduced from the example shown in Fig. 3.1, it is also the least efficient in its use of transmission capacity.

Since in many data communication situations actual information frames (I-frames) will be flowing in both directions simultaneously, to discriminate between the sender (source) and receiver (sink) of I-frames at each side of a link, the notion of a *Primary* (P) and a *Secondary* (S) are used respectively. Initially, however, for clarity only a unidirectional flow of I-frames is considered. The following should be noted when interpreting the operation of the example in the figure:

1. P can have only one I-frame outstanding (awaiting an acknowledgment or ACK-frame) at a time;
2. when P initiates the transmission of a frame it starts a timer;
3. if S receives an I-frame or P receives an ACK-frame containing transmission errors, the frame is discarded;
4. on receipt of an error free I-frame, S returns an ACK-frame to P;
5. on receipt of an error free ACK-frame, P can transmit another I-frame;
6. if P does not receive an ACK-frame within a predefined time interval – the *timeout interval* – P retransmits the waiting I-frame (part (b)).

The above scheme is also known as *Send-and-Wait* and it will ensure that S receives at least one copy of each frame transmitted by P. Clearly, however, if an ACK-frame is itself corrupted and hence ignored by P (part (c)), it is possible for S to receive two (or more) copies of a particular I-frame. These are known as *duplicates* and, to allow S to discriminate between a valid I-frame and a duplicate, each frame transmitted by P contains a unique identifier (N, $N+1$, etc.). S thus retains a record of the identifier contained within the last frame it correctly received and discards any frames already correctly received. To allow P to resynchronise, however, S returns an ACK-frame for each correctly received frame.

It can be deduced from Fig. 3.1 that the Idle RQ method is inefficient in its use of the available transmission capacity since, in the best case, P must wait a total time of:

$$(T_{FX} + T_{FP} + T_{AX} + T_{AP})$$

before transmitting the next I-frame, even if the previous I-frame was correctly received by S. In the worst case, this will be the same time plus the timeout interval which clearly must be selected to be longer than the worst case delay anticipated for P to receive a valid ACK-frame from S. It is for this reason that some Idle RQ schemes utilise an *additional negative acknowledgment (NACK) frame* to allow S to report the receipt of a corrupted I-frame immediately rather than waiting for the timeout mechanism to initiate the retransmission of another copy of the frame. Such a scheme is the Binary Synchronous Control (BSC) protocol which is described in Chapter 5.

The major advantage of Idle RQ is that it requires a minimum of buffer storage for its implementation since both P and S need only contain sufficient storage for one frame. In addition, S must retain a record of the identifier of the last correctly received frame to enable it to detect duplicates. In general, the various retransmission schemes trade buffer storage requirements for transmission efficiency.

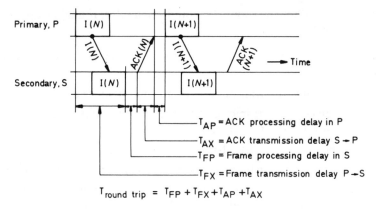

$$T_{round\ trip} = T_{FP} + T_{FX} + T_{AP} + T_{AX}$$

(a)

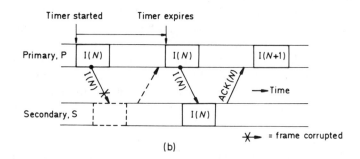

(b)

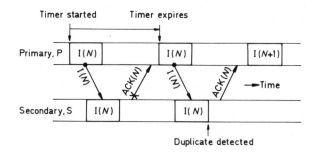

(c)

Fig. 3.1 Idle RQ frame sequences: (a) no transmission errors [*Note:* Transmission delay is the time interval between the first bit of a frame leaving the sender (P or S) and the last bit of the frame being received by the receiver (S or P)]; (b) I-frame corrupted; (c) ACK-frame corrupted

3.2.2.2 Protocol specification methods
Although the three frame sequence diagrams shown in Fig. 3.1, coupled with the descriptive text, are probably sufficient to illustrate the operation of an Idle RQ protocol, with more sophisticated protocols it is often not practicable

to describe fully the operation of the protocol using just this method. Indeed, as will be seen in this and later chapters of the book, to define fully the operation of a protocol allowing for all the possible events and error conditions that may arise can be very complex. In general, therefore, protocols are specified using one of a number of more precise methods and formalisms, and frame sequence diagrams of the type shown in Fig. 3.1 are normally used simply to illustrate selected aspects of a protocol rather than as a means of specifying the protocol.

The three most common methods used for specifying a communications protocol are: state transition diagrams, state transition tables, and high-level structured programs. In many instances, however, a protocol is defined as a combination of these coupled where appropriate with frame (or, more generally, time) sequence diagrams to highlight selected aspects of its operation.

Irrespective of the specification method used, a protocol is treated as a *finite state machine* or *automaton* that can assume, at any instant of time, just one of a number of defined *states*; for example, 'waiting to send a frame' or 'waiting to receive an acknowledgment'. Transitions between states take place as a result of an *event* occurring; for example, a frame becoming ready to send or a timer expiring. The various specification methods then use different techniques to define the states and enabling transitions associated with the automaton. The principles of the three methods listed above are now described.

State transition diagrams
The traditional method used to define the operation of a communications protocol is the *state transition diagram*. Using this method the various possible states of the automaton are given names and are shown in the form of circles. Directional arrows are then used to indicate the possible transitions between states together with the event causing the transition stated alongside it. As an example, a state transition diagram for the Primary and Secondary side of a link operating with an Idle RQ protocol is shown in parts (a) and (b) of Fig. 3.2 respectively.

As can be seen, the Primary has two defined states: Idle (that is, there are no new I-frames ready to send and the previous frame has been correctly acknowledged) and Waiting Acknowledgment which is self explanatory. Transitions between these two states are shown by means of the arrows with the event causing the transition alongside the arrow. Thus if the automaton is in the Idle State and an I-frame becomes ready to send, for example, the frame will be transmitted (this is known as the *action* and is often not shown on the diagram for space reasons) and the automaton will enter the Waiting Acknowledgment state. Also, notice that an event need not necessarily result in a change of state. Typically, such events will cause a certain action to occur (for example, the timer expiring will result in an I-frame being retransmitted) but the automaton will remain in the same state.

It can be deduced from this description that although a state transition diagram provides a convenient method for diagrammatically representing the possible states and transitions and enabling events associated with a protocol, considerable additional explanatory information is required to define the protocol completely. This includes not only a description of the actions that take place as a result of certain events but also a definition of any additional conditions that are associated with a state and which must be met before a particular transition can occur. Also, if the protocol is complex, the state transition diagram(s) used to define the protocol can become very cluttered, especially if all the possible events are shown on the diagram(s). It is for these reasons that, when using a state transition diagram to define a protocol, a substantial amount of supplementary documentation must be provided.

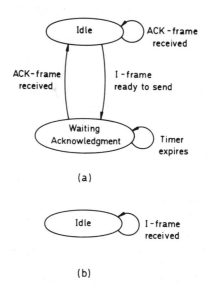

Fig. 3.2 Idle RQ state transition diagrams: (a) Primary; (b) Secondary

State transition tables
A development of the state transition diagram which effectively presents the same information but in a more concise way is the *state transition table*. Using this method, the various automaton states and interface events are represented in the form of a table: each event that may occur is assigned to a specific column in the table and each of the possible automaton states to a row in the table. A state transition table thus contains entries corresponding to all the possible automaton states and, for each state, entries for each possible interface event. Each entry in the table then defines firstly any conditions that must be satisfied, secondly the necessary action to be performed as a result of the event, and thirdly the new state to which the automaton will enter. As an example, a state transition table defining the operation of the Primary and Secondary with an Idle RQ link protocol is shown in Fig. 3.3.

To describe its interpretation, assume the automaton is in the Idle State (first row) and an I-frame becomes ready to send (second column). The entry in the table then indicates that the frame should be transmitted – the Action – and the automaton enter the Waiting Acknowledgment state – the New State. Similarly, if the automaton is in the Idle State and an ACK-frame is received, this indicates an error condition and hence, typically, its occurrence will be noted in an *error log* and the automaton will remain in the same state.

Clearly, a state transition table contains more information about the operation of a protocol than a simple state transition diagram. Moreover, since the information is in tabular form it is easy to assimilate and hence understand. Normally, however, associated with the automaton (*protocol entity*) is a set of variables which hold information relating to the current state of the automaton, for example, the identifier to be assigned to the next in-sequence I-frame. Clearly, since certain events and actions will cause these variables to change, it is also necessary to define precisely the effect of each event and action on them. This is done using either additional descriptive comments or, more usually, program segments – written in a structured programming language – which define unambiguously the steps to be taken to implement each action. The latter will be expanded upon in the next section.

Structured programs
Structured programs are frequently used in protocol specification documents, in collaboration with state transition tables, to describe the detail actions which are identified in the state transition table. This has the advantage that not only can the actions be precisely defined but also the implementation of

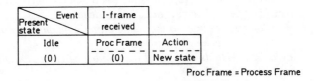

Event Present state	Timer expires	I-frame ready to send	ACK-frame received	
Idle	N A	TxFrame	Error	Action
(0)	0	1	0	New state
Waiting Acknowledgment	Retx Frame	Delay	ProcAck	Action
(1)	1	1	0	New state

TxFrame = Transmit Frame
RetxFrame = Retransmit Frame
ProcAck = Process Acknowledgment
NA = No Action

(a)

Event Present state	I-frame received	
Idle	Proc Frame	Action
(0)	(0)	New state

Proc Frame = Process Frame

(b)

Fig. 3.3 Idle RQ state transition tables: (a) Primary; (b) Secondary

the actions in actual program code is made more straightforward. In addition to using a structured programming language to specify the actions associated with the state transition table, however, it is also possible to represent the complete contents of the state transition table in the form of a high-level data structure as well. This then has the added advantage that the complete protocol specification is in a form which is readily implemented in program code.

To illustrate this, Fig. 3.4 shows how the Primary side of the Idle RQ protocol may be specified in the form of a structured program and Fig. 3.5 the Secondary side. The programming language used is a form of *Pascal* which has been selected because of its general acceptance and relative clarity. To improve readability, however, as is the case in many specification documents a high-level pseudo code is used rather than pure code which means that the implementor must normally make additional refinements to produce the executable code. Wherever possible, however, the names used in the various pseudo code program segments are the same as those used in the accompanying state transition tables.

For the Primary, it is assumed that the main body of the program is executed whenever one of the defined events occurs – *FrameToSend*, *AckReceived*, or *Timeout* – and, once activated, the program runs to completion. Also, it is assumed that the various variables associated with the program have been initialised prior to the first event occurring. Thus the contents of the *EventStateTable* array are assumed to be initialised to contain the appropriate actions and new states as defined in Fig. 3.3 and *PresentState* set to the Idle state.

program   *IdleRQ_Primary*;

type   *Events* = (*FrameToSend, AckReceived, Timeout*);
                {*List of possible events*}
        States = (*Idle, WaitAck*); {*List of automaton states*}
        Actions = (*NA, TxFrame, Error, RetxFrame, Delay, ProcAck*);
                {*List of actions*}

var   *EventStateTable* = **array** [*States, Events*] **of** {*Contains the Event State Table*}
                    record *Action*:   *Actions*;
                            Newstate: *States*
                    end;
        PresentState: *States*; {*Holds the current automaton state*}
        EventType: *Events*; {*Specifies the event that has invoked the program*}
        NextIdentifier; {*The next insequence identifier*}
        RetxPointer; {*Pointer to the frame buffer containing the I-frame awaiting acknowledgment*}
        ErrorLog; {*Holds a count of the number of error conditions that have occurred*}

(continued)

procedure *NoAction*;
    begin *Do nothing* **end**;

procedure *TransmitFrame*;
    begin *Insert NextIdentifier into frame*; *Output frame to line*;
        Save frame pointer in RetxPointer; *Start timer* **end**;

procedure *ErrorCondition*;
    begin *Add 1 to EventLog* **end**;

procedure *RetransmitFrame*;
    begin *Get frame pointer from RetxPointer*; *Output frame to line*:
        Start timer **end**;

procedure *WaitAwhile*
    begin *Delay a short time interval* **end**;

procedure *ProcessAcknowledgment*;
    begin *Remove frame pointer from RetxPointer*; *Increment NextIdentifier*;
          Reset timer **end**;

begin   *{Start of main body}*
    with *EventStateTable* [*PresentState, EventType*] **do**
     begin case *Action* **of** *{List of possible actions}*
         NA :   *NoAction*;
         TxFrame : *TransmitFrame*;
         Error : *ErrorCondition*;
         RetxFrame : *RetransmitFrame*;
         Delay : *WaitAwhile*;
         ProcAck : *ProcessAcknowledgment*;
      end; *{Case}*
      PresentState:= NewState; *{Present state is updated}*
    end;

end.

Fig. 3.4 Specification of Idle RQ Primary in the form of a structured program

program *IdleRQ__Secondary*;

var   *LastIdentifier*; *{Identifier contained within the last correctly received*
     I-frame}

begin *{Start of main body}*
    Create ACK-frame with Identifier = Identifier from received I-frame;
    Output ACK-frame to line;
    if *Identifier = LastIdentifier* **then** *Discard the received I-frame*;
     else begin *LastIdentifier:= Identifier from the received I-frame*;
        Pass on frame for further processing;
     end;

end.

Fig. 3.5 Program specification of the Idle RQ Secondary

The event causing the program to be run is assumed to be assigned to *EventType* before the main body is run. Hence, on receipt of each event, the current contents of *PresentState* and *EventType* are used as indices to the *EventStateTable* array to allow the required action and new state to be accessed from the array. A Case statement is then used to initiate the execution of the selected action from the list of action procedures. For clarity, the latter have also been defined in the form of descriptive pseudo code.

The listing of the Secondary is perhaps self explanatory: whenever an I-frame is received, an ACK-frame is first created with the same identifier as that contained within the received I-frame and this is output to line. The identifier from the I-frame is then compared with the identifier from the last correctly received frame – *LastIdentifier*. If they are equal, the frame is discarded as a duplicate; if they are not equal, the frame is passed on for further processing and *LastIdentifier* is updated to be the same as the identifier from the accepted frame.

3.2.2.3 Continuous RQ

With a Continuous RQ scheme the link utilisation is much improved at the expense of increased buffer storage requirements. An example illustrating the transmission of a sequence of I-frames and their returned ACK-frames is shown in Fig. 3.6. The following points should be noted:

1. P sends I-frames continuously without waiting for an ACK-frame to be returned;
2. P retains a copy of each I-frame transmitted in a *Retransmission List*;
3. the Retransmission List operates on a first-in, first-out queue discipline;
4. S returns an ACK-frame for each correctly received I-frame;
5. each I-frame contains a unique identifier which is returned in the corresponding ACK-frame;
6. S retains an ordered list – the Receive List – containing the identifiers from the last correctly received I-frames;
7. on receipt of an ACK-frame the corresponding I-frame is removed from the Retransmission List by P.

A more precise definition of the Continuous RQ protocol can now be derived and this is shown in Figs. 3.7 (Primary) and 3.8 (Secondary). Again a form of descriptive pseudo code is used to improve readability. Also, as will be expanded upon later, a timeout mechanism similar to that used with an Idle RQ protocol must be associated with each frame and hence this is shown as one of the possible events.

The illustrated example assumes no transmission errors occur. When an error does occur, two alternative procedures may be followed;

either: P detects the out-of-sequence ACK-frame and retransmits just the unacknowledged frame(s) – *Selective Retransmission*,

or: S detects the receipt of an out-of-sequence I-frame and requests P to retransmit all outstanding unacknowledged I-frames from the last correctly received, and therefore acknowledged, frame – *Go-Back*-N.

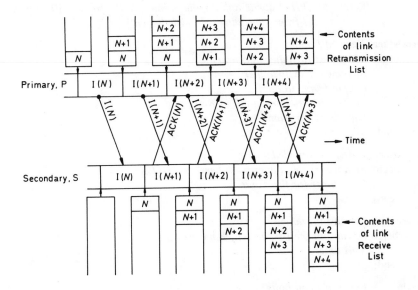

Fig. 3.6 Continuous RQ frame sequence

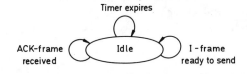

(a)

Present state	I-frame ready to send	ACK-frame received	Timer expires	
Idle	Tx Frame	ProcAck	Retx Frame	Action
(0)	0	0	0	New state

(b)

```
program    ContinuousRQ__Primary;

type       Events = (FrameToSend, AckReceived); {List of possible events}
           Actions = (TxFrame, ProcAck, RetxFrame); {List of actions}

var        EventStateTable = array [Events] of
                                        Action : Actions;
           EventType : Events ; {Specifies the event that has invoked the program}
           NextIdentifier ; {The next insequence identifier}
           RetxList ; {FIFO queue holding the pointers to the frame buffers of the
                       I-frames awaiting acknowledgment}

procedure  TransmitFrame;
    begin  Insert NextIdentifier into frame;
           Increment NextIdentifier;
           Output frame to line;
           Insert frame pointer at tail of RetxList;
           Start timer for frame
      end;

procedure  ProcessAcknowledgment;
    begin  Remove frame pointer from head of RetxList;
           Reset timer for the frame
      end;

procedure  RetransmitFrame;
    begin  Retransmit the I-frame which has timed out;
           Start timer
      end;

begin      {Start of main body}
           with EventStateTable [EventType] do
                begin case Action of {List of possible actions}
                          TxFrame :    TransmitFrame;
                          ProcAck :    ProcessAcknowledgment;
                          RetxFrame : RetransmitFrame;
                      end; {Case}
                end;

end.
```

Fig. 3.7 Continuous RQ protocol – Primary: (a) state transition diagram;
(b) state transition table; (c) program segment

Selective retransmission
An example illustrating the effect of a corrupted I-frame with a Selective
Retransmission control strategy is shown in part (a) of Fig. 3.9. Its operation
is as follows:

1. assume I-frame $N + 1$ is corrupted;
2. S returns an ACK-frame for each correctly received I-frame as before;

3. S returns an ACK for frames $N - 1$, N, $N + 2$, ...;

4. on receipt of the ACK for frame $N + 2$, P detects this is out of sequence and that frame $N + 1$ has not been acknowledged;

5. P removes I-frame $N + 2$ from the Retransmission List and retransmits I-frame $N + 1$ before transmitting frame $N + 5$.

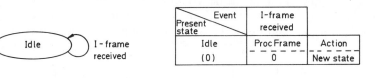

(a)   (b)

program   *ContinuousRQ_Secondary*;

var   *RxList*; {*A list of the Identifiers of the last n correctly received I-frames*}

begin   {*Start of main body*}
              Create ACK-frame with Identifier = Identifier from received I-frame;
              Output ACK-frame to line;
              Add Identifier from received frame to RxList;
              Pass frame on for further processing;

end.

(c)

Fig. 3.8 Continuous RQ protocol – Secondary: (a) state transition diagram;
(b) state transition table; (c) program segment

The effect of the above on the general protocol description presented earlier in Fig. 3.7 is that the ProcessAcknowledgment procedure must be expanded to determine if there are any frames awaiting acknowledgment ahead of the acknowledged frame and, if there are, to initiate their retransmission. The appropriate additions are thus as shown in part (b) of Fig. 3.9.

The above example assumed that an I-frame was corrupted and that the acknowledgment frames were received correctly. Clearly it is possible for the I-frames to be received correctly by S but the subsequent ACK-frame(s) to be corrupted. An example illustrating the effect of this on the frame transmission sequence is shown in part (a) of Fig. 3.10. The following points should be noted:

1. S receives each transmitted I-frame correctly;

2. assume ACK-frame N is corrupted;

3. on receipt of ACK-frame $N + 1$, P detects there is an outstanding I-frame in the Retransmision List (N) and hence retransmits it;

4. in the example, on receipt of the retransmitted frame (N), S searches the Receive List and determines N has already been correctly received and is therefore a duplicate;

5. S discards the frame but returns an acknowledgment to P to ensure N is removed from the Retransmission List.

The effect of the above on the protocol description presented earlier in Fig. 3.8 is that the Secondary, on receipt of each I-frame, must search the Receive List to determine if the frame is a valid new frame or a duplicate. The necessary addition is readily achieved and is shown in part (b) of Fig. 3.10.

It is apparent from the first example that although S receives a correct copy of each frame sent by P, the order of reception is not maintained – for example, S receives I-frames $N + 2$, $N + 3$ and $N + 4$ before frame $N + 1$.

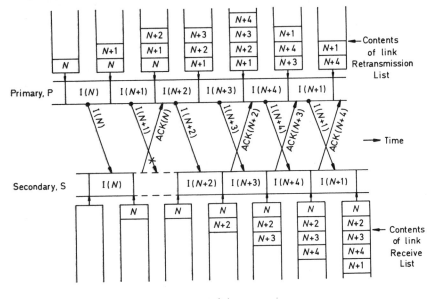

(a)

procedure *ProcessAcknowledgment; {Initiates retransmission of unacknowledged Frames}*

begin   **repeat** *Read Identifier from the frame at the head of the RetxList;*
                 if *Identifier = Identifier in ACK-frame*
                 then *Remove frame from RetxList*
                 else begin *Retransmit the frame;*
                            Start timer for the frame;
                            Insert frame pointer at tail of RetxList;
                 end;
          until *Identifier = Identifier in ACK-frame;*

end;

(b)

Fig. 3.9 Selective retransmission I: (a) corrupted I-frame [*Note:* $\times\!\!\to$ indicates frame corrupted during transmission]; (b) protocol modification I

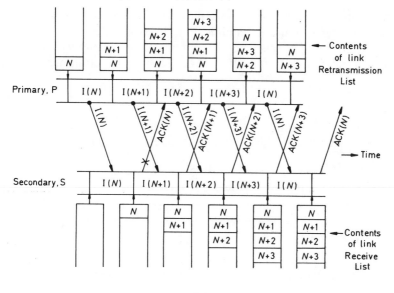

(a)

program   *ContinuousRQ__Secondary*;

var   *RxList; {A list of Identifiers of the last n correctly received I-frames}*

begin   *{Start of main body}*
        Create ACK-frame with Identifier = Identifier from received I-frame;
        Output ACK-frame to line;
        if *Identifier from received frame is in the RxList* **then** *Discard the frame;*
            else begin *Add Identifier from received frame to RxList;*
                        Pass frame on for further processing;
                end;

end.

(b)

Fig. 3.10 Selective retransmission II: (a) corrupted ACK-frame [*Note:* ✗⟶ indicates frame corrupted during transmission]; (b) protocol modification II

This approach, therefore, is primarily used when the frames being transmitted are self-contained entities with no correlation to other frames and hence the order of reception is not important. As will be seen in later chapters, however, this is not always the case since large messages are often broken into smaller frame segments for transmission through a communications network. The frames relating to each message must therefore be reassembled in the correct sequence prior to delivery of the complete message to the destination DTE. In order to achieve this with a selective retransmission control scheme, it is necessary for S to buffer any frames it receives out of sequence until the missing frame(s) is received. Since this may have to be performed for a number of messages simultaneously, the number of frame buffers required can become large and is of course non-deterministic. For this type of communication requirement, therefore, it is more usual to adopt the alternative Go-Back-N retransmission control scheme.

Go-Back-N

An example illustrating a typical frame sequence using a Go-Back-N scheme is shown in part (a) of Fig. 3.11. The following should be noted:

1. assume I-frame $N + 1$ is corrupted;
2. S receives I-frame $N + 2$ out of sequence;
3. on receipt of I-frame $N + 2$, S returns a negative acknowledgment (NACK) for this frame indicating the identity of the last correctly received I-frame (N in the example);
4. S discards I-frame $N + 2$ and all other I-frames received ($N + 3$ and $N + 4$ in the example) until the next in-sequence I-frame is received ($N + 1$ in the example);
5. on receipt of I-frame N + 1, S continues as before.

The effect of the above on the general protocol descriptions presented earlier in Figs. 3.7 and 3.8 are firstly, the *ProcessAcknowledgment* procedure

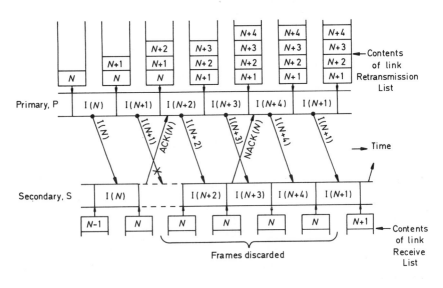

(a)

(continued)

procedure *ProcessAcknowledgment*; *{Allows for both ACK and NACK frames}*

begin   *FrameType:= Type of acknowledgment frame received*;

  case *FrameType* **of**
    ACK: *{As Figure 3.7}*
    NACK: **repeat** *Read Identifier from frame at head of RetxList*;
          if *Identifier > Identifier in NACK frame*
            then begin *Retransmit the frame*;
                    Start timer for frame; **end**;
        until *All entries in RetxList have been processed*;
    end; *{Case}*

end;

program *ContinuousRQ__Secondary*; *{Creates either an ACK or a NACK frame}*

var   *RxList*; *{Holds Identifier of last in-sequence I-frame accepted}*

begin   *Read Identifier from received frame*;

  if *Identifier = Identifier in the RxList + 1*
    then begin *Create ACK-frame with Identifier = Identifier from RxList*;
            Output ACK-frame to line;
            Put Identifier into link RxList;
            Pass frame on for further processing; **end**;
      else begin *Create NACK-frame with Identifier = Identifier from*
            RxList;
            Output NACK-frame to line;
            Discard received frame; **end**;

end.

(b)

Fig. 3.11 Go-Back-*N* I: (a) corrupted I-frame; (b) modification to Primary;
(c) modification to Secondary

in the Primary must be expanded to allow for the received acknowledgment frame being either a positive acknowledgment (ACK) or negative acknowledgment (NACK) and secondly, the Secondary must be modified to allow a NACK-frame to be generated whenever an out-of-sequence I-frame is received. The two modifications are as shown in parts (b) and (c) of Fig. 3.11.

Again, in the above example it was assumed that an I-frame was corrupted and that the acknowledgment frames were received correctly. An example illustrating the effect of a corrupted acknowledgment on the frame transmission sequence is shown in part (a) of Fig. 3.12. The following points should be noted:

1. S receives each transmitted I-frame correctly;
2. assume ACK-frames N and $N + 1$ are both corrupted;
3. on receipt of ACK-frame $N + 2$, P detects there are two outstanding I-frames in the Retransmision List – N and $N + 1$;

4. since it is an ACK rather than a NACK frame, P implies that the two ACK frames for I-frames N and $N + 1$ have both been corrupted and hence accepts ACK $(N + 2)$ as an acknowledgment for the two outstanding frames also.

It can be deduced from this that the procedure *ProcessAcknowledgment* in the general protocol description defined earlier in Fig. 3.7 must be modified to allow a number of I-frames to be acknowledged by a single ACK-frame. The necessary change is given in part (b) of Fig. 3.12.

It can be deduced from this example that with a Go-Back-N strategy, the correct frame sequence is maintained, thus minimising the amount of buffer storage required for its implementation. But, since some already correctly received frames must be retransmitted, it is less efficient in its use of the available transmission capacity than a Selective Retransmission scheme.

3.2.3 Sequence numbers I

The three retransmission schemes just described all assume that each I-frame transmitted can be both uniquely identified and also its correct sequence relative to other I-frames deduced. Also, that ACK and NACK (where appropriate) frames carry similar identification information. In the examples illustrated, this was accomplished by the use of arbitrary identifiers N, $N + 1$, $N + 2$, etc. In practice these are known as *sequence numbers* since, as the examples illustrate, their main function is to allow the Primary and Secondary to deduce from the identifier the position or sequence of a frame relative to other frames.

To implement the control functions to be performed at each side of a link, in addition to the sequence numbers contained within each frame, it is necessary for both the Primary and Secondary sides of a link to retain a record of the identifiers of the previously correctly received frames on the link. Thus the Primary maintains a *Send State Variable*, $V(S)$, which indicates the sequence number it will assign to the next I-frame to be transmitted, and the Secondary maintains a *Receive State Variable*, $V(R)$, which indicates the next in-sequence I-frame it expects to receive. Their use is as follows:

1. each I-frame transmitted by P is assigned a *Send Sequence Number*, $N(S)$, which is equal to its current $V(S)$;
2. each I-frame received by S with an $N(S)$ equal to its current $V(R)$ is accepted by S which then increments its $V(R)$ by 1;
3. when S returns an ACK or NACK frame it contains a *Receive Sequence Number*, $N(R)$, which is equal to its current $V(R)$;
4. since $V(R)$ is incremented at S prior to the ACK or NACK being transmitted, on receipt of an ACK or NACK by P, the $N(R)$ contained within it acknowledges those I-frames in the Retransmission List up to and including $N(R) - 1$.

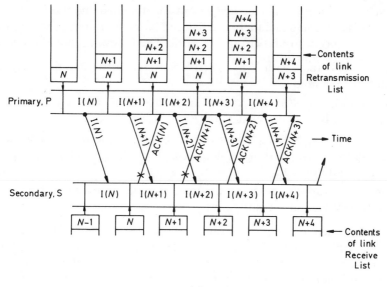

(a)

procedure *ProcessAcknowledgment*; {*Allows a single ACK frame to acknowledge multiple frames*}

begin   *FrameType*:= *Type of acknowledgment frame received*;
             case *FrameType* **of**
                 ACK: **repeat** *Read Identifier from the frame at the head of the RetxList*;
                               Remove frame from RetxList
                         until   *Identifier = Identifier in ACK-frame*;
                 NACK: **repeat** *Read Identifier from frame at head of RetxList*;
                               if *Identifier > Identifier in NACK-frame*
                               then begin *Retransmit the frame*;
                                             Start timer for the frame; **end**;
                         until   *All entries in RetxList have been processed*;
             end; {*Case*}

end;

(b)

Fig. 3.12 Go-Back-*N* II: (a) corrupted ACK-frame; (b) modification to Primary

To illustrate the implementation of the above in a diagrammatic form, consider the frame sequence shown in part (a) of Fig. 3.13. It is based on a Go-Back-*N* control strategy. The following additional points should be noted:

1. the two state variables $V(S)$ and $V(R)$ are initialised to zero prior to the transmission of any frames on the link;

2. no transmission errors are assumed to have occurred.

Now consider the same example but this time assume the I-frame with $N(S) = 1$ is corrupted and therefore ignored (discarded) by S. The new frame sequence is shown in part (b) of Fig. 3.13. The following should be noted:

1. since the I-frame with $N(S) = 1$ $(I[N(S)=1])$ is corrupted, the $V(R)$ at S is not incremented;

2. on receipt of $I[N(S)=2]$, $N(S)$ is not equal to $V(R)$ and hence the frame is discarded by S and a NACK $[N(R)=1]$ is returned to P;

3. on receipt of NACK$[N(R)=1]$, the two outstanding unacknowledged I-frames in the Retransmission List (I $[N(S)=1]$ and $I[N(S)=2]$) are retransmitted by P;

4. in the example each is assumed to be received correctly and acknowledged in the normal way.

It can be deduced from the example illustrated in Fig. 3.13 that the loss of the frame $I[N(S)=1]$ was detected only after the next (out-of-sequence) frame $I[N(S)=2]$ was correctly received by S. Clearly, this necessitates other frames waiting and therefore being transmitted on the link since, if P did not have another frame awaiting transmission, S would not know that frame $I[N(S)=1]$ was corrupted until another I-frame became ready and was successfully transmitted to S.

To allow for this possibility, as has been indicated, P normally employs an additional timeout mechanism similar to the one outlined earlier with the Idle RQ control scheme. A number of alternative timeout schemes are possible but the one selected in the earlier protocol definitions assumes a separate timer is started each time an I-frame is transmitted by P and this is stopped (reset) when an acknowledgment indicating its correct receipt is received. Then, if an acknowledgment for a frame is not received before the timeout interval expires, the frame is retransmitted. This is shown diagrammatically in Fig. 3.14.

Clearly, the timeout interval selected must be greater than the worst-case propagation delay between transmitting a frame and receiving the associated acknowledgment. Also, with a timeout mechanism, as was indicated earlier, it is possible for S to receive duplicate copies of a frame: the frame may be successfully received by S but the resulting acknowledgment frame corrupted on its return to P; in the absence of an acknowledgment, P would assume the initial frame had been corrupted and hence erroneously retransmit another copy. With a Go-Back-N control scheme, this does not create a problem since the $N(S)$ in the duplicate frame(s) will not be equal to the current $V(R)$ held by S and hence it will be discarded automatically. With a Selective Retransmission scheme, however, as was indicated earlier, to allow for the possibility of one or more duplicate frames being sent by P, it is necessary for S to retain an ordered list – the Receive List – containing the sequence numbers of the last N correctly received I-frames so that it may check if a received frame is a duplicate of an already correctly received (and therefore acknowledged) frame or a new frame. The number of frames to be retained,

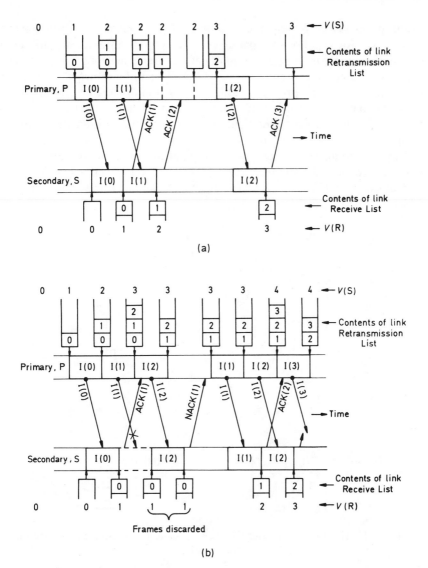

Fig. 3.13 Sequence numbers: (a) normal operation; (b) corrupted I-frame

N, is influenced by the flow control algorithm being employed and this is considered in more detail in the next section.

For clarity, all of the above examples assumed that information frames flowed in one direction only and that the return path was used simply for acknowledgment purposes. Normally, however, most communication links carry information frames in both directions. To accommodate this, therefore, each side of such links contains both a Primary and a Secondary: the first controlling the sequence of I-frames being transmitted and the second controlling the sequence of I-frames being received. Thus each side of the link contains both a Send Sequence Variable – $V(S)$ – which is controlled by the

Primary and a Receive Sequence Variable – $V(R)$ – which is controlled by the Secondary. Also, although separate ACK and NACK frames are utilised as above, since there is also the possibility of an I-frame awaiting transmission in the reverse direction when an ACK or NACK is to be returned, to improve link efficiency some protocols utilise the I-frames flowing in the return direction to carry acknowledgment information relating to the transmission of I-frames in the forward direction. Each I-frame transmitted then contains both an $N(S)$ indicating the send sequence number as was described previously and also an $N(R)$ containing acknowledgment information for the reverse direction. This is then referred to as a *piggy-back acknowledgment* and an example of a protocol which uses this technique is the HDLC protocol which will be described in Chapter 5.

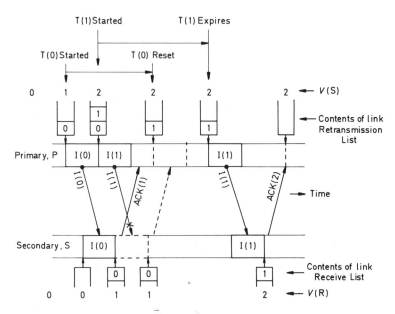

Fig. 3.14 Timeout mechanism [*Note:* ✗⟶ indicates frame corrupted during transmission]

3.3 FLOW CONTROL

As was indicated earlier, error control is only one component of a communication protocol. Another important and related component is *flow control*. This, as the name implies, is concerned with controlling the rate of transmission of elements – characters or frames – on a link so that the receiver always has sufficient buffer storage resources to accept each element sent to it prior to processing. With a character oriented terminal-to-computer link for example, if the remote computer is servicing many terminals it may become temporarily overloaded and hence be unable to process all characters sent to it at the available transmission rates. Similarly, with a frame oriented Selective Retransmission scheme, the receiver may run out of buffer storage capacity if it is endeavouring to buffer an indeterminate number of frames. Two of the more common flow control schemes will now be considered.

3.3.1 X-ON/X-OFF

It may be deduced from the earlier discussion concerning the communication between a terminal and a remote computer over an asynchronous link that echo checking is in many ways self regulating since, if the remote computer runs out of buffer storage, it will cease echoing characters back to the user screen and hence the user will automatically stop keying further characters on the keyboard. Normally, however, the lack of echoed characters from the computer is due to the computer becoming temporarily overloaded and hence, if the user does not cease transmitting new characters, the computer incurs further and unnecessary processing overheads simply reading each character and then discarding it.

It is for this reason that an additional automatic flow control facility is often invoked to ensure that if the computer becomes overloaded, the terminal does not send any further characters until the overload condition is cleared. This is achieved by the computer, when it becomes overloaded, returning a special control character, X-OFF, to the controlling device within the terminal instructing it to cease transmission. On receipt of the X-OFF character, the terminal then ignores any further characters entered at the keyboard and hence the computer does not incur any unnecessary processing overheads associated with them. Then, when the overload condition decays and the computer becomes able to accept further characters, it returns a companion control character, X-ON, to indicate to the terminal control device that it may restart sending characters.

3.3.2 Window mechanisms

With a frame oriented link, it may be remembered that an Idle RQ error control scheme, although inefficient in its use of transmission bandwidth, requires a minimum of buffer storage capacity for its implementation since, after a frame is transmitted by P, it must wait until an acknowledgment is returned by S before transmitting the next frame. The flow of I-frames across the link is therefore automatically tightly controlled.

With a Continuous RQ error control scheme, however, P may send I-frames continuously before receiving any acknowledgments and hence, with this type of scheme, it is clearly possible for the destination to run out of available buffer storage if, for example, it is unable to pass on the frames at the rate they are being received. In order to allow for this possibility, therefore, it is usual to introduce an additional regulating action into such schemes. The approach has many similarities to the one inherent in the Idle RQ control scheme since it essentially sets a limit on the number of I-frames P may send before receiving an acknowledgment signalling correct receipt of a previously transmitted frame. This is accomplished by P monitoring the number of outstanding (unacknowledged) I-frames currently held in the

Retransmission List. Then, if the destination side of a link becomes unable to pass on the frames sent to it, S will stop returning acknowledgment frames, the Retransmission List at P will build up and this in turn can be interpreted as a signal for P to stop transmitting further frames until acknowledgments start to flow again.

To implement this scheme a maximum limit is set on the number of I-frames that can be outstanding in the Retransmission List. This is referred to as the *Send Window* for the link. Clearly, if this is set to unity the transmission control scheme reverts to Idle RQ with the consequential drop in transmission efficiency. The limit is normally selected, therefore, so that providing the destination is able to pass on or absorb all frames it receives, the Send Window does not impair the flow of I-frames across the link. Such factors as the maximum frame size, the amount of buffer storage available, and the transmission bit rate must all be considered when selecting the Send Window to be used.

Before describing the additional steps in pseudo program code, it is perhaps helpful to first consider how the higher-level (user) software normally communicates with the communications protocol software. Until now it has been assumed that whenever the higher-level software has an I-frame ready to send, the Primary is run. Similarly, whenever the Secondary receives a valid in-sequence I-frame, this is simply passed on to the higher-level software for further processing.

In practice, the interface between the higher-level software and the communications protocol software normally takes the form of two first-in, first-out (FIFO) queues similar to those used for the Retransmission List. This is shown in schematic form in part (a) of Fig. 3.15. Again only a unidirectional flow of I-frames is considered for clarity.

Thus, whenever the higher-level software wishes to send a frame, it simply inserts the address pointer to where the frame contents are stored in memory into the Primary Input Queue. This, in turn, is interpreted as an event – frame ready to send – and the main body of the Primary is therefore run. Similarly, whenever a received frame is to be passed to the higher-level software by the Secondary, the latter inserts the frame address pointer at the tail of the Output Queue which, in turn, causes the higher-level software to be run.

The necessary additions to the pseudo program code for the Primary are thus as shown in part (b) of Fig. 3.15. Whenever a new frame pointer is placed in the Input Queue of the Primary, before initiating the transmission of the frame, the program first determines if the current number of frame pointers in the Retransmission List awaiting acknowledgment – RetxCount – is less than the Send Window for the link. If it is, the frame is transmitted and the frame pointer transferred to the Retransmission List; if it is not, the frame is not transmitted and the pointer is left in the Input Queue. Then, whenever an ACK-frame is received, in addition to the normal acknowledgment processing, a check is made to determine if there are any frames awaiting transmission in the link Input Queue. If there are, one of the queued frames is sent for each frame pointer that is removed from the Retransmission List.

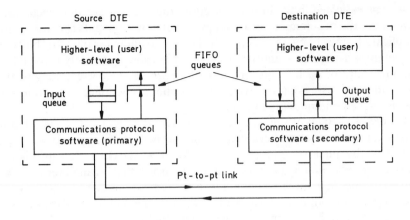

Source DTE

Destination DTE

(a)

.
.
.

procedure *TransmitFrame*; {*Transmits a frame only if Send Window still open*}

    begin if *RetxCount* < *SendWindow* **then**
           begin *Transmit frame at head of InputQueue*; *Start timer*;
           Transfer frame pointer to RetxList;
           Increment RetxCount; **end**;

    end;

procedure *ProcessAcknowledgment*; {*Transmits any frame(s) held up by Send Window*}
    begin *Remove acknowledged frame from RetxList*;
    Reset timer for frame;
    Decrement RetxCount;
    if *InputQueue non-empty* **then**
           begin *Transmit frame from top of InputQueue*;
           Start timer;
           Transfer frame pointer to RetxList;
           Increment RetxCount; **end**;

    end;

.
.
.

(b)

Fig. 3.15 Implementation of send window: (a) communications software interface; (b) modifications to pseudo code

As was indicated in the previous section, the use of a timeout mechanism to overcome the problem of lost (corrupted) acknowledgments can also result in duplicate frames being received by S. Hence, to allow for this possibility, S must retain a list of the identifiers of the last N frames correctly received so that, on receipt of each frame, it can deduce whether a correct copy of the frame had previously been received. The number of identifiers, n, is referred to as the *Receive Window* for the link.

With a Go-Back-N control scheme, n need only be 1 since, if any out-of-sequence frames are received, S will simply discard them and wait until it receives the next in-sequence frame. With a Selective Retransmission scheme, however, n must be large enough to ensure that S can determine if a received frame had already been received some time before. It may be deduced that the adoption of a maximum limit on the number of I-frames that P may send before receiving any acknowledgments – the Send Window – means that the number of identifiers to be retained by S need only be the same. Thus with Selective Retransmision, it is normal to operate the link with equal Send and Receive Windows so that in the worst case, S can always determine if a received frame is a valid retransmitted frame or a duplicate.

3.3.3 Sequence numbers II

Until now it has been assumed that the sequence number inserted into each frame by P is simply the previous sequence number plus one and that the range of numbers available is infinite. Another effect of defining a maximum limit to the number of I-frames that may be in the process of being transferred across a link, however, is that it then becomes possible to limit the range of sequence numbers required to identify uniquely each frame. The number of identifiers required is a function of both the type of retransmission control scheme being used and the size of the Send and Receive Windows.

For example, with an Idle RQ control scheme, the Send and Receive Windows are both one and hence only two identifiers are required to allow S to determine whether a particular I-frame received is a new frame or a duplicate copy of the last frame correctly received. Typically, the two identifiers would be 0 and 1 – thus requiring just a single binary digit for its implementation – and the Send and Receive Variables would then be incremented modulo 2 by P and S respectively.

With a Go-Back-N control scheme and a Send Window of, say, K, the number of identifiers must be at least $K + 1$. This can best be seen by considering the example shown in Fig. 3.16. The following should be noted:

1. the Send Window used in the example is 3;
2. P sends its full window of 3 I-frames;
3. the 3 I-frames are correctly received by S;
4. the 3 ACK-frames returned by S are all corrupted;
5. P times out each I-frame and retransmits them;

6. S discards each duplicate I-frame and acknowledges all of them with a single ACK frame.

Now, if only 3 identifiers were being used – the same as the Send Window – S would not be able to determine whether I-frame I[0] was a new frame or a duplicate since 0 would then be the next in-sequence identifier. Hence with 4 identifiers (the Send Window + 1) S would know that the next in-sequence I-frame would have an identifier of 3 whereas the retransmitted (duplicate) frame would have an identifier of 0. It would therefore correctly discard the latter.

With a Selective Retransmission scheme and a Send and Receive Window of K, the number of identifiers must not be less than $2K$. Again this can be deduced by considering the case when P sends a full window of K frames and all the subsequent acknowledgments are corrupted. S must be able to determine if any of the next K frames are new frames – that is, all the acknowledgments returned were correctly received – or retransmissions of the previous batch of correctly received frames – all acknowledgments were corrupted. The only way of ensuring S can deduce this is to assign a completely new set of K identifiers to the next window of I-frames transmitted thus necessitating at least $2K$ identifiers for correct operation.

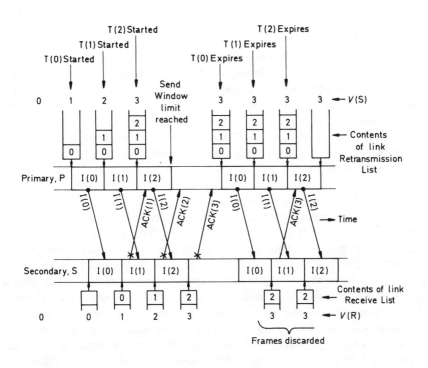

Fig. 3.16 Window mechanism [*Note*: ✗→ indicates frame corrupted during transmission]

In practice, since the identifier of a frame is in binary form, a set number of binary digits must be reserved for its use. For example, with a Send Window of, say, 7 and a Go-Back-*N* control scheme, 3 binary digits would be required for the Send and Receive Sequence Numbers yielding 8 possible identifiers: 0 through 7. The Send and Receive Variables would then be incremented modulo 8 by P and S respectively.

3.4 LINK MANAGEMENT

Error and flow control are both concerned with the correct transfer of characters or frames across an imperfect communication link and, for the schemes outlined to function correctly, it has been assumed that both communicating parties have been primed so that they are ready to exchange information. With a frame oriented link, for example, it is necessary to ensure that both sides of a link start with the same Send and Receive Variables before any information frames are transmitted. In general, this is known as the initialisation or *link setup phase* and, after all data have been exchanged across a link, this is normally followed by the *link disconnection phase*. Since the link setup and disconnection phases are not concerned with the actual transfer of user data, they are collectively referred to as *link management* and some aspects of this are now described.

For a link between a terminal and a computer, providing the separation of the two devices is relatively short (up to, say, 20 m, for example), the management functions can be achieved by means of exchanging signals on additional control lines. This is often known as a *handshake procedure*: when the user wishes to open a dialogue with the computer, he first switches the terminal on and this results in one of the control lines becoming set (active) thus indicating to the computer that the terminal is ready to send characters. The terminal must then wait until the computer responds by setting a corresponding response control line to indicate that it is ready to receive characters. The exchange of characters as outlined previously can then commence. There are in fact internationally agreed standards laid down for this type of interconnection and these will be discussed in the next chapter.

When the two communicating devices are, say, computers and a frame oriented link is being used, the link is established (set up) by the link-level protocol within each computer exchanging an agreed set of *control* or *supervisory frames*. In the previous example, the link was established as a result of the user switching on the terminal. In the case of a computer-to-computer link, however, the setting up of the link is normally initiated as a result of some higher-level software in one of the computers – an application program for example – signalling to the communications software that it wishes to open a dialogue with a remote computer. Typically this might take the form of a Send or Transfer Request primitive being executed in the application program which, in turn, causes the communications software to be invoked. In practice, as will be seen in later chapters, the communications software is normally made up of a number of separate protocol layers each responsible for a specific function in the overall communications strategy but, as an example, a typical set of messages used by a higher (user) software layer together with their interpretation by the lower communications (link-level protocol) software are shown in Fig. 3.17.

In the example, the initial primitive issued by the user software is assumed to be a Connect Request which results firstly in a Connect Request message being passed to the communications software and, in turn, a (link) SETUP frame being sent to the communications software in the destination DTE. On receipt of this, the latter passes a Connect Indication message to the user software in the destination DTE. Then, assuming the latter is ready to accept a message, it issues a Connect Response primitive. This results in an ACK-frame being returned to the source DTE and, in turn, a Connect Confirmation message being passed to the user software. A logical communications path between the two user software layers has now been established and the various variables associated with the underlying link-level protocol initialised.

The data associated with the message are then transferred by the communications software within one or more I-frames, as has been described earlier, using one of the selected link-level protocols. Finally, after all data have been transferred – a unidirectional flow is assumed for clarity – the

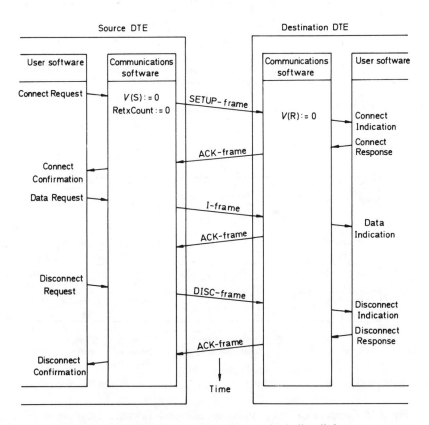

Fig. 3.17 Time (frame) sequence diagram including link set up

logical communications path between the two user software layers is disconnected following a similar procedure as has been outlined for the setup phase.

The addition of a link setup and disconnection phase into the state transition diagrams and tables introduced earlier is readily achieved and the updated versions for the Primary are shown in Fig. 3.18. A Continuous RQ protocol is assumed although the link management section is in many ways independent of the type of protocol being used to control the flow of I-frames. For clarity, only those entries in the state transition table which result in an action taking place are shown. Typically, all the other entries would correspond to no action taking place and the protocol entity remaining in the same state.

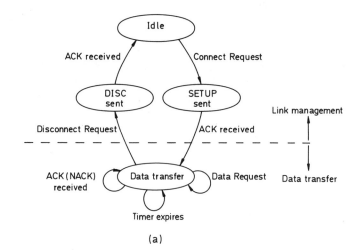

(a)

Event Present state	Connect Request	Data Request	Disconnect Request	ACK received	Timer expires	
Idle	Setup	— — —	— — —	— — —	— — —	Action
(0)	1					New state
Setup sent	— — —	— — —	— — —	ProcAck	Retx Frame	Action
(1)				2	1	New state
Data transfer	— — —	TxFrame	Disc	ProcAck	Retx Frame	Action
(2)		2	3	2	2	New state
Disc sent	— — —	— — —	— — —	ProcAck	RetxFrame	Action
(3)				0	3	New state

Messages from   Frames   Internal
user interface   received   event
                  from link

(b)

Fig. 3.18 Communications protocol specification: (a) state transition diagram; (b) state transition table

As has been shown earlier, it is also possible to derive from the state transition table definition a specification for the protocol written in a high-level programming language. Since in this instance the user software, in addition to originating requests (Connect, Data, Disconnect), must also receive the corresponding responses (Connect and Disconnect Confirmation) from the communications software, two queues would be used: an Input Queue for the requests and an Output Queue for the responses. Typically, the user request would be written into a message buffer in memory by the user software and the address pointer of the buffer inserted into the Input Queue. Then, when the communications software is invoked, the type of request would first be decoded before consulting the array containing the event state table definitions to determine the necessary action and new state. Similarly, whenever a response is to be passed from the communications software to the user software, the address pointer of the memory buffer containing the response message is inserted into the Output Queue. An outline structure of the pseudo-code definition of the Primary is given in Fig. 3.19. In practice, since in many instances I-frames flow in both directions simultaneously, on receipt of a frame from the communications link the software must first determine the type of frame before consulting the event state table array.

It can be concluded from these descriptions that the user and communications software in each computer is organised into layers and that each layer operates independently. Thus in the example, the higher software layers communicate by exchanging messages using the resources provided by the lower communications layer. The types of frames and messages used by each layer vary since they each perform a different and complementary function. The function and operation of the various protocol layers normally used for computer communication will be described in subsequent chapters of the book.

program   *ContinuousRQ__Primary*; {*Modifications to incorporate link management*}

type   *Events = (ConnectRequest, DataRequest, DisconnectRequest,*
   ACKReceived, Timeout);
   States = (Idle, SetupSent, DataTransfer, DiscSent);
   Actions = (NA, Setup, Disc, TxFrame, ProcAck, RetxFrame);
   IncomingMessage = (Connect, Data, Disconnect); {List of user
   messages}

var
   {*As Figure 3.4*}
   .
   .
   .
   {*List of Action procedures*}
   .
   .
   .

(continued)

```
begin        {Start of main body}
             case IncomingMessage of
                     Connect:    EventType:= ConnectRequest;
                     Data:       EventType:= DataRequest;
                     Disconnect: EventType:= DisconnectRequest;
             end; {Case}
             with EventStateTable [PresentState, EventType] do
                 begin case Action of {List of action procedure calls}
                     NA :
                     Setup :
                     TxFrame :
                     Disc :
                     ProcAck :
                     RetxFrame :
                         end; {Case}
                         PresentState:= NewState;
                 end;

end.
```

Fig. 3.19 Protocol specification in pseudo code form

Problems

3.1 Assume a terminal is connected to a computer. Explain the two techniques which are used to achieve error control and flow control. Clearly outline the effect of each mechanism on the user of the terminal.

3.2 a) With the aid of frame sequence diagrams, describe the difference between an Idle RQ and a Continuous RQ error control procedure. For clarity, assume no frames are corrupted during transmission.

   b) Using a Continuous RQ error control scheme as an example, describe how the operation of the Primary and Secondary side of a link may be defined in the form of a finite state machine and:

   i) a state transition diagram;
   ii) a state transition table;
   iii) a high-level language program segment written in pseudo-code.

3.3 a) With the aid of frame sequence diagrams and assuming an Idle RQ error control procedure, describe the following:

   i) the factors influencing the minimum time delay between the transmission of two consecutive information frames;
   ii) how the loss of a corrupted information frame is overcome;
   iii) how the loss of a corrupted acknowledgment frame is overcome.

   b) Use the frame sequence diagrams of part (a) to define the operation of the Primary and Secondary sides of a link which is operating with an Idle RQ error control scheme using:

   i) a state transition diagram;
   ii) a state transition table;
   iii) a program segment written in a pseudo high-level language.

3.4 a) With the aid of frame sequence diagrams and assuming a Selective Retransmission error control scheme, describe how the following are overcome:

   i) a corrupted information frame;
   ii) a corrupted acknowledgment frame.

b) Use the frame sequence diagrams of part (a) to define the operation of the Primary and Secondary sides of a link, which is operating with a Continuous RQ and Selective Retransmission error control scheme, using:

   i) a state transition diagram;
   ii) a state transition table;
   iii) a program segment written in pseudo high-level code.

Deduce the factors which influence the maximum size of the link Receive List with a Selective Retransmission strategy.

3.5 With the aid of frame sequence diagrams and assuming a Go-Back-N error control scheme, describe how the following are overcome:

   i) a corrupted information frame;
   ii) a corrupted acknowledgment frame;
   iii) a corrupted NACK frame.

Include in your diagrams the contents of the link Retransmission and Receive Lists and also the state of the Send and Receive Sequence Variables as each frame is transmitted and received.

3.6 What is the function of a timeout mechanism? Use frame sequence diagrams to illustrate how a timeout may be used to overcome the effect of a corrupted information frame assuming:

   i) a Selective Retransmission control scheme,
   ii) a Go-Back-N control scheme.

Deduce the factors which determine the duration of the timeout interval to be used for a link.

How are duplicates handled with each scheme?

3.7 a) Discriminate between the Send Window and Receive Window for a link and how they are related with;

   i) a Selective Retransmission scheme;
   ii) a Go-Back-N control scheme.

b) With the aid of frame sequence diagrams, illustrate the effect of a Send Window flow control limit being reached. Assume a Send Window of 2 and a Go-Back-N error control procedure.

3.8 Assuming a Send Window of K, deduce the minimum range of sequence numbers (frame identifiers) required with each of the following error control schemes:

    i) Idle RQ;
    ii) Selective Retransmission;
    iii) Go-Back-N.

Clearly identify the condition when the maximum number of identifiers is in use.

3.9 a) Explain what is meant by the term link management. Use an example set of user primitives and a time sequence diagram to show how a logical communications path is established (set up) between two systems and subsequently cleared (disconnected).

    b) Assuming the user primitives used in part (a) and an Idle RQ error and flow control mechanism, derive

        i) a state transition diagram,
        ii) a state transition table,

    for the protocol.

    Outline how the protocol could be defined in a pseudo high-level programming language form.

Chapter 4 **The Electrical Interface**

Objectives:
When you have completed studying the material in this chapter you should be able to:

- know the different types of physical transmission media which are used to transmit data from a source DTE to a destination DTE;

- appreciate the characteristics and limitations of each type of medium;

- explain the different forms of electrical signal that are used with some of the alternative transmission media;

- appreciate that standards have been defined for connecting a DTE to a PTT supplied data communications equipment (DCE) which include the type of transmission medium, the form of the electrical signals to be used, and additional control lines to regulate the flow of data across the interface;

- know and understand the function of a number of the additional control lines which are used with some of the more common standards and be aware that the same standards are often used for defining the interface between a computer and a peripheral equipment which operates in a serial mode;

- appreciate that when data are to be transmitted using the public switched telephone network a modem must be used;

- describe some of the alternative designs for the modulator and demodulator sections of a modem.

4.1 INTRODUCTION

In Chapter 2 the basic principles of data transmission were described together with a description of the various integrated circuits that are now available for interfacing data terminal equipments to transmission lines. Essentially, because of the serial mode of transmission of data on a line, these circuits are used to perform the necessary synchronisation and error detection functions at the receiver. In the discussions relating to the operation of these circuits, it was assumed that the bit patterns transmitted by the sending device were logically received by the destination device as similar bit patterns with occasional corruptions caused by transmission errors.

In order to transmit data over a transmission line, however, it is necessary to convert the binary digits which make up each character or frame into physical electrical signals. For example, a binary 1 may be transmitted by applying a voltage signal or level of amplitude $+V$ volts to the sending end of a line and a binary 0 by applying $-V$ volts. Then, providing the transmission line is perfect, the receiving device on receipt of $+V$ volts would interpret this as a binary 1 and on receipt of $-V$ volts as a binary 0. In practice, because of the imperfect nature of the physical transmission medium, the transmitted electrical signals can become *attenuated* (smaller) and *distorted* (misshaped) with the effect that in the limit the receiver is unable to discriminate between the binary 1 and 0 signals. Some of the different effects of attenuation and distortion are shown in Fig. 4.1. The degree of each effect is strongly influenced by such factors as the type of transmission medium, the bit rate of the data being transmitted, and the distance between the two communicating devices.

Because the effects caused by attenuation and distortion can be quantified for different types of transmission media and physical separations, there are now sets of well-defined, internationally agreed standards laid down for the electrical interface between pieces of equipment. These standards include not only a definition of the electrical signal levels to be used but also the use and meaning of any additional control signals and conventions that are used at the physical level. The two bodies that formulate standards for interconnecting equipments are the *Consultative Committee of the International Telegraph and Telephone* (*CCITT*) in Europe and the *Electrical*

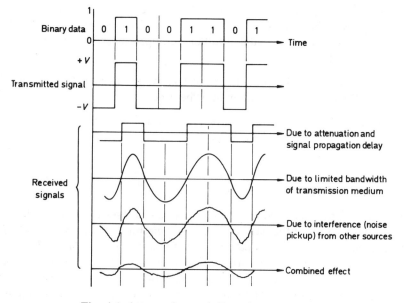

Fig. 4.1 Attenuation and distortion effects

Industries Association (EIA) in the United States. Although the standards defined by both bodies use slightly different terminology, the basic signals and their meaning are the same.

The chapter is divided into three sections: the first describes some of the alternative transmission media which are currently in widespread use, the second the different forms of electrical signal in use, and the third some of the additional aspects of a number of the more common physical level protocols.

4.2 TRANSMISSION MEDIA

The transmission of an electrical signal from a source to a destination point requires the use of a transmission medium generally called a *transmission line*. In most cases this takes the form of a pair of conductors or wires but in some instances transmission is achieved by the use of a beam of light passing through a piece of glass fibre or an electromagnetic wave being transmitted through free space. Some of the more common types of transmission media are now discussed.

4.2.1 Two-wire open lines

A two-wire open line – that is, although each wire is insulated from the other they are both open to free space – is the simplest type of transmission medium. It is perfectly adequate for connecting two equipments with short physical separation between them (less than, say, 50 m) and for modest bit rates (less than, say, 19.2 kbps). The signal – typically a voltage or current level relative to some ground reference – is applied to one wire and the ground reference to the other.

Although this type of line may be used to connect two DTEs together directly, it is mainly used for connecting a DTE to a local piece of *data communications equipment (DCE)* – a modem, for example. As will be seen, such connections usually utilise multiple lines and the most common arrangement is to use a separate insulated wire for each signal and a single wire for the common ground reference. The complete set of wires is then either enclosed in a single protected cable – *multicore cable* – or moulded into the form of a *flat ribbon cable* as shown in part (a) of Fig. 4.2.

With this type of line care is needed to avoid cross coupling of electrical signals from one wire to another, adjacent wire in the same cable. This is known as *crosstalk* and is caused by *capacitive coupling* between the two wires. Also, the open structure of this type of line means that it is susceptible to the pick-up of spurious *noise signals* from other electrical signal sources caused by *electromagnetic radiation*. The main problem is that interference signals of this type may be picked up in just one wire – the signal wire for example – and not the ground wire. This means there can be an additional difference signal created between the two wires and hence, since the receiver normally operates using the difference signal between the two wires, this can give rise to erroneous interpretation of the combined (signal plus noise)

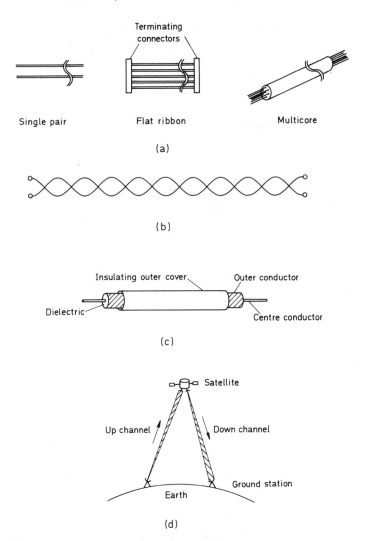

Fig. 4.2 Some alternative transmission media: (a) 2-wire open lines; (b) twisted-pair; (c) coaxial; (d) microwaves

received signal. These factors all contribute to the limited lengths of line and bit rates that can reliably be used.

4.2.2 Twisted-pair lines

Much better immunity to spurious noise signals – *noise immunity* – can be obtained by the use of a pair of wires which are twisted together. This is then known as a *twisted-pair* line. The resulting close proximity of both the signal and ground reference wires means that any interference caused by extraneous signal sources is picked up by both wires and hence its effect on the difference signal is reduced. Also, if multiple twisted pairs are enclosed within the same cable, then the twisting of each pair within the cable also reduces interference

effects caused by crosstalk. A schematic of a twisted-pair line is shown in part
(b) of Fig. 4.2.

Twisted-pair lines are suitable, with appropriate line driver and receiver
circuits which exploit the potential advantages gained by using such a
geometry, for bit rates up to in the order of 1 Mbps over short distances (less
than 100 m) and lower bit rates for longer distances. With some twisted-pair
cables an additional protective screen is used to reduce further the effects of
extraneous interference signals.

4.2.3 Coaxial cable

The main limiting factor of a twisted-pair line is caused by a phenomenon
known as *skin-effect*: as the bit rate (and hence frequency) of the transmitted
signal increases, the current flowing in the wires tends to flow only on the
outside surface of the wire, thus using less of the available cross section. This
has the effect of increasing the electrical resistance of the wires for higher
frequency signals which in turn causes more attenuation of the transmitted
signal. Also, at higher frequencies an increasing amount of signal power is
lost due to radiation effects. For those applications which demand a higher bit
rate than 1 Mbps it is normal to use other transmission media rather than
simple twisted-pair wires. One type of transmission line which minimises both
of the above effects is *coaxial cable*.

In a coaxial cable the signal and ground reference wires are implemented
in the form of a solid centre conductor running concentrically (coaxially)
inside a solid (or braided) outer circular conductor as shown in part (c) of Fig.
4.2. The space between the two conductors should ideally be filled with air
but in practice is normally filled with a dielectric insulating material with
either a solid or honeycomb structure.

Because of its geometry, the centre conductor is effectively shielded from
external interference signals and also only minimal losses occur due to
electromagnetic radiation and skin-effect. Coaxial cable can be used with a
number of different signal types, but typically 10 or even 20 Mbps over
several hundred metres is perfectly feasible. Also, as will be expanded upon
in Chapter 8, coaxial cable is applicable to both point-to-point and multipoint
topologies.

4.2.4 Optical fibre

Although the geometry of a coaxial cable significantly reduces the various
limiting effects mentioned previously, like twisted-pair lines, the maximum
signal frequency – and hence information rate – that can be transmitted using
coaxial cable, although very high, is also limited. Optical fibre cable,
however, carries the transmitted information in the form of a fluctuating
beam of light in a glass fibre rather than an electrical signal in a piece of wire.
It can be used, therefore, for transmitting very high bit rates – hundreds of
megabits per second. Also, the use of a light beam means that it is immune to
the effects caused by spurious electromagnetic interference signals and

crosstalk effects. Fibre optic cable is therefore also extremely useful for the transmission of lower bit rate signals through extremely noisy electrical environments – in steel plants, for example, which employ much high-voltage and current switching equipments. Also, since it is difficult to physically tap an optical fibre cable, they are being used increasingly in environments which demand a high level of security.

An optical fibre cable consists of just a single glass fibre, for each signal to be transmitted, contained within a protective cover which also shields the fibre from any external light sources. The light signal is first generated by a special optical transmitter unit which performs the conversion from normal electrical signals as used in the DTE. Similarly, at the other end of the line a special optical receiver module is used to perform the reverse function. Typically, the transmitter uses a *light emitting diode* (*LED*) to perform the conversion operation and the receiver a light sensitive *photo diode* or *photo transistor*. The majority of the light produced by the LED remains inside the fibre because it is coated with a reflective film and hence the attenuation effect is low. In general, optical fibre cable systems are more expensive than coaxial cable and hence they are only considered when either very high bit rates are required or enhanced levels of noise immunity are needed.

4.2.5 Microwaves

Although all the transmission media so far mentioned have used a physical line to carry the transmitted information, data can also be transmitted using electromagnetic (radio) waves through free space. One example is by means of *satellites*: a collimated *microwave beam* is transmitted to the satellite from the ground and this is then received and retransmitted (relayed) by the satellite to the predetermined destination(s). A typical satellite channel has an extremely high bandwidth and can provide many hundreds of high bit rate data links using a technique known as *multiplexing*. This will be described in more detail in the next chapter but essentially, the total available capacity of the channel is divided into a number of subchannels each of which can support a high bit rate link.

Satellites used for communication purposes are normally *geostationary*, which means the satellite is orbiting the earth once every 24 hours and hence from the ground appears stationary. The orbit of the satellite is chosen so that it provides a line-of-sight communications path to both the transmitting station(s) and the receiving station(s). The degree of the collimation of the microwave beam retransmitted by the satellite can be either coarse so that the signal may be picked up over a wide geographical area or it may be finely focussed so that it may only be picked up over a limited area. With the latter the signal power is higher and hence smaller diameter receivers – *antennas* or *dishes* – can be used. Satellites are in widespread use as a data transmission medium and the applications range from interconnecting different national computer communication networks to providing high bit rate interconnecting paths to link communications networks located in different parts of the same country. A schematic of a typical satellite system is shown in part (d) of Fig. 4.2.

Microwave links are also widely used to provide communication links when it is impractical or too expensive to use physical transmission media; for example, across a river or perhaps a busy motorway or street. Since with this type of application the collimated microwave beam travels through the earth's atmosphere, it can therefore be disturbed by such things as man-made structures and weather conditions. With a satellite link, of course, the beam travels most of its path through free space and hence it is less affected by these effects. Nevertheless, line-of-sight microwave communication through the earth's atmosphere can be used reliably over distances up to 50 km.

4.3 SIGNAL TYPES

When the two items of communicating equipment are situated relatively close to one another and only modest bit rates are being used, then all that is necessary to transmit the data are two-wire open lines and simple interface circuits to change the signal levels used within the equipment to a suitable level for use on the interconnecting cable. As the physical separation between the two items and the bit rate increases, however, more sophisticated circuits and techniques must be employed. Moreover, if the two items are situated in, say, different parts of the country (or world) and there are no public data communications facilities available, the only cost effective approach is to use lines provided by the various PTT authorities for telephone purposes. When using this type of communications medium, therefore, it is necessary to convert the electrical signals output by the source DTE into a form analogous to the signals used to convey spoken messages. Similarly, on receipt of these signals it is necessary to convert them back again into a form suitable for use by the destination DTE. The equipment used to perform these functions is known as a modem and some of the different signal types used by modems and also other forms of transmission lines are now discussed.

4.3.1 RS-232C/V.24

The RS-232C interface (defined by the EIA) and the V.24 interface (defined by the CCITT) were originally defined as a standard interface for connecting a DTE to a PTT supplied (or approved) modem to allow the manufacturers of different equipment to use the transmission facilities available in the switched telephone network. The physical separation between the DTE and the modem is therefore relatively short and, because of the characteristics of the switched telephone network, the maximum possible bit rate is relatively low (9600 bps). Since their original introduction, however, these standards have been adopted as the standard interface for connecting any character oriented peripheral (VDU, printer etc.) to a computer, thus allowing peripherals from a number of different manufacturers to be connected to the same computer.

Because of the very short distances (less than 1 m) between neighbouring subunits within a DTE, the signal levels used to represent the binary data are often quite small. For example, a common logic family used in digital equipment is *transistor transistor logic* or *TTL*. This uses a voltage signal of between 2.0 V and 5.0 V to represent a binary 1 and a voltage of between 0.2 V and 0.8 V to represent a binary 0. Voltages between these two levels can yield an indeterminate state and hence, in the worst case, if the voltage level is near one of the limits, the effect of even modest levels of signal attenuation or electrical interference can be very disruptive. The voltage levels used when connecting two separate pieces of equipment together, therefore, are normally greater than those used to connect subunits together within the equipments.

The signal levels defined for use with the RS-232C (V.24) interface together with the appropriate interface circuits are shown in Fig. 4.3. As can be seen, the voltage signals used on the lines are symmetric with respect to the signal ground reference and are at least 3 V: +3 V for a binary 0 and −3 V for a binary 1. In practice, the actual voltage levels used are determined by the supply voltages applied to the interface circuits and + and − 12 V or even + and − 15 V are not uncommon. The transmit circuits convert the low-level signal voltages used within the equipments to the higher voltage levels used on the transmission lines. Similarly, the receive circuits perform the reverse function. Also, the interface circuits – known as line drivers and line receivers respectively – perform the necessary voltage inversion functions.

The relatively large voltage levels used means the effect of signal attenuation and noise interference are much improved over normal, say, TTL logic levels. RS-232C (V.24) normally uses a flat ribbon cable or multicore cable with a single ground reference wire for connecting the pieces of equipment together and hence the effect of noise picked up in a signal wire can be troublesome. Also, to reduce the effect of crosstalk, it is not uncommon to connect a *capacitor* across the output of the transmitter circuit. This has the effect of rounding off the transition edges of the transmitted signals which in turn removes some of the troublesome higher-frequency

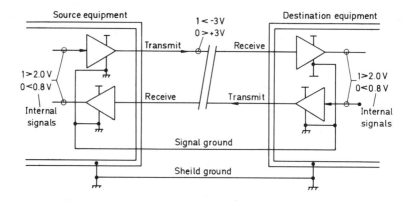

Fig. 4.3 RS-232C/V.24 signal levels

components in the signal. As the length of the lines or the bit rate of the signal increases, then the attenuation effect of the line reduces the received signal levels to the point that any external noise signals of even low amplitude produce erroneous operation. The RS-232C and V.24 standards specify maximum physical separations of less than 15 m and bit rates lower than 9.6 kbps although larger values than these are often used when connecting a peripheral to a computer.

4.3.2 20 mA current loop

An alternative type of electrical signal that is sometimes used instead of that defined by RS-232C is the 20 mA current loop. This, as the name implies, utilises a current signal rather than a voltage as defined in the RS-232C standard and, although not extending the available bit rate, substantially increases the potential physical separation of the two communicating devices. The basic approach is shown in Fig. 4.4.

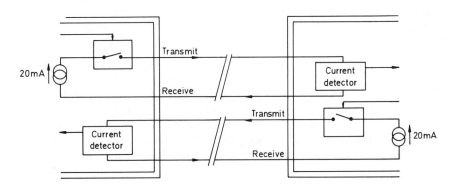

Fig. 4.4 20 mA current loop

Essentially, the state of a switch (relay or other similar device) is controlled by the bit stream to be transmitted: the switch is closed for a binary 1 – thus passing a current (pulse) of 20 mA – and opened for a binary 0 – thus stopping the current flow. At the receiver, the flow of the current is detected by a matching current sensitive circuit and the transmitted binary signal reproduced.

The noise immunity of a current loop interface is much better than a basic voltage driven interface since, as can be seen in the figure, it uses a pair of wires for each signal. This means any external noise signals are normally picked up in both wires – often referred to as *common-mode noise* or *pickup* – which have minimal effect on the basic current sensitive receiver circuit. This means 20 mA current loop interfaces are particularly suitable for driving long lines – up to 1 km – at modest bit rates; the latter due to the limited operational rate of the switches and current sensitive circuits. It is for this reason that some manufacturers very often provide two separate RS-232C output interfaces with a piece of equipment: one which produces voltage output signals and the other 20 mA current signals. The user can then decide which interface to use depending on the physical separation of the two items.

4.3.3 RS-422/V.11

If the physical separation and the bit rate are both to be increased, then the alternative RS-422/V.11 signal definitions should be used. These are based on the use of twisted-pair cable and a pair of *differential* (also referred to as *double-ended*) *transmitter and receiver circuits*. A typical circuit arrangement is as shown in Fig. 4.5.

A differential transmitter circuit produces two signals of equal and opposite polarity for every binary 1 or 0 signal to be transmitted. Also, a differential receiver is sensitive only to the difference between the two signals on its two inputs. Hence, any noise picked up in both wires – common mode noise – will not affect the operation of the receiver. Differential receivers are therefore said to have good *common-mode rejection* properties and a derivative of RS-422 called RS-423 can be used to accept the single-ended voltages output by an RS-232C interface with a differential receiver. RS-422 is suitable for use with twisted-pair cable for physical separations of, say, 100 m at 1 Mbps or greater distances at lower bit rates.

An important parameter of any transmission line is its *characteristic impedance*, Z_0, since only if the line is terminated by a resistor equal to Z_0 is all the received signal power absorbed by the receiver. If this is not the case *signal reflections* will occur which in turn cause the received signals to be further distorted. It is for this reason that lines are normally terminated by a resistor equal to Z_0, values from 50 to 200 ohms being common.

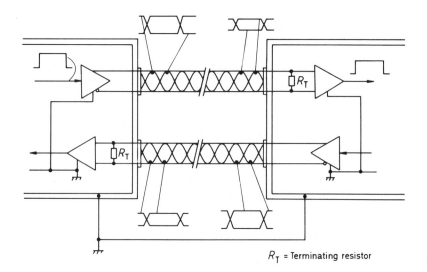

R_T = Terminating resistor

Fig. 4.5 RS-422 signal levels

4.3.4 Coaxial cable signals

Although coaxial cable is normally driven from a single-ended voltage source, its geometry of construction means that the effect of external interference is very low. There are a number of matching transmit and receive interface circuits available for use with coaxial cable and their connection is shown in Fig. 4.6. The figure also shows the effect of terminating the line with the correct value of terminating resistance (that is Z_0). Such arrangements are suitable for transmitting data at up to 10 Mbps over a distance of several hundred metres.

4.3.5 Optical fibre signals

There are a variety of forms of optical signal encoding but one example based on a bipolar encoding scheme is shown in Fig. 4.7. This type of encoding produces three-level optical output which makes it suitable for operating the cable from d.c. (zero frequency equivalent to a continuous string of binary 0s or 1s) up to 50 Mbps. The three optical power output levels are zero, half maximum power and maximum power respectively. The transmit module performs the necessary conversion from the internal binary voltage levels being used to the three-level optical signal which is applied to the fibre using special connectors and a high-speed light emitting diode (LED).

At the receiver, the fibre is terminated with a special connector to a high-speed photodiode housed within a special receiver module. This contains the necessary control electronics to convert the electrical signal output by the photodiode – proportional to the light level – into internal voltage levels corresponding to binary 1s and 0s.

4.3.6 Modem signals

When data are to be transmitted using lines from the public switched telephone network (PSTN) as the transmission medium, it is first necessary to convert the electrical signals output by the interface circuits used within the

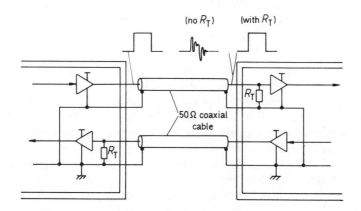

Fig. 4.6 Coaxial cable signals

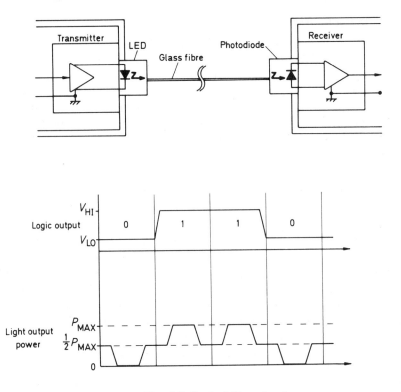

Fig. 4.7 Optical fibre signals

DTE into a form which is acceptable by the various items of equipment used in the PSTN. The latter was of course designed for speech communications which is assumed to be made up of a mix of (audio) frequencies in the range 400 to 3400 Hz. This is shown in diagrammatic form in Fig. 4.8.

The range of signal frequencies that a circuit will pass is known as the *bandwidth* of the circuit. Thus the PSTN is said to have a bandwidth of from 400 to 3400 Hz or simply 3000 Hz. This means that a telephone line cannot handle – that is, will not pass – very low frequency signals which may arise, for example, if the data stream to be transmitted is made up of a continuous string of binary 1s or 0s. For this reason it is not possible to simply apply two voltage levels to the telephone line since zero output would be obtained for both levels if the binary data stream was all 1s or all 0s. Instead, it is necessary to first convert the binary data into a form compatible with a speech signal at the sending end of the line and to reconvert this signal back into its binary form at the receiver. The circuit to perform the first operation is known as a *modulator* and the circuit to perform the reverse function a *demodulator*. Since each side of a data link must normally both send and receive data, the combined device is known as a *modem*.

Using modems, data can be transmitted through the PSTN either by first dialling and thereby setting up a switched path through the network as with a normal telephone call or by leasing a *dedicated line* from the PTT authorities.

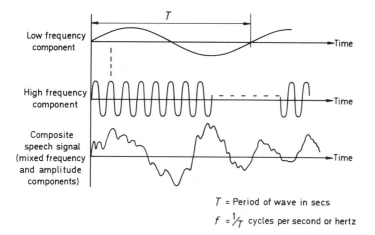

T = Period of wave in secs

$f = \frac{1}{T}$ cycles per second or hertz

Fig. 4.8 Speech waveform

This is also known as a *leased line* and such circuits bypass the normal switching equipments (exchanges) in the network. They are therefore set up on a permanent or long-term basis and hence are only economically justifiable for those applications which have a high utilisation factor. An added advantage of a leased line, however, is that because it is permanently set up, its operating characteristics can be more accurately quantified than for a short-term switched circuit and hence higher signalling (bit) rates are possible with a leased line. For clarity, the modulation and demodulation functions will be considered separately.

4.3.6.1 Modulation

There are three basic types of modulation which may be employed for the conversion of a binary signal into a form suitable for transmission on the PSTN. These are amplitude modulation (AM), frequency modulation (FM), and phase modulation (PM). The general principle of each is illustrated in Fig. 4.9.

With *amplitude modulation* the level or amplitude of a single frequency audio tone – known as the *carrier* frequency and selected to be within the acceptable range of frequencies for use in the PSTN – is switched or *keyed* between two levels at a rate determined by the transmitted binary data signal. This type of modulation, although the simplest, is prone to the varying effect of signal attenuation caused, for example, by varying propagation conditions as different routes through the PSTN are selected. In its basic form, therefore, this type of modulation is not often used although it is used in conjunction with phase modulation in more sophisticated modem designs primarily for use on leased lines.

With *frequency modulation* the frequency of a fixed amplitude carrier signal is changed according to the binary stream to be transmitted. Since there are only two frequencies (audio tones) required for binary data, this type of modulation is also known as *digital FM* or *frequency shift keying (FSK)*. This

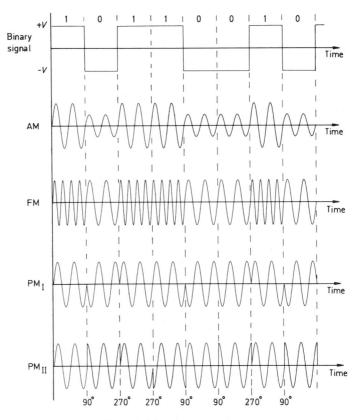

Fig. 4.9 Modulation methods

type of modulation is the method most frequently used for use with lower bit rate modems (300 baud to 1200 baud) designed to operate with switched connections across the PSTN since the demodulation circuitry needed is relatively simple and the bandwidth requirements low.

With *phase modulation* the frequency and amplitude of the carrier signal are kept constant but the carrier is shifted in phase as each bit in the data stream is transmitted. The first example illustrates a PM scheme which uses two fixed carrier signals for binary 1 and binary 0 with a 180° phase difference (equivalent to a signal reversal) between them. This is known as *phase shift keying* or *PSK*. With this type of PM a reference carrier signal must be maintained at the receiver against which the phase of the received signal is compared and it is therefore also known as *phase coherent PSK*. In practice, this can involve complex demodulation circuitry and also this type of modulation is very susceptible to random phase changes in the transmitted waveform. It is for these reasons that an alternative form of PM is often used which employs shifts in phase at each bit transition determined by the state of the next bit to be transmitted relative to the current bit. Thus in the second example, a phase shift of 90° relative to the current signal indicates a binary 0 is being transmitted and a phase shift of 270° a binary 1. In this way the demodulation circuitry need only determine the magnitude of each phase shift rather than the absolute value. This type of PM is therefore known as *differential PSK*.

4.3.6.2 Demodulation

To understand how the various modulated signals shown in Fig. 4.9 are demodulated at the receiver to reproduce the transmitted data stream, it is necessary to understand some basic properties of these types of signal. It is outside the scope of this book to derive mathematical expressions for the waveforms produced by the different modulation methods – they are in fact complex – and the aim here is to outline in a qualitative way the various effects that must be considered during the demodulation process. Some of these effects are shown in diagrammatic form in Fig. 4.10. The following should be noted when interpreting the figure:

a) When a carrier signal of fixed frequency, f_c, is modulated by a second fixed frequency signal, f_m, a number of additional frequency components known as *sidebands* are produced (part (a)). With AM just two sidebands are produced at $f_c + f_m$ and $f_c - f_m$ each containing a fraction of the power contained within the carrier; note, however, it is the sidebands which contain the information we require, f_m. With both FM and PM there are many sidebands produced at multiples of f_m from the carrier ($f_c + f_m$, $f_c + 2f_m$, etc.) whose amplitude is derived using *Bessel functions*.

b) Using a mathematical technique known as *Fourier analysis*, it can be shown that a *square wave* – equivalent to a repetitive binary data string of 0, 1, 0, 1, 0, 1 etc. – is made up of an infinite number of sinusoidal frequency components comprising a *fundamental frequency*, f_n, equal to one half the bit rate in *cycles per second* or *hertz*, and multiples of this frequency ($3f_n$, $5f_n$, $7f_n$, etc.) known as *harmonics* the amplitude of which decreases with increasing frequency.

c) When transmitting a binary data stream the bit pattern is continuously changing and hence the fundamental frequency (and the associated harmonics) will also continuously change. At one extreme the data stream may be a square wave – repetitive 0s and 1s as before – and at the other it may be a zero frequency (d.c.) signal equivalent to a continuous string of 0s or 1s.

It can be concluded from the above that the signal produced after modulating a sinusoidal carrier signal with a binary data stream is made up of the carrier plus a possibly infinite number of additional frequency components which contain the required information. Because most power is contained in the fundamental frequency of the modulating bit stream and the primary sidebands of the resulting modulated signal, in practice it is possible to determine the transmitted information by detecting just a limited band of frequencies either side of the carrier and ensuring that this band embraces the primary sidebands produced by the maximum modulation frequency. This, in turn, is determined by the maximum bit rate being used since the sidebands

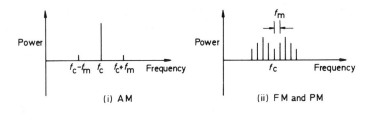

(a)

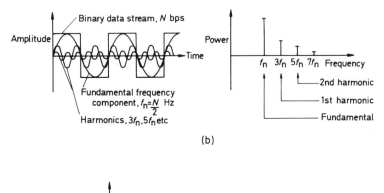

(b)

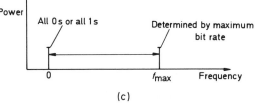

(c)

Fig. 4.10 Modulation: (a) power-frequency spectrum; (b) square wave frequency components; (c) fundamental frequency of binary data stream

produced by any lower bit rate signals in the transmitted data stream will automatically be nearer to the carrier and hence within this band.

For example, an FSK modulated signal can be considered as being made up of two separate carrier frequencies – one for binary 0 and the other for binary 1 – each of which is being keyed on and off at the maximum bit-rate frequency as shown in part (a) of Fig. 4.11. The *frequency spectrum* of this type of signal is therefore as shown in part (b) of the figure. Now, if the maximum bit rate is, say, 300 bps, this has a maximum fundamental frequency component of 150 Hz and hence the frequency spectrum will contain primary sidebands spaced at 150 Hz on each side of the carriers. Hence, if a frequency separation between the two carriers of, say, 200 Hz is selected, this would embrace the primary sidebands of each carrier.

Similarly, if the maximum bit rate is 1200 bps, this has a maximum fundamental frequency component of 600 Hz and hence a frequency separation in the order of 1000 Hz is normally selected. It should be noted, however, that a bit rate of 9600 bps has a maximum fundamental frequency component of 4800 Hz which exceeds the bandwidth of a line through the PSTN and hence this rate of operation cannot be accomplished with the basic modulation techniques outlined.

An example illustrating how a pair of channels is obtained in practice from a single pair of wires derived from a connection through the PSTN is

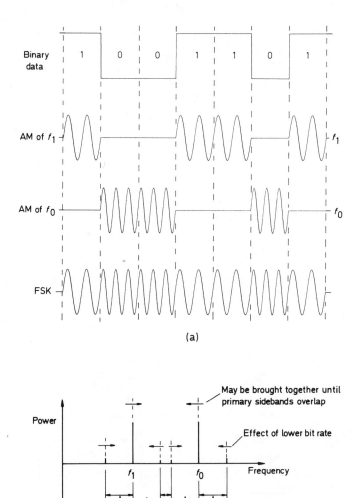

Fig. 4.11 FSK frequency components: (a) FSK modulation components; (b) power-frequency spectrum

shown in part (a) of Fig. 4.12. The two channels would be used, typically, to provide a full duplex 300 bps link between two DTEs. This type of modem uses FSK and the lower pair of frequencies carries data in one direction and the higher pair data in the reverse direction. The actual frequencies used for

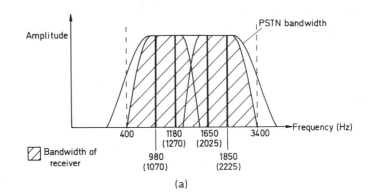

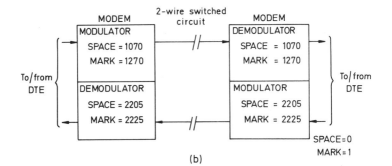

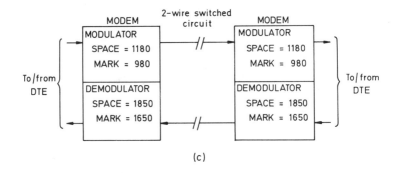

Fig. 4.12 300 bps full-duplex modem: (a) frequency spectrum; (b) US frequency assignments; (c) CCITT frequency assignments

this type of modem differ from one country (and hence PTT) to another but parts (b) and (c) of the figure show two alternative frequency assignments.

4.3.6.3 Hybrid modulation techniques

In order to derive higher bit-rate channels from a normal telephone line, it is necessary to use more sophisticated modulation techniques. In the examples discussed so far the bit rate was the same as the *signalling rate* being used; that is, the number of times per second the amplitude, frequency, or phase of the transmitted signal changes per second. The signalling rate is measured in *baud* and hence in the examples the bit rate has been equal to the baud rate. It is possible, however, when transmitting a signal across a PSTN line to utilise more than two different values and four or eight are not uncommon. This means that each signal element may contain two (4 values) or three (8 values) bits of encoded information and hence the resulting bit rate is two or three times the baud rate.

As an example, with phase modulation four different phase changes may be employed (0°, 90°, 180° and 270°) instead of just two and hence the phase change of each signal can convey two bits. This is shown in two diferent forms in parts (a) and (b) of Fig. 4.13. Also, the different modulation techniques may be combined to produce, for example, *amplitude modulated-phase shift keying* (*AM-PSK*) as shown in schematic form in part (c) of the figure. It should be noted, however, that although it is possible to increase the information content of the signal by increasing the number of signal changes per transmitted element, the bandwidth of the line always imposes a maximum limit on the information (bit) rate. The other factor that restricts the information rate of a line is the level of *noise* – random perturbations that produce signals on the line even when no information is being transmitted. Clearly, as the number of different signal levels increases the magnitude of the minimum level reduces and, in the limit, becomes indistinguishable from the line noise. The theoretical maximum information rate – also known as *channel capacity* – of a line (channel) can be derived using the *Shannon-Hartley Law* which states:

$$C = B \log_2 \left(1 + \frac{S}{N}\right) \text{ bps}$$

where C = information rate in bps
 B = bandwidth of the line
 S = signal power
 N = random (white) noise power.

The term S/N is known as the *signal-to-noise ratio* and is often quoted in *decibels* (*dB*):

$$\left(\frac{S}{N}\right) \text{dB} = 10 \log_{10} \left(\frac{S}{N}\right)$$

As an example, the PSTN has a bandwidth of 3000 Hz and a typical signal-to-noise ratio of 20 dB and hence the maximum theoretical information rate that can be obtained is derived as follows:

$$20 = 10 \log_{10} \left(\frac{S}{N}\right)$$

Therefore,

$$\frac{S}{N} = 100$$

and

$$C = 3000 \log_2 (1 + 100)$$

that is,

$$C = 19\ 963 \text{ bps.}$$

It should be stressed, however, that this is the theoretical limit and other forms of noise – for example crosstalk – reduce this figure further. Thus 9600 bps is nearer the maximum limit that can be obtained from a PSTN line and then only on good-quality leased lines.

4.4 PHYSICAL LEVEL PROTOCOLS

The previous sections have been concerned with some of the alternative transmission media and associated electrical signals that may be used to transmit a binary data stream between two DTEs. The various standards that were introduced earlier, however, in addition to defining the form of the electrical signals to be used, also define a complete range of additional control signals which must be used to control the order and timing of data transfers across the appropriate interfaces. Collectively these are said to form the *physical level protocol* which in many ways performs an analogous set of functions to the link level protocol discussed in Chapter 3. Although it is not practicable in a book of this type to give a description of the complete range of signal definitions presented in the various standards documents, some of the additional control signals used with the various interface standards introduced previously will now be described.

4.4.1 RS-232C/V.24

As was mentioned earlier, RS-232C and V.24 were originally defined as a standard interface for connecting a DTE to a PTT supplied (or approved) modem. The latter is more generally referred to as a data communications equipment or DCE and a schematic diagram indicating the position of the interface standard with respect to the two equipments is shown in part (a) of Fig. 4.14. Some of the additional control signals which have been defined for use with RS-232C are shown in part (b) of the figure.

The Transmit Data (TxD) and Receive Data (RxD) are the lines on which the data are transmitted and received respectively and the other lines collectively perform the timing and control functions associated with the

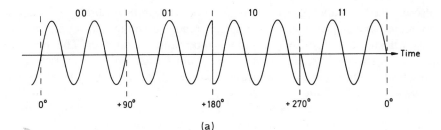

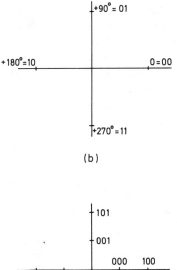

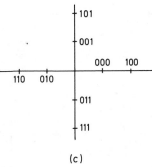

Fig. 4.13 Alternative modulation techniques: (a) phase–time; (b) phase diagram; (c) AM–PSK

setting up and clearing down of a switched connection through the PSTN. All the lines shown use the same electrical signal levels as were described earlier. The function and sequence of operation of the various signals is outlined in the example shown in Fig. 4.15. In order to illustrate the function of each line, the example shows how a connection (call) is first established and a half-duplex data interchange carried out. It assumes the calling DTE is a user at a terminal and the called DTE is a remote computer with automatic (auto) answering facilities. The latter is normally switch selectable on the modem.

The connection is first established by the user dialling the number associated with the remote computer in the usual way – *autodial* facilities can also be used – and waiting for the call to be answered. Assuming the remote computer line is free and the computer ready to communicate, the ringing tone will stop and a single audio tone wil be heard by the user. The user then presses a special button known as the *data button* on the handset which initiates the connection of the terminal to the setup line and the local modem responds by setting the Data Set Ready (DSR) line on. There is normally a small indicator lamp associated with this line and hence this now comes on indicating a link has been established with the remote computer.

At the remote computer, when the number is dialled the local modem sets the Ring Indicator (RI) line on and, assuming the computer is ready to receive a call – Data Terminal Ready (DTR) on – it responds by setting the Request-to-Send (RTS) line on. This has two effects: first it results in the modem sending a carrier signal – a single audio tone – to the calling modem to indicate the call has been accepted by the remote computer and second, after a short delay to allow the remote modem to prepare to receive data, the modem responds by setting the Clear-to-Send (CTS) line on to indicate to the called computer that it may start sending data.

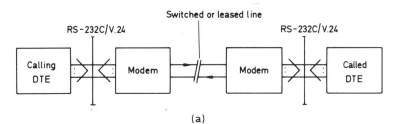

(a)

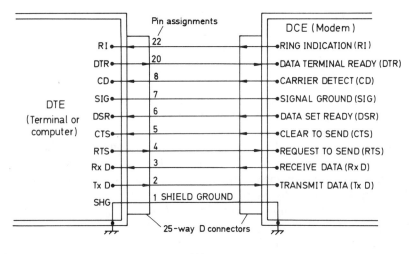

(b)

Fig. 4.14 RS-232C/V.24 signal definitions: (a) interface function; (b) signal definitions

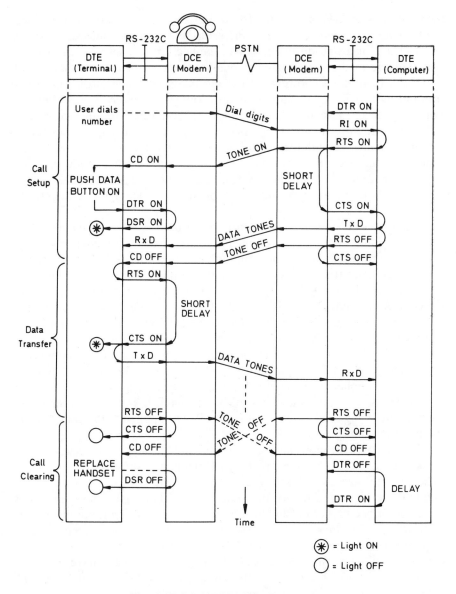

Fig. 4.15 RS-232C/V.24 call procedure

Typically the called computer will then respond by sending a short invitation-to-type message or character to the calling terminal via the setup link. The computer will then prepare to receive the user's response by switching the RTS line off, which in turn results in the carrier signal being switched off. The calling modem in turn detects the carrier being switched off and sets the Carrier Detect (CD) line off. The terminal then sets the RTS line on and, on receipt of the CTS signal from the modem – a lamp is normally associated with this signal and hence when this comes on – the user types his response message. Finally, after the complete transaction has taken place, both carriers are switched off and the setup link (call) is released (cleared).

The use of a half-duplex switched connection was selected in order to illustrate the meaning and use of some of the control lines available with RS-232C. In practice, however, the time taken to change from receive to transmit mode with a half-duplex circuit – known as the *turn-around time* – is not insignificant and for this reason it is preferable to operate with a full-duplex circuit whenever possible even if only half-duplex working is required. When a full-duplex circuit is being used, the transmit and receive functions can, of course, take place simultaneously and hence the RTS line from both devices is normally left permanently set and, under normal operation, both modems maintain CTS on and a carrier signal to the remote modem.

When synchronous transmission is being used it is necessary to have a clock signal for bit synchronisation purposes. If a synchronous modem is being used, the modulation and demodulation functions both require a clock signal to perform the signal encoding and decoding functions and hence it is necessary for the modem to supply the transmit and receive clocks to the interface control circuits (USRTs) in the DTEs (terminal and computer). The clock signal is passed from the modem to the DTE using the Transmit Signal Element Timing (DCE source) control line and Receive Signal Element Timing line. These are assigned Pins 15 and 17 respectively in the connector. If a single bit per signalling element is being used by the modem, then the clock signal supplied to the DTE for control of the transmission and reception rates is the same as the baud rate of the channel. If two bits per signalling element are being used, however, then the clock supplied to the DTE is twice the baud rate and so on.

With an asynchronous modem the baud and bit rates are the same and no clock is used within the modem. If synchronous transmission is being used, therefore, it is necessary for the clock to be extracted by the interface circuits within the DTE from the incoming data stream. The digital phase-lock-loop circuit described earlier in Chapter 2 is an example of a circuit suitable for use with an asynchronous modem. Also, to minimise the additional circuitry required to interface a terminal (or computer) to a modem, the interface control circuits described – UARTs and USRTs – normally have a modem control section which automatically handles the RTS/CTS and DSR/DTR control lines.

4.4.1.1 The null modem

With the signal assignments shown in Fig. 4.14, the terminal and computer both receive and transmit data on the same lines since the modem provides the same function for both devices. Since its original definition, however, RS-232C has been adopted as a standard interface for connecting character oriented peripherals – VDUs, printers etc. – to a computer. For this type of use of RS-232C, therefore, it is necessary to decide which of the two devices –

peripheral or computer – is going to emulate the modem since clearly both devices cannot transmit and receive data on the same lines.

There are three possible alternatives: either the terminal emulates the modem and the appropriate line definitions are used accordingly, or the computer emulates the modem, or both the terminal and computer remain unchanged and the interconnecting wiring is modified. The disadvantage of the first two alternatives is that the terminal or computer cannot then be used directly with a modem. Nevertheless, a common approach is for the computer RS-232C port to be wired to emulate a modem and hence an unmodified terminal can be connected directly to it. The third alternative is also widely used, however, and this necessitates the use of a *null modem* – also known as a *switch box* – inserted between the terminal and the computer to perform the necessary modifications to the interconnecting lines. The line modifications performed by a null modem are as shown in Fig. 4.16.

As can be seen, in addition to reversing the transmit and receive data lines, some of the control lines are also reversed. For example, since a computer and terminal normally operate in a full-duplex mode, the RTS and CTS lines are connected together at each end and this signal is then connected to the CD input line of the other device. Similarly, the DSR and RI lines are connected together at each end and these signals are cross-connected to the DTR inputs. The signal and shield ground lines are of course connected directly.

When the two devices communicate via a synchronous data link, normally the transmit clock from each device is cross-connected to be used as the receive clock by the other device. In some instances, however, neither device contains a clock source and the clock to be used by both devices is generated within the null modem. The latter is then known as a *modem eliminator*.

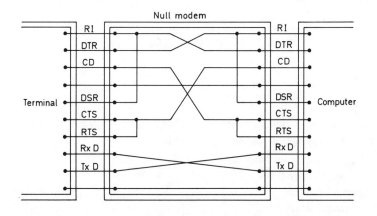

Fig. 4.16 Null modem connections

4.4.2 RS-449/V.35

The interface used when RS-422 electrical signals are being used is RS-449/V.35. Some of the control signals used with this standard are shown in Fig. 4.17. The differential signals used with RS-422 mean that each line requires a pair of wires. As can be seen, some of the control signals are the same as those used with RS-232C. Also, the Data Mode and Receiver Ready lines correspond to the DSR and DTR lines in RS-232C. Test Mode is a new mandatory signal specific to RS-449 which is intended to provide a means for testing the communications equipment. Essentially, this provides a facility for looping the output of the DTE (terminal or computer) back again through the DCE (modem); that is, the Transmit Data output line is automatically looped back onto the Receive Data input line. In this way a series of tests can be carried out by the DTE to determine which (if any) piece of communications equipment (DCE) is faulty.

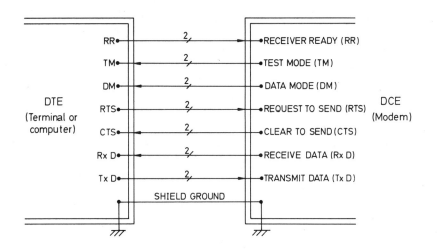

Fig. 4.17 RS-449/V.35 signal definitions

Problems

4.1 Give a brief description of the application and limitations of the following types of transmission medium:

two-wire open lines,
twisted-pair lines,
coaxial cable,
optical fibre,
microwaves.

4.2 Make a sketch showing the interface circuits and associated signal levels used to transmit binary data between two DTEs using the following signal types and transmission media:

RS-232C/V.24 and open lines,
20 mA current loop and open lines,
RS-422 and twisted pair,
coaxial cable,
optical fibre.

Outline the properties of each signal type.

4.3 a) Why must a modem be used to transmit binary data through the public switched telephone network?

Use sketches and additional text to describe the following modulation methods:

i) amplitude modulation,
ii) frequency modulation,
iii) phase-coherent PSK,
iv) differential PSK.

b) Discuss the factors which influence the choice of carrier frequency and the bandwidth used by the demodulator section of a modem.

4.4 List the main signals used with the RS-232C/V.24 standard interface and state their function.

Derive a time sequence diagram to show the use of each line. Use as an example a user at a terminal establishing a half-duplex connection through the public switched telephone network to carry out a transaction involving the exchange of data between the terminal and a remote computer.

4.5 a) What is the function of a Null Modem?

Show the internal connections used within a Null Modem and explain the significance of each connection.

b) List the main signals used with the RS-449/V.35 standard interface and state their function.

Chapter 5 **Terminal-Based Networks**

Objectives:

When you have completed studying the material in this chapter you should:

- know the most commonly used information codes used in terminal-based networks;

- understand the role of the additional communications devices which are used in interactive character-mode terminal networks and explain their operation;

- understand the role of the additional communications devices which are used in block-mode terminal networks and explain their operation;

- be able to describe the Binary Synchronous Control protocol as used in poll-select networks and appreciate its limitations;

- understand the alternative modes of operation of the High-level Data Link Control protocol and describe selected aspects of its operation.

5.1 INTRODUCTION

Terminal-based networks in their various forms are probably the most prevalent type of distributed system in use today. They range from systems comprising a small number of relatively unintelligent character-mode terminals linked directly to a locally situated computer, to systems containing a large number of sophisticated block-mode terminals linked through a network of additional communications equiment to a powerful central computing complex. There is a common thread which links the different forms of system together, however, and that is there is normally just a single central computer or computing complex, to which all the terminals in the network require access. Also, because of the limited intelligence associated with a terminal, the communications protocols used in such networks are relatively simple, certainly in comparison with those used in computer-to-computer communication networks. This chapter is concerned with the range of communications equipment which is used in such networks and also with the communications protocols which are used for their operation.

5.2 TERMINAL CHARACTERISTICS

Since the advent of the microprocessor in the mid 1970s all terminals have a degree of local intelligence – processing capability – associated with them. The level of intelligence varies, however, from one type of terminal to another and is determined by both the amount of local processing to be performed and also the type of communications protocol being used to control the flow of information to and from the terminal. Essentially, therefore, the local processor performs two functions: firstly, it controls the operation of the terminal – that is, the reception and processing of characters entered at the terminal keyboard and the output of characters to the terminal display screen – and secondly, it controls the exchange of characters or blocks of characters between the terminal and the remote computer or its agent. A terminal can be represented in diagrammatic form, therefore, as shown in Fig. 5.1.

The different classes of terminal in common use, listed in order of increasing processing capability, are:

1. single character (also known as scroll-mode) interactive terminals,
2. screen-mode interactive terminals,
3. data entry/point-of-sale terminals,
4. remote job entry terminals.

For the purpose of this chapter, however, terminals are perhaps best classified according to the type of communications protocol they are able to support. In general, both scroll- and screen-mode interactive terminals incorporate just a basic UART within them and utilise a simple asynchronous character-mode protocol, normally with an echo checking error control procedure. Also, since interactive screen-mode terminals may at times generate a complete string of characters rather than a single character, an X-ON/X-OFF flow control mechanism is often used with this type of terminal to enable the central computer to regulate the flow of characters from the terminal.

On the other hand, data entry and remote job entry terminals normally utilise a more sophisticated synchronous block-mode protocol with an ARQ

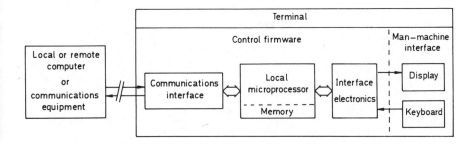

Fig. 5.1 Generalised terminal schematic

error control procedure. Both character oriented and bit oriented protocols are in widespread use. Also, as will be seen later, many character-mode terminal networks incorporate additional communications equipment which also uses a block-mode protocol.

5.3 INFORMATION EXCHANGE CODES

A feature of terminal-based systems is that most of the information is exchanged in the form of either single characters or strings (blocks) of characters. There are two main character codes which have been adopted for this function. They are the American Standards Committee for Information Interchange code (*ASCII*) and the Extended Binary Coded Decimal Interchange Code (*EBCDIC*). Also, a third code called International Alphabet Number 5 (*IA5*) is the standard code defined by the CCITT and recommended by the International Standards Organisation, ISO. In practice, IA5 is almost exactly the same as ASCII since the latter is basically the American national version of IA5.

The ASCII/IA5 code is a 7-bit code and the bit-pattern definitions used are shown in Fig. 5.2. As can be seen, the code caters for all the normal alphabetic and numeric (collectively referred to as *alphanumeric*) characters plus a range of additional control and graphical characters.

The EBCDIC code is an 8-bit code used with all equipment – terminals and computers – manufactured by IBM. As such it is a proprietary code but, owing to the widespread use of IBM equipment in the computer industry, it is frequently used. The bit-pattern definitions used are shown in Fig. 5.3. As can be seen, EBCDIC covers most of the characters used in ASCII/IA5. Also, because of the large number of possible bit combinations (256), a number of combinations are not defined in EBCDIC.

								0	0	0	0	1	1	1	1
								0	0	1	1	0	0	1	1
								0	1	0	1	0	1	0	1
Bits	b_7	b_6	b_5	b_4	b_3	b_2	b_1	Row							
				0	0	0	0	0	NUL	(TC$_7$) DLE	SP	0	@	P		p
				0	0	0	1	1	(TC$_1$) SOH	DC$_1$	!	1	A	Q	a	q
				0	0	1	0	2	(TC$_2$) STX	DC$_2$	"	2	B	R	b	r
				0	0	1	1	3	(TC$_3$) ETX	DC$_3$	£	3	C	S	c	s
				0	1	0	0	4	(TC$_4$) EOT	DC$_4$	$	4	D	T	d	t
				0	1	0	1	5	(TC$_5$) ENQ	(TC$_8$) NAK	%	5	E	U	e	u
				0	1	1	0	6	(TC$_6$) ACK	(TC$_9$) SYN	&	6	F	V	f	v
				0	1	1	1	7	BEL	(TC$_{10}$) ETB	'	7	G	W	g	w
				1	0	0	0	8	FE$_0$ (BS)	CAN	(	8	H	X	h	x
				1	0	0	1	9	FE$_1$ (HT)	EM	)	9	I	Y	i	y
				1	0	1	0	10	FE$_2$ (LF)	SUB	*	:	J	Z	j	z
				1	0	1	1	11	FE$_3$ (VT)	ESC	+	;	K		k	
				1	1	0	0	12	FE$_4$ (FF)	IS$_4$ (FS)	,	<	L		l	
				1	1	0	1	13	FE$_5$ (CR)	IS$_3$ (GS)	–	=	M		m	
				1	1	1	0	14	SO	IS$_2$ (RS)	.	>	N	^	n	—
				1	1	1	1	15	SI	IS$_1$ (US)	/	?	O	—	o	DEL

Fig. 5.2 ASCII/IA5 code

EBCDIC	Bit Configuration	EBCDIC	Bit Configuration	EBCDIC	Bit Configuration	EBCDIC	Bit Configuration
NUL	0000 0000	SP	0100 0000		1000 0000		1100 0000
SOH	0000 0001		0100 0001	a	1000 0001	A	1100 0001
STX	0000 0010		0100 0010	b	1000 0010	B	1100 0010
ETX	0000 0011		0100 0011	c	1000 0011	C	1100 0011
PF	0000 0100		0100 0100	d	1000 0100	D	1100 0100
HT	0000 0101		0100 0101	e	1000 0101	E	1100 0101
LC	0000 0110		0100 0110	f	1000 0110	F	1100 0110
DEL	0000 0111		0100 0111	g	1000 0111	G	1100 0111
	0000 1000		0100 1000	h	1000 1000	H	1100 1000
RLF	0000 1001		0100 1001	i	1000 1001	I	1100 1001
SMM	0000 1010	[	0100 1010		1000 1010		1100 1010
VT	0000 1011	.	0100 1011		1000 1011		1100 1011
FF	0000 1100	<	0100 1100	⌐	1000 1100	⌐	1100 1100
CR	0000 1101	(	0100 1101		1000 1101		1100 1101
SO	0000 1110	+	0100 1110	⌙	1000 1110	⌙	1100 1110
SI	0000 1111	|	0100 1111		1000 1111		1100 1111
DLE	0001 0000	&	0101 0000		1001 0000		1101 0000
DC1	0001 0001		0101 0001	j	1001 0001	J	1101 0001
DC2	0001 0010		0101 0010	k	1001 0010	K	1101 0010
TM	0001 0011		0101 0011	l	1001 0011	L	1101 0011
RES	0001 0100		0101 0100	m	1001 0100	M	1101 0100
NL	0001 0101		0101 0101	n	1001 0101	N	1101 0101
BS	0001 0110		0101 0110	o	1001 0110	O	1101 0110
IL	0001 0111		0101 0111	p	1001 0111	P	1101 0111
CAN	0001 1000		0101 1000	q	1001 1000	Q	1101 1000
EM	0001 1001		0101 1001	r	1001 1001	R	1101 1001
CC	0001 1010	]	0101 1010		1001 1010		1101 1010
CU1	0001 1011	$	0101 1011		1001 1011		1101 1011
IFS	0001 1100	*	0101 1100		1001 1100		1101 1100
IGS	0001 1101	)	0101 1101		1001 1101		1101 1101
IRS	0001 1110	;	0101 1110		1001 1110		1101 1110
IUS	0001 1111	¬	0101 1111		1001 1111		1101 1111
DS	0010 0000	–	0110 0000	—	1010 0000		1110 0000
SOS	0010 0001	/	0110 0001		1010 0001		1110 0001
FS	0010 0010		0110 0010	s	1010 0010	S	1110 0010
	0010 0011		0110 0011	t	1010 0011	T	1110 0011
BYP	0010 0100		0110 0100	u	1010 0100	U	1110 0100
LF	0010 0101		0110 0101	v	1010 0101	V	1110 0101
ETB	0010 0110		0110 0110	w	1010 0110	W	1110 0110
ESC	0010 0111		0110 0111	x	1010 0111	X	1110 0111
	0010 1000		0110 1000	y	1010 1000	Y	1110 1000
	0010 1001		0110 1001	z	1010 1001	Z	1110 1001
SM	0010 1010	,	0110 1010		1010 1010		1110 1010
CU2	0010 1011		0110 1011		1010 1011		1110 1011
	0010 1100	%	0110 1100		1010 1100		1110 1100
ENQ	0010 1101	–	0110 1101		1010 1101		1110 1101
ACK	0010 1110	>	0110 1110		1010 1110		1110 1110
BEL	0010 1111	?	0110 1111		1010 1111		1110 1111
	0011 0000		0111 0000		1011 0000	0	1111 0000
	0011 0001		0111 0001		1011 0001	1	1111 0001
SYN	0011 0010		0111 0010		1011 0010	2	1111 0010
	0011 0011		0111 0011		1011 0011	3	1111 0011
PN	0011 0100		0111 0100		1011 0100	4	1111 0100
RS	0011 0101		0111 0101		1011 0101	5	1111 0101
UC	0011 0110		0111 0110		1011 0110	6	1111 0110

(continued)

EBCDIC	Bit Configuration	EBCDIC	Bit Configuration	EBCDIC	Bit Configuration	EBCDIC	Bit Configuration
EOT	0011 0111		0111 0111		1011 0111	7	1111 0111
	0011 1000		0111 1000		1011 1000	8	1111 1000
	0011 1001		0111 1001		1011 1001	9	1111 1001
	0011 1010	:	0111 1010		1011 1010		1111 1010
CU3	0011 1011	#	0111 1011		1011 1011		1111 1011
DC4	0011 1100	@	0111 1100		1011 1100		1111 1100
NAK	0011 1101	'	0111 1101		1011 1101		1111 1101
	0011 1110	=	0111 1110		1011 1110		1111 1110
SUB	0011 1111	"	0111 1111		1011 1111		1111 1111

Fig. 5.3 EBCDIC code

5.4 CHARACTER-MODE NETWORKS

An example of a very simple character-mode terminal network is shown in part (a) of Fig. 5.4. Typically, the terminals would be visual display units (VDUs) each connected to a locally situated central computing complex by means of a point-to-point data link. Each terminal would be either a character or screen-mode device operating in an interactive mode and the data link a low bit-rate – typically less than 9600 bps – asynchronous link operating using simple echo checking and an X-ON/X-OFF flow control protocol similar to that described in Chapter 3.

This type of organisation is perfectly adequate providing the terminals are all locally situated relative to the central computer or if there is a single terminal at each remote location. If the terminals are remotely situated, then either simple line drivers are required or, if the terminals are in a remote location, PTT approved modems. This is shown in part (b) of the figure.

In a large establishment, a common requirement is to have more than one terminal at each remote location. Clearly, an organisation similar to that shown in Fig. 5.4 with additional communication lines could be used for each terminal but a more efficient, and ultimately more flexible, arrangement is to provide a single high bit-rate line between each remote location and the central computer and to share its data bandwidth between the various lower bit-rate terminals. If all the terminals are within the same establishment, a device known as a *terminal multiplexer* may be used. Alternatively, if the remote terminals are in a different establishment and modems are required, a device known as a *statistical multiplexer* is often more appropriate. These and other types of communications equipment used in this type of network will now be described.

5.4.1 Terminal multiplexer

A schematic diagram illustrating a typical application of a terminal multiplexer is shown in part (a) of Fig. 5.5. As can be seen, a similar multiplexer is normally used at both ends of the link and this has the effect that each terminal operates as if it were connected directly to a terminal port on the computer. The presence of the multiplexers is therefore said to be *transparent* to both the terminal user and the computer.

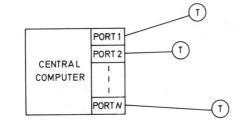

(a)

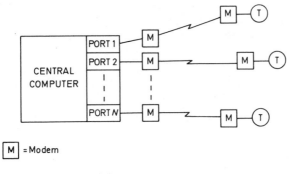

(b)

Fig. 5.4 Simple terminal networks: (a) local; (b) remote

A schematic of the internal organisation of a terminal multiplexer is shown in part (b) of the figure. As can be seen, each terminal is allocated a separate UART and the controlling microprocessor continuously *polls* each UART in turn to determine if a character has been received from the terminal; that is, the status byte in each UART is read to determine if the Receive Buffer Full status bit is set. If it is, the received character is read and prepared for transmission on the outgoing data link to the remote computer; if it isn't, the status byte in the next UART is read and so on. Similarly, on receipt of each character from the data link, it is transferred to the Transmit Buffer register of the appropriate UART for forwarding to the terminal.

It can readily be deduced from the previous paragraph that, with a terminal multiplexer, the bit rate of the common data link must be at least N times that used for each terminal where N is the number of terminals. For example, if the bit rate used for each terminal is 1200 bps and the multiplexer is servicing 8 such terminals, the bit rate of the common data link must be greater than 8 times 1200; that is, greater than 9600 bps.

Since the controlling microprocessor polls each UART in turn, it automatically knows from which terminal or computer port any received characters have come. As characters are received from the data link, however, it must be able to determine for which UART – and hence terminal or computer port – they are intended. This may be achieved in a number of ways but a typical arrangement is as shown in part (c) of the figure. In this scheme each UART – and hence terminal or computer port – is assigned a specific character slot relative to the start of each *frame*. Typically, each frame has the same number of character slots as there are UARTs and, to allow the controlling microprocessor to determine the start of each slot, each frame is preceded by a synchronising control character such as SYN. It is for this

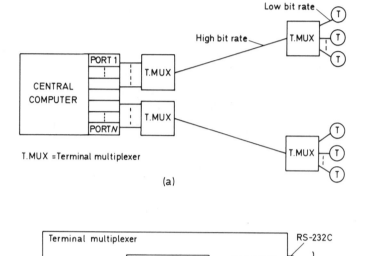

T.MUX = Terminal multiplexer

(a)

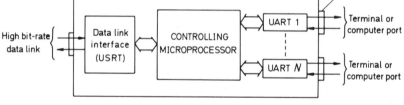

(b)

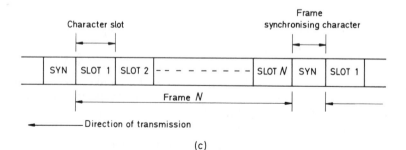

(c)

Fig. 5.5 Terminal multiplexer principles: (a) network schematic; (b) multiplexer schematic; (c) data link organisation

reason that the bit rate of the common data link must be greater than the aggregate bit rate of each terminal. This type of multiplexing arrangement is known as *Time Division Multiplexing (TDM)* since the available transmission capacity of the data link is being time-shared between the various terminals.

If the multiplexer is servicing only a small number of low bit-rate terminals – for example, four VDUs each operating at 1200 bps – the aggregate bit rate of the common data link is still only low and hence an asynchronous transmission control scheme can be used. As the aggregate data rate increases, however, then a synchronous control scheme must be used. In fact, terminal multiplexers of the type just described can be purchased which are designed to service up to 32 terminals each operating at up to 9600 bps. Clearly, therefore, the aggregate data rate is then in excess of 300 kbps and hence this type of multiplexer can only be used where special high bit-rate data links can be laid and transmission media such as fibre optics used. This type of multiplexer is normally constrained for use, therefore, within a single private establishment.

5.4.2 Statistical multiplexer

It can be concluded from the above that with a terminal multiplexer each terminal is allocated a fixed character slot in each frame. If the terminal or computer has no character ready to transmit when the controlling microprocessor polls the associated UART, therefore, the microprocessor must insert a NULL character in the reserved character slot, thus leading to inefficiencies in the use of the available transmission bandwidth. If the data link being used is a private line this is not necessarily important but, if PTT supplied lines are being used, this can be very costly. An alternative and more efficient method is to use a device known as a *statistical multiplexer* or *stat mux*.

Statistical multiplexers operate on the principle that the mean data rate of characters entered at a terminal keyboard is often much lower than the nominal available transmission capacity of the line – this is certainly the case with a human user, for example. Hence, if the mean user data rate is used rather than the transmission line rate, the bit rate of the common data link can then be much lower, with the effect that transmission line costs are substantially reduced. For example, assume a remote location has eight terminals which need to be connected to a single remote central computer by means of a PTT supplied line. Also, assume a maximum line rate of, say, 4800 bps. Using a basic multiplexer and a single line, the nominal operating rate of each terminal would therefore have to be less than 600 bps – say 300 bps – with the effect that the response time of the computer to each character keyed in at the terminal would be relatively slow or, if a block of characters was being transmitted to the terminal, the delay would be very noticeable. Alternatively, if the mean data rate of the terminal is say 300 bps, then with a statistical multiplexer, the data produced by a terminal when active could be transmitted at the maximum available bit rate of 4800 bps, with the effect that the average response time to each keyed character is much improved.

To implement this scheme, the controlling microprocessor within a statistical multiplexer, in addition to performing the normal polling function associated with the terminal UARTs as described earlier, must also provide and manage a limited amount of buffer storage facilities in order to allow for possible transient overload conditions on the common data link when a number of terminals are active simultaneously. Also, because characters are being transmitted on the common data link on a statistical rather than a preallocated basis, each character or group of characters transmitted must also carry some identification information.

Another function which must be performed by the microprocessor in a stat mux is related to error control. With a normal terminal multiplexer since each terminal and computer port is allocated a fixed character slot in each frame, simple echo checking is often a perfectly acceptable mode of working. Because of the statistical mode of working of a stat mux, however, this is not the case and hence it is more common to introduce a separate ARQ-based error control scheme on the shared data link. A typical statistical multiplexer arrangement is shown in part (a) of Fig. 5.6. As can be seen, in this example the link between the stat mux and the computer is shown as a single high speed link since, if echo checking is not used, there is no advantage in performing a demultiplexing function on behalf of the computer.

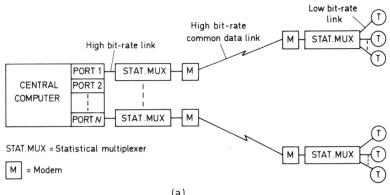

(a)

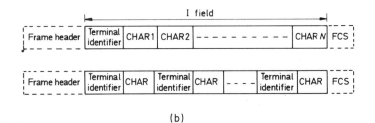

(b)

Fig. 5.6 Statistical multiplexer principles: (a) network schematic;
(b) framing alternatives

It may be remembered from Chapter 3 that with an ARQ error control scheme each block of data transmitted is separately identified for retransmission purposes. Hence, in order to reduce the overheads associated with each transmitted character, it is usual to group a number of characters together for transmission on the shared data link. This can be done in a number of ways and two examples are shown in part (b) of the figure. In the first, the controlling microprocessor waits until it has a number of characters from a single terminal – a string of characters making up a single line, for example – and then transmits them as a complete block with a single terminal (channel) identifier at its head. In the second, each block contains a mix of characters from those terminals which are currently active with a separate terminal identifier associated with each. Also, as can be seen from part (b), the assembled characters collectively occupy the I-field of each block or frame transmitted on the shared data link. The communications control protocol used on the link is normally either a character oriented or a bit oriented synchronous protocol and details of both of these will be described in more detail later in the chapter.

5.4.3 Terminal switching exchange

Although most terminal networks contain a single central computer to which all the terminals require access, it is rapidly becoming common practice in many larger establishments to have a number of computers physically distributed around the establishment and for users to require access to more than one of them. This is the case, for example, if the various computers each offer different user services such as word processing, electronic mail, special application packages, and so on. To meet this type of requirement a device known as a *terminal switching exchange* or *TSE* has evolved and a typical character-mode terminal network based on such a device is shown in Fig. 5.7.

Essentially, a TSE has a number of asynchronous terminal access ports and also a number of asynchronous computer ports. To gain access to a particular computer (port), the user first keys in the address of the required computer at the terminal keyboard analogous to dialling a person's telephone

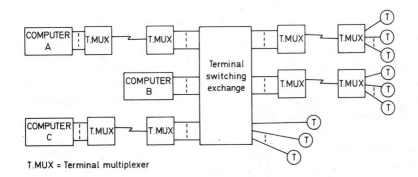

Fig. 5.7 Terminal switching exchange

number with the PSTN. Then, assuming there is a free port available on the required computer, the TSE establishes a logical connection between the terminal and the required computer port. The user then goes through the normal logging-in procedure and the presence of the TSE – and indeed terminal multiplexer should this be present – is transparent to the user and computer alike. Finally, at the end of the transaction, the user initiates the clearing of the connection by pressing a specific control character on the keyboard and the released computer port is then made available to another user.

5.5 BLOCK-MODE NETWORKS

As was mentioned earlier, more sophisticated terminals such as those used in a bank for data entry or point-of-sale terminals as used in a department store normally operate in a block mode rather than a character mode; that is, as each character is keyed in at the terminal it is echoed onto the display screen directly by the local processor within the terminal and only when a complete block of data (a message) has been assembled is this passed to the central computing complex for processing. Because of this, such terminals normally support a more sophisticated block oriented communications protocol to control the transfer of messages between the terminal and the central computer. Also, because the acceptable response time to each transmitted message can often be much slower than that expected with an interactive character-mode network, equipment aimed at reducing communications line costs at the expense of response time is often used in block-mode terminal networks. Some of the techniques and equipment used in such networks are now described.

5.5.1 Multidrop lines

A common method which is used to reduce transmission line costs in block-mode terminal networks is to use *multidrop* (also known as *multipoint*) *lines*. A schematic of a network which uses multidrop lines is shown in part (a) of Fig. 5.8. As can be seen, instead of each terminal being connected directly to the central computer by means of a separate line, a number of terminals share the same line. In this way, the number of lines and hence modems – or line drivers depending on the geographical scope of the network – is much reduced. Clearly, however, with only one line for each community of terminals, only one message block at a time can be sent, either by a terminal or the central computer. To achieve this, all transmissions on each line are controlled by the central computer itself and an arbitration procedure known as *poll-select* is used.

5.5.2 Poll-select

To ensure only one message is being transmitted at any instant of time on each shared communications line, the central computer – or its agent – either *polls* or *selects* each terminal connected to the line in a particular sequence.

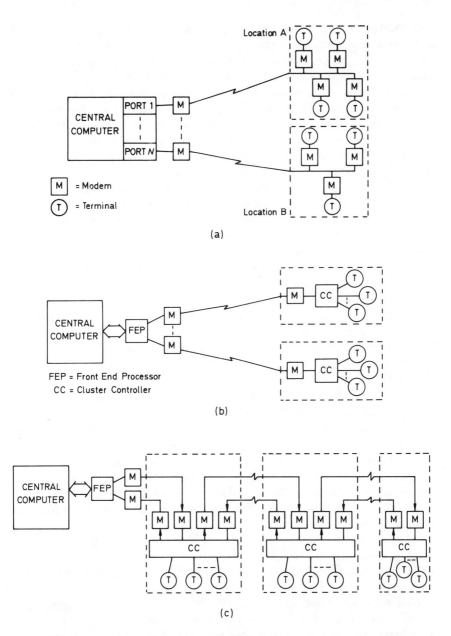

Fig. 5.8 Polling network alternatives: (a) multidrop; (b) cluster controllers; (c) hub polling

Each terminal connected to the shared line is allocated a unique identifier and the central computer communicates with a terminal by sending it messages with the identity of the terminal at the head of the message. Messages are either control messages or data messages.

At periodic intervals, the central computer sends each terminal in turn a

Poll control message which effectively invites the polled terminal to send a message should it have one waiting. If it has, it returns the message in a Data message; if it hasn't, it responds with a *Nothing-to-Send* control message. Similarly, whenever the central computer wishes to send a message to a terminal, it first sends a *Select* control message addressed to the particular terminal and, assuming the selected terminal is able to receive a message, it responds by returning a *Ready-to-Receive* control message. The central computer then continues by sending the data message. Finally, the terminal acknowledges its correct receipt of the data message and the central computer continues by either polling or selecting another terminal.

This type of polling is known as *roll call polling* and it can be deduced from the previous paragraph that since each terminal in the network must be polled or selected before it can send or receive a message, the response time of larger networks can be quite long. Also, the communications overheads imposed on the central computer can be very high.

To overcome these problems, a more common type of multidrop network uses firstly a device known as a *cluster controller* to reduce the response time of the network, and secondly a device known as a *Front-End Processor (FEP)* to reduce the communications overheads on the central computer. An example of such a network is then as shown in part (b) of Fig. 5.8. Effectively, each cluster controller manages all message transfers to and from the terminals which are connected to it and hence the central computer – the FEP in practice – instead of having to poll or select each terminal, needs only to poll or select each controller. The latter thus acts as an agent on behalf of the central computer by polling and selecting the terminals connected to it. In this way the polling overheads imposed on the central computer are much reduced.

A front-end processor is typically a small computer which is closely coupled to the central computer. It is programmed to handle all the above polling and selection procedures and hence allows the central computer to be devoted to the main task of application processing rather than communications processing.

The use of an FEP has the advantage that only when a data message has been received or is to be sent need the central computer be involved. Also, since all the communications overheads associated with each message transfer are handled by the FEP, the central computer need only initiate the transfer of each message to and from the FEP.

If very large physical distances separate each terminal cluster, an alternative to roll-call polling known as *hub-polling* is sometimes cost justified. This is shown in diagrammatic form in part (c) of Fig. 5.8. As can be seen, instead of each cluster controller being connected to the central computer directly – with the associated high communications line costs – it is connected to its nearest neighbour. As before, the central computer via the FEP manages all transfers to and from the cluster controllers. Thus the central computer is able to select and send a data message to any of the controllers at any time by means of the top line in the figure.

To receive messages from the controllers, the central computer first sends a Poll control message – again by means of the top line – to the furthest controller. The latter then responds by sending either a Data message or a Nothing-to-Send control message on the bottom (return) line. This is sent not to the central computer directly, however, but to its nearest neighbour controller. Then, on receipt of this message, the next controller interprets this as a Poll message and, if it has a message waiting, it responds by adding its own Data message to the tail of the received message from its upstream neighbour. It then forwards the composite message to its own downstream neighbour again on the return line. This procedure continues down the chain, each controller adding its own response message as it relays the message towards the central computer. Finally, on receipt of the composite response message, the FEP disassembles the message and passes on any valid Data messages contained within it to the central computer for further processing.

5.6 TERMINAL NETWORK PROTOCOLS

In a character-mode terminal network, all transmissions on the link between the terminal and the remote computer or piece of communications equipment are normally carried out using an asynchronous transmission control scheme. Also, because the terminals in such networks are normally used in an interactive mode, an echo checking error control procedure is used with an X-ON, X-OFF flow control mechanism to regulate the rate of flow of characters between the terminal and the computer should this be required. Both these techniques were introduced earlier in Chapters 2 and 3 of the book and hence the reader is referred back to these for more information about their operation.

As has just been described, however, in a block-mode terminal network, the terminals communicate using complete messages and hence they must be able to support a more sophisticated block oriented link control protocol. There are two such protocols in widespread use: *Binary Synchronous Control* (also known as *Bisync* or simply *BSC*) which is a character oriented protocol, and *High-level Data Link Control* (*HDLC*) which is a bit oriented protocol. Both have been designed to control the exchange of blocks of data (information) across a synchronous transmission line although the character definitions and sequences used in BSC are also sometimes used to transfer message blocks across an asynchronous line. Aspects of both protocols are now described.

5.6.1 Binary synchronous control

Binary Synchronous Control – or BSC as it will be referred to – is in fact the terminology adopted by IBM for the ISO character oriented link-level protocol known as *Basic Mode*. Because of the prevalence of IBM equipment, however, BSC is the term most widely used and hence will be used in this chapter to refer to the ISO Basic Mode protocol. It is a practical example of the Idle RQ protocol discussed earlier in Chapter 3 with the addition that a negative acknowledgment is used to improve the link efficiency.

It may be remembered from Chapter 3 that any link-level protocol can be considered as being made up of three sections: the first concerned with the initial setting up of the link to ensure both parties are ready to exchange information, the second concerned with the ordered exchange of data blocks or messages across the link, and the third concerned with the orderly release or clearing of the link. It can therefore be deduced from this that, in addition to normal data blocks or messages, a number of additional control messages are needed to perform the various functions associated with link management. Also, it may be remembered that, with a synchronous link, it is necessary for the receiver to be able to achieve both character (byte) and frame synchronisation.

To achieve these functions, with a character oriented protocol like BSC some of the control characters defined in ASCII/IA5 (or EBCDIC if this is being used) are provided for this purpose. The role of some of these characters was described earlier in Chapter 3 but a more complete list of those used with BSC, together with their functions, is as follows:

SYN   two or more such characters provide the means for the receiver to achieve character synchronisation;

SOH   indicates the start of the header of a block (when a header is present);

STX   indicates the start of a string (block) of text (data) characters;

ETX   indicates the end of the text string started with STX;

ETB   indicates the end of a data block which is one of a sequence of blocks;

EOT   indicates the end of a complete transmission sequence and effectively clears the link;

DLE   this is used to achieve data transparency when pure binary data instead of characters are being transmitted;

ENQ   this is used in the link setup and polling procedures;

ACK   positive acknowledgment to a data block or to a poll request control message;

NACK   negative acknowledgment to a data block or to a poll request control message.

5.6.1.1 Block formats

Some examples of the different types of data block used in BSC illustrating the use of some of these characters are shown in part (a) of Fig. 5.9. All blocks transmitted are preceded by at least two SYN characters to allow the receiver to achieve character synchronisation. The header field contains such information as the destination address and an identifier (sequence number) for use in the error control procedure. In addition, all data blocks have a block check character (BCC) after the end-of-block delimiter – ETX or ETB – which is a longitudinal (column) parity check – see Chapter 2 – on the block contents. It starts the check with the STX character and ends with the particular end-of-block delimiter character being used. Parity has, of course, only limited error detection properties and hence there is a maximum number of characters allowed in each data block transmitted. Longer messages must therefore be transmitted as a sequence of shorter fixed-sized data blocks. The last data block in a sequence is then terminated with an ETX control character.

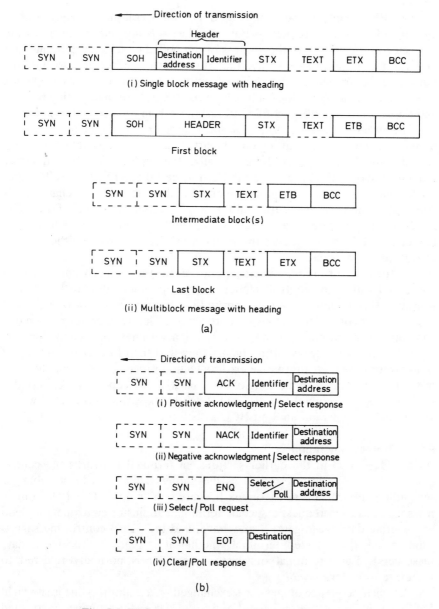

Fig. 5.9 BSC message formats: (a) data; (b) control

Four different control messages associated with the BSC protocol are shown in part (b) of the figure. The ACK and NACK control characters have two functions: the first is for acknowledgment purposes – one or other is returned in response to a previously transmitted data block and hence contains an identifier – the second is as a response to a Select control message – an ACK indicates the selected station is able to receive a data block, a NACK indicates it is not able – and carries the address of the selected terminal.

The ENQ control character is used as both a Poll and a Select control message. The type of request – Poll or Select – is defined in the following character(s) together with the address of the polled or selected terminal in a multidrop configuration. Finally, the EOT control character also has two functions: the first signals the end of a complete message exchange sequence and effectively clears the logical link between the two communicating parties, and the second as a Nothing-to-Send response from a polled terminal.

The use of the Data Link Escape character (DLE) to achieve data transparency when transmitting pure binary data rather than character strings was described in Chapter 2. Essentially, the various framing character sequences shown in Fig. 5.9 are modified to be DLE.STX, DLE.ETX, etc. Also, whenever a binary pattern corresponding to a DLE character is detected in the text by the transmitter, it adds (inserts) an extra DLE. The receiver then performs a similar check and, whenever it detects two consecutive DLEs, it removes the inserted DLE before passing the data on for further processing.

A further difference when operating in the transparent mode is concerned with error control. Under normal operation, the 8th bit of each transmitted character is used as a parity bit – transverse or row parity – and hence features in the error detection procedure. Clearly, therefore, if a block contains a transparent sequence of 8-bit binary values this cannot then be used. Hence, when transmitting binary data and therefore operating in the transparent mode, an alternative error detection procedure is normally used: instead of a simple 8-bit longitudinal parity check per block, a more sophisticated polynomial code is used. Each block is thus terminated with a 16-bit CRC rather than an 8-bit BCC as before.

5.6.1.2 Protocol operation

As was described in the earlier sections, in terminal networks the central computer – normally referred to as the *master station* – is responsible for scheduling all transmissions on each shared data link. The Poll control message is used to request a specific terminal (or cluster controller) to send any waiting data message(s) it may have, and the Select control message is used to ask the selected terminal whether it is ready to receive a data message(s). Each terminal or cluster controller is normally referred to therefore as a *slave station*.

A typical sequence of messages exchanged on a multidrop line is shown in Fig. 5.10. In part (a) a successful and an unsuccessful sequence associated

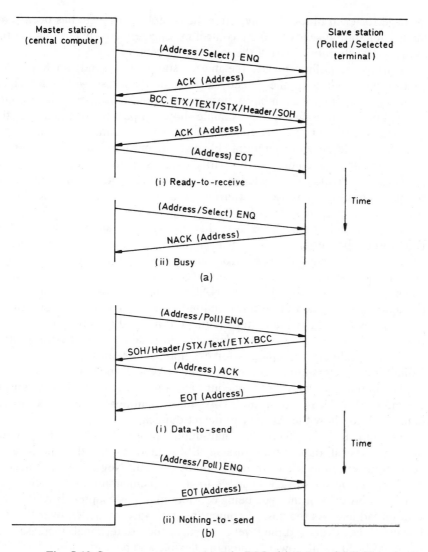

Fig. 5.10 Some message sequences in BSC: (a) Select; (b) Poll

with a select operation is shown and in part (b) two sequences associated with a poll operation. For clarity, only single-block data messages are shown.

To select a particular slave station (terminal), the master station (central computer) sends an ENQ control message with the slave station address within it. Then, assuming the selected station is ready to receive a message, it responds with an ACK control message. The master station then sends the message either as a single data block – as shown in the figure – or as a sequence of data blocks with the last block terminated with an ETX character. As each data block is being received and stored, the slave station recomputes the parity check sequence – transverse and longitudinal – and, assuming there are no transmission errors, responds with an ACK control message for each block. Finally, after the complete message has been sent, the master station sends an EOT control message effectively terminating the message transfer and clearing the logical connection.

During the polling phase, the master station first sends an ENQ Poll control messsage with the polled slave station address within it. Then, assuming the polled station has a message awaiting transmission, it responds by sending the message. In the example shown in part (b) of the figure, the message is assumed to be contained within a single data block and longer messages would be sent as multiple blocks. The master station, on receipt of each data block, recomputes the parity check sequence and, assuming no transmission errors, acknowledges its correct receipt. Finally, after the complete message has been transferred and acknowledged, the logical connection is cleared with an EOT control message.

It can be deduced from Fig. 5.10 that BSC is in fact an example of an Idle RQ protocol because, after sending each data block, the transmitter waits for either an ACK or a NACK control message before sending the next block and, in the case of the latter, the sending station retransmits the corrupted block. The use of an additional NACK control message means that a corrupted data block will be retransmitted sooner; that is, on receipt of the NACK message rather than after the timeout interval as is the case with the basic Idle RQ protocol. As was described in Chapter 3, if the transmitted block is completely corrupted – for example, if the start- or end-of-frame delimiter characters are corrupted or if the NACK or indeed ACK messages are corrupted – an additional timeout mechanism is still required to ensure the affected block is retransmitted. A single identifier is then used in each data block to allow the receiver to detect duplicates.

Because BSC is effectively a half-duplex protocol, even if the physical link supports full-duplex transmission, BSC cannot exploit this and hence is very inefficient in its use of transmission bandwidth. Nevertheless, it needs a minimum of buffer storage facilities for its implementation, and hence, for terminal networks of the type being considered in this chapter, BSC is still in widespread use. As the cost of computing hardware has fallen over the past few years, however, and the level of sophistication of terminals increased , so there has been a shift towards the more flexible and potentially more efficient HDLC protocol. This is certainly the case for computer-to-computer communication networks which normally require full-duplex, transparent working.

5.6.2 High-level data link control

Like BSC, HDLC is a link-level protocol which has been defined by the International Standards Organisation (ISO) for use on both point-to-point and multipoint (multidrop) data links. It supports full-duplex, transparent-mode operation and is now extensively used in both terminal-based networks of the type being considered here and also computer networks to be described in subsequent chapters. Although the acronym HDLC is now widely accepted, a number of large manufacturers and other standards bodies still use their own acronym. These include SDLC (Synchronous Data Link Control) by IBM, and ADCCP (Advanced Data Communications Control Procedure) used by the American National Standards Institute (ANSI).

Because HDLC has been defined as a general purpose data link control protocol, when the data link is first set up a specific mode of operation is selected. The two most prevalent modes are:

Unbalanced Normal Response (UNR)   this is mainly used in terminal-based networks since in this mode slave stations – known as *secondaries* in HDLC – can only transmit when specifically instructed by the master – known as the *primary* – station. The link may be point-to-point or multidrop but in the case of the latter, only one primary station is allowed.

Asynchronous Balanced Mode (ABM)   this is mainly used on point-to-point links for computer-to-computer communication or for connections between, say, statistical multiplexers. In this mode, each station has an equal status and performs both primary and secondary functions.

5.6.2.1 Frame formats

Unlike BSC, HDLC is a bit oriented protocol which, for reasons given in Chapter 2, is more efficient than a byte (character) oriented protocol. With HDLC, both data and control messages are carried in a standard format block which is referred to as a *frame*. The standard format of a frame is shown in Fig. 5.11 together with the different frame types which are defined in the Control field of the frame header. There are three different classes of frame used in HDLC:

Unnumbered frames   these are used for such functions as link setup and disconnection and hence do not contain any acknowledgment information. Since the latter is contained in sequence numbers, these frames are known as *unnumbered frames*.

Information frames   these are used to carry the actual information or data; they are normally referred to simply as I-frames. Also, as will be seen, I-frames may be used to piggyback acknowledgment information relating to the flow of I-frames in the reverse direction when the link is being operated in the ABM mode.

Supervisory frames   these are used for error and flow control purposes and hence contain send and receive sequence numbers.

The use of the *Flag field* as a start- and end-of-frame delimiter, together with zero bit insertion and deletion to achieve data transparency, was described in Chapter 2 and hence will not be repeated here.

The *Frame Check Sequence* (*FCS*) is a 16-bit cyclic redundancy check for the complete frame contents enclosed between the two flag delimiters. The generator polynomial used with HDLC is:

$$x^{16} + x^{12} + x^5 + 1$$

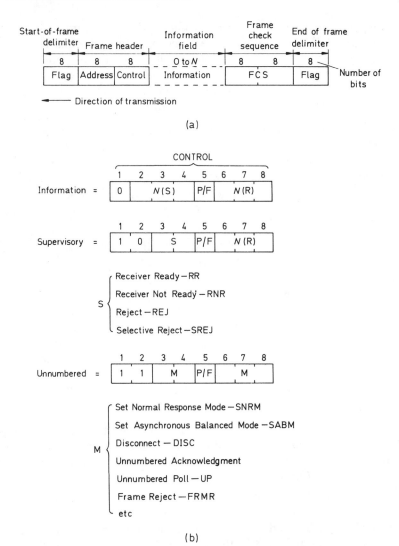

Fig. 5.11 Frame format and types: (a) standard frame format;
(b) control field bit definitions

The FCS is generated using the procedure described in Chapter 2 except that additional procedures, such as adding 16 ones to the tail of the dividend prior to division and inverting the remainder, are used in order to make the check more robust. This has the effect that the remainder when computed by the receiver is not all zeros but a special bit pattern – 0001 1101 0000 1111.

The contents of the *Address field* depends on the mode of operation being used. In the Unbalanced Normal Response Mode as used on a multidrop line, for example, every secondary station is assigned a unique address and, whenever the primary station – the central computer – communicates with a particular secondary, the Address field contains the address of the secondary. In addition, certain addresses may be assigned to more than one secondary station. These are known as *Group Addresses* and all frames transmitted with a Group Address within them will be received by all stations in that group. Also, an address containing all ones is known as a *Broadcast Address* since it is used to transmit a frame to all secondary stations on the link.

When a particular secondary station returns a response message (frame) back to the primary, the Address field always contains the unique address of the secondary. Also, for large networks containing possibly a large number of secondaries, the Address field may be extended beyond 8 bits. The least significant bit of each 8-bit field is then used to indicate whether there is another octet to follow (l.s. bit = 0) or whether it is the last or only octet (l.s. bit = 1).

The use of the Address field when Asynchronous Balanced Mode is being used is different because only direct point-to-point links are involved. It is used instead, therefore, to indicate the direction of Commands and their associated Responses. This will be expanded upon later.

The various Control field bit definitions are defined in part (b) of Fig. 5.11. The S-field in Supervisory frames and the M-field in Unnumbered frames are used to define the specific frame type. The Send and Receive Sequence Numbers – $N(S)$ and $N(R)$ – are used in conjunction with the error and flow control procedures and will be expanded upon later.

The P/F bit is known as the *Poll/Final bit*. A frame of any type is called a *Command frame* if it is sent by the primary station and a *Response frame* if it is sent by a secondary station. The P/F bit is called the *Poll bit* when used in a Command frame and, if set, indicates that the receiver must acknowledge this frame. The receiver then acknowledges this frame by returning an appropriate response frame with the P/F bit set; it is then known as the *Final bit*. Again, this will be expanded upon later.

5.6.2.2 Frame types
Before describing the operation of the HDLC protocol, it is perhaps helpful first to list some of the different frame types and to outline their function. As has been mentioned, there are three classes of frame used – Unnumbered, Information, and Supervisory – and some of the different types of frame in each class are listed in part (b) of Fig. 5.11.

The Unnumbered frames are used for link management purposes. Thus the SNRM and SABM frames are used firstly, to set up a logical link between the primary and a secondary station and secondly, to inform the secondary station of the mode of operation to be used. A logical link is then subsequently cleared by the primary station sending a DISC frame. The UA frame is used as an acknowledgment to the other frames in this class.

Although there are four different types of Supervisory frame – RR, RNR, REJ and SREJ – only the first two are used in both the NRM and ABM modes. The RR and RNR frames are used, firstly to indicate the willingness or otherwise of a secondary station to receive an I-frame(s) from the primary station, and secondly for acknowledgment purposes. The REJ and SREJ frames are used only in the ABM mode. This mode permits two-way-simultaneous communication across a point-to-point link and the two frames are used to indicate to the other station that a sequence error has occurred; that is, an I-frame containing an out-of-sequence $N(S)$ has been received. The SREJ frame is used when a Selective Retransmission procedure is being used whereas the REJ frame is used when a Go-Back-N procedure is being used. The use of some of the different types of frame will now be illustrated as some aspects of the operation of the protocol are described.

5.6.2.3 Protocol operation

The aim of this section is not to produce a full description of the operation of the HDLC protocol, but rather to highlight some of its more important features. The two basic functions of link management and data transfer (including error and flow control) will be considered.

5.6.2.4 Link management

Before any information (data) may be transmitted, either between the primary and a secondary station on a multidrop link, or between two stations connected by a point-to-point link, a logical connection between the two communicating parties must first be established (set up). This is accomplished by the exchange of two Unnumbered frames as shown in Fig. 5.12.

In part (a), a multidrop link is assumed and in part (b) a point-to-point link. Thus in part (a), an SNRM frame is first sent by the primary station with the Poll bit set to one and the address of the appropriate secondary in the Address field. The secondary then responds with a UA frame with the Final bit set and its own address in the Address field. Also, as can be seen, the setup procedure also has the effect of initialising the sequence variables held by each station. These, as will be described, are used in the error and flow control procedures. Finally, after all data have been transferred, the link is cleared by the primary sending a DISC frame and the secondary responding with a UA.

The procedure followed to set up a point-to-point link is the same as that used for a multidrop link. In the example shown in part (b), however, the Asynchronous Balanced Mode has been selected and hence an SABM frame instead of an SNRM is first sent. In this mode, both sides of the link may initiate the transfer of I-frames independently and hence each station is often referred to as a *Combined Station* since it must act as both a primary and a secondary. For this mode either station may initiate the setting up or clearing of the link. In the example, station A initiates the setup of the link and station B initiates the clearing of the (logical) connection. A single exchange of frames sets up the link in both directions. Also, as can be seen, the address field is being used to indicate the direction of the command frame – SABM/DISC – and its associated response.

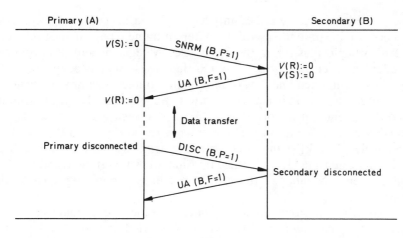

(a)

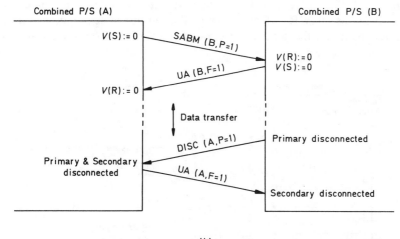

(b)

Fig. 5.12 Link management procedure: (a) Normal Response Mode – multidrop link; (b) Asynchronous Balanced Mode – point-to-point link

5.6.2.5 Data transfer

In the NRM mode all data (I-frames) are transferred under the control of the primary station. The Unnumbered Poll (UP) frame with the P bit set to 1 is normally used by the primary to poll a secondary. If the secondary has no data to transmit, it returns an RNR frame with the F bit set. If it has data waiting, it transmits the data – typically as a sequence of I-frames – with the F bit set to 1 in the last frame of the sequence.

The two more important aspects associated with the data transfer phase are error control and flow control. Essentially, error control is accomplished by means of a *Continuous RQ* procedure, with either a *Selective Retransmission* or a *Go-Back*-N retransmission strategy, and flow control is accomplished by means of a window mechanism. The basic operation of both these procedures was described in Chapter 3 and hence only typical frame sequences to illustrate the use of the different frame types will be given here.

An example illustrating the basic acknowledgment and retransmission procedure is given in Fig. 5.13. A Go-Back-N strategy is assumed. In the figure just a unidirectional flow of information frames is shown and hence all acknowledgment information must be returned using specific acknowledgment supervisory frames. As can be seen, each side of the link maintains both a *Send* and a *Receive Sequence Variable* – $V(S)$ and $V(R)$ respectively. The $V(S)$ indicates the next *Send Sequence Number*, $N(S)$, which will be allocated to an I-frame transmitted by that station, and $V(R)$ the Send Sequence Number of the next in-sequence I-frame expected by that station.

Each RR – positive acknowledgment – supervisory frame contains a *Receive Sequence Number*, $N(R)$, which acknowledges correct receipt of all previously transmitted I-frames up to and including that with an $N(S)$ equal to $[N(R) - 1]$. Similarly, each REJ – negative acknowledgment – supervisory frame contains an $N(R)$ which indicates that an out-of-sequence I-frame has been received and the sender must start to retransmit from the I-frame with $N(S)$ equal to $N(R)$.

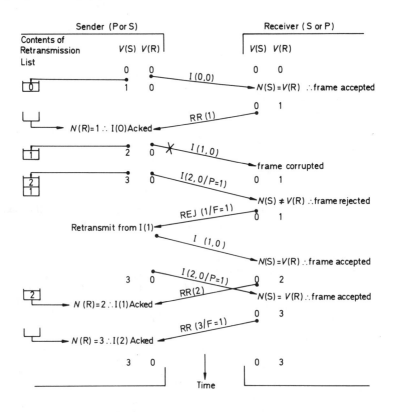

Fig. 5.13 Use of acknowledgment frames

As can be seen from the example, the sequence numbers are incremented modulo 8. Also, when the receiver detects frame I(2,0) – that is, the last frame in the sequence hence P=1 – is out-of-sequence, it returns an REJ frame with the F bit set. The sender then retransmits frames I(1,0) and I(2,0) with the P bit again set to 1 in frame I(2,0). The receiver then acknowledges correct receipt of each frame with the F bit set to 1 in the last RR frame. If Selective Retransmission were being used, then frame I(2,0) would be accepted and an SREJ frame returned to request frame I(1,0) retransmitted.

The frame sequence shown in Fig. 5.13 is typical of an information transfer over a multidrop link operating in the NRM mode. For a point-to-point link being operated in the ABM mode, however, a bidirectional flow of I-frames is possible and hence acknowledgment information relating to the flow of I-frames in one direction can be *piggybacked* in I-frames flowing in the reverse direction. An example illustrating this is given in Fig. 5.14. For clarity, no transmission errors are shown.

As each I-frame is received, both the $N(S)$ and $N(R)$ contained within it are read. The $N(S)$ is first compared with the receivers $V(R)$ and, if they are equal, the frame is in the correct sequence and hence is accepted (if they were not equal then the frame would be discarded and an REJ or SREJ frame returned). The $N(R)$ is then examined and this is used to acknowledge any outstanding frames in the *Retransmission List*. Finally, as no further I-frames are awaiting transmission, an RR frame is used to acknowledge the outstanding unacknowledged frames in each Retransmission List.

Flow control is particularly important when two-way simultaneous working is being used and hence the link is being operated in the ABM mode. Clearly, with the NRM mode, if the primary experiences some transient overload conditions it can simply suspend the polling operation, thereby allowing the overload to subside. When both sides of the link are operating independently, however, an alternative mechanism must be used. The flow control procedure used in HDLC is based on a *window mechanism* similar to that already discussed in Chapter 3.

As has been seen in the examples, the Send and Receive Sequence Numbers are incremented modulo 8 and hence the maximum *Send Window*, K – that is, the maximum number of I-frames that can be awaiting acknowledgment in the Retransmission List at any time – that can be used is 7. Each side of the link maintains a separate variable known as the Retransmission Count (*RetxCount*) which is initialised to zero when the logical link is first set up. It is incremented each time an I-frame is transmitted – and hence each time a frame is placed in the Retransmission List – and is decremented whenever a positive acknowledgment is received – and hence each time a frame is removed from the Retransmission List. The primary then stops sending I-frames if the Retransmission Count reaches K until a positive acknowledgment is received either as a separate RR supervisory frame or piggybacked in an I-frame flowing in the reverse direction. It can be concluded, therefore, that transmission of I-frames is stopped when

$$V(S) = \text{last } N(R) \text{ received} + K$$

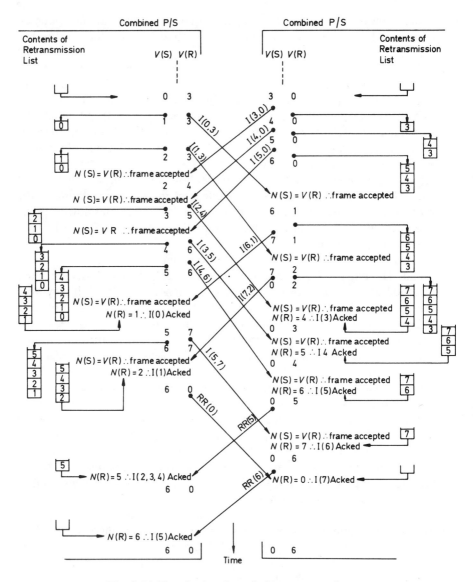

Fig. 5.14 Piggyback acknowledgment procedure

It should be noted, that the window mechanism controls the flow of I-frames in only one direction and also that supervisory and unnumbered frames are not affected and hence may still be transmitted when the window is operating. An example illustrating this is shown in Fig. 5.15. In the example, for clarity only the flow of I-frames in one direction is affected.

The application of a window mechanism means that the sequence numbers in all incoming frames – $N(S)$ and $N(R)$ – must lie within certain boundaries. On receipt of each frame, therefore, the secondary may check to establish that this is the case and, if not, take corrective action. It can readily be deduced that each received $N(S)$ and $N(R)$ must satisfy the following conditions:

$$V(R) - 1 \leqslant N(S) < V(R) + K$$

and

$$V(S) > N(R) \geqslant V(S) - \text{RetxCount}$$

Clearly, if $N(S)$ equals $V(R)$ then all is well and the frame is accepted. Also, if $N(S)$ is not equal to $V(R)$ but is still within the above range, then a frame has simply been corrupted and hence an REJ – Go-Back-N – or an SREJ – Selective Retransmission – frame is returned indicating to the primary a sequence error has occurred and from which frame to start retransmission. This was illustrated in Fig. 5.13.

If $N(S)$ or $N(R)$ is outside of the above range, however, then the sequence numbers at both ends of the link have become unsynchronised and

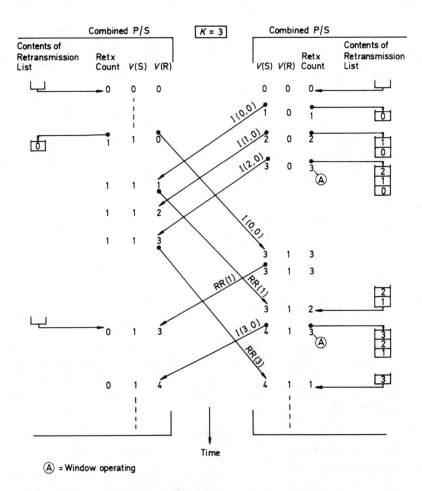

Fig. 5.15 Window flow control procedure

hence the link must be re-initialised (set up) again. This is accomplished by the secondary, on detecting an out-of-range sequence number, discarding the received frame and returning an FRMR – also known as a *Command Reject* or *CMDR* – frame to the primary. The latter then discards all waiting frames and proceeds to set up the link again by sending an SABM and waiting for a UA response. On receipt of the latter, both sides of the link will have reset their sequence and window variables and hence the flow of I-frames can be resumed. In fact, this is only one reason why a link may be reset; others include the receipt of an unnumbered frame such as a UA when in the data transfer phase since this also indicates the primary and secondary have become unsynchronised.

The above flow control procedure is controlled by the primary side of the link controlling the flow of I-frames according to the Send Window. In addition, however, it may be necessary for the secondary to stop the flow of I-frames as a result of some event occurring at its side – that is, the secondary side – of the link. For instance, with a Go-Back-N retransmission strategy the Receive Window is unity and hence it is reasonably straightforward to ensure there are sufficient memory buffers available at the receiver. If Selective Retransmission is being used, however, it is possible for the secondary to run out of free buffers to store any new frames. Hence, if this occurs, when the secondary approaches a point when all its buffers are likely to become full, it returns an RNR (Receiver-Not-Ready) supervisory frame to the primary to instruct the latter to stop sending any more I-frames. Acknowledgment frames are not affected, of course, and hence when the number of full buffers drops below another preset limit, the secondary returns an RR frame to the primary with an $N(R)$ indicating from which frame to restart transmission.

Problems

5.1 a) Explain the principle of operation of a terminal multiplexer and sketch an example terminal network which uses a number of such devices.

b) Sketch a schematic diagram showing the internal organisation of a terminal multiplexer and explain its operation. Describe the organisation of the shared data link and how the controlling device determines the destination of each received character.

5.2 Explain the principle of operation of a statistical multiplexer and sketch an example terminal network which uses such a device. Derive typical data rates for both the user links and the shared data link and list the advantages and disadvantages of such a device against a basic terminal multiplexer.

5.3 Outline the function of a terminal switching exchange and sketch a typical terminal network which is based on such a device.

5.4 Sketch a typical block-mode terminal network which uses multidrop lines and a poll-select control protocol. Explain the operation of the network and how the computer sends and receives messages to and from each terminal.

5.5 a) Explain the function of:

  i) a cluster controller, and
  ii) a front-end processor

  as used in block-mode terminal networks, and sketch a typical network schematic which uses such devices. List the advantages of using these devices.

  b) Distinguish between roll-call and hub polling. Sketch a typical network schematic for each polling method and explain their operation.

5.6 a) Form a list of the main control characters used in the Binary Synchronous Control (BSC) protocol and explain their function.

  b) Show how the various characters listed in part (a) are incorporated into BSC messages and illustrate typical message sequences to show their use in both the poll and select modes.

5.7 Assuming the HDLC protocol, distinguish between the Normal Response Mode and the Asynchronous Balanced Mode of working.

Sketch typical frame sequences to show how a link is first set up (established) and then cleared (disconnected) for each mode. Show clearly the different frame types used and the use of the Address and Poll/Final bit in each frame.

5.8 Define the supervisory frames used for acknowledgment purposes in the HDLC protocol. Assuming a undirectional flow of I-frames, sketch a typical frame sequence diagram to illustrate the acknowledgment procedure used in the HDLC protocol. Include in your diagram the contents of the link Retransmission List and the state of the Send and Receive Sequence Variables as each frame is transmitted and received. Also show the Send and Receive Sequence Numbers contained within each frame and the state of the Poll/Final bit where appropriate.

5.9 What is understood by a piggyback acknowledgment? Sketch a typical frame sequence diagram to illustrate how piggyback acknowledgments are used in the HDLC protocol. Clearly show the Send and Receive Sequence Numbers contained within each frame transmitted and the contents of the Retransmission Lists and Send and Receive Variables at each side of the link.

5.10 a) Outline the operation of a window flow control mechanism. Assuming a Send Window of K and a Send Window Variable $V(W)$, deduce the range within which the Send and Receive Sequence Numbers contained within each received frame should be, assuming both sides of the link are in synchronism.

b) Assuming a Send Window of 3 and a unidirectional flow of I-frames, sketch a frame sequence diagram to illustrate the operation of the window flow control mechanism used with the HDLC protocol.

Chapter 6 **Computer-to-Computer Communication Protocols**

Objectives:

When you have completed studying the material in this chapter you should be able to:

- appreciate the structure and aims of the ISO Reference Model for open systems interconnection;

- understand the different techniques which are used in the various standards documents to describe the services and operation of the protocol layers making up the Reference Model;

- describe a typical set of services and the operation of the Transport Layer;

- describe the basic set of services provided by the Session Layer and understand the operation of the associated protocol;

- explain the function of the various optional services associated with the Session Layer; define a typical set of services provided by the Presentation Layer and describe their function;

- understand how a simple application layer service interacts with the underlying communications oriented protocol layers to carry out a network-based transaction.

6.1 INTRODUCTION

Communication between distributed communities of computers is required for many reasons. At a national level, for example, computers located in different parts of the country use public data communication services to exchange electronic messages (mail) and to transfer files of information from one computer to another. Similarly, at a local level within, say, a single building or establishment, distributed communities of computer-based workstations use local data communication networks to access expensive shared resources – printers, copiers, etc. – which are also managed by computers. Clearly, as the range of computer-based products and associated public and local data communication networks proliferate, computer-to-computer communication will expand rapidly and ultimately dominate the field of distributed systems.

Although the physical separation of the communicating computers in the above examples may vary considerably from one type of application to another, in general, a computer communication network can be represented diagrammatically as shown in Fig. 6.1. At the heart of any computer communication network is the data communication facility which, as has just been outlined, may be a public switched data network, a private local area data network, or perhaps a number of such networks interconnected together. Irrespective of the type of data communication facility, however, an amount of hardware and software is required within each attached computer to handle the appropriate network-dependent protocols. Typically, these are concerned with the establishment of a communications channel across the network and with the control of the flow of messages across this channel. Providing these facilities is only part of the requirements, however, since in many applications the communicating computers may be of different types. This means that they may use different programs and, more important, different operating systems and types of data representation. Also, the interface with programs within each system may be different: one computer may be a small single-user computer, for example, and another a large time-sharing system.

In the earlier days of computer communication these issues meant that only closed communities of computers – that is, computers from the same manufacturer – could communicate with each other in a meaningful way. IBM's Systems Network Architecture (SNA) and DEC's Digital Network Architecture (DNA) are just two examples of communication software

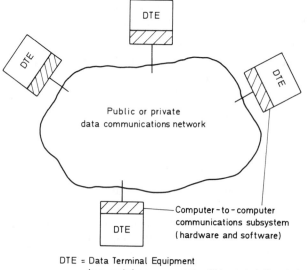

DTE = Data Terminal Equipment
(e.g. mainframe computer, office workstation etc)

Fig. 6.1 Computer communication schematic

packages produced by manufacturers to allow their systems to be interconnected together. These proprietary packages, however, of which there are still many in existence, do not address the problem of universal interconnectability – open systems interconnection – and hence, in the late 1970s, in an attempt to alleviate this problem, the International Standards Organisation (ISO) formulated a reference model for such packages to provide a common basis for the coordination of standards developments and to allow existing and evolving standards activities to be placed into perspective with one another. The ultimate aim of the various standards activities is to allow any computer which supports the applicable standards to freely communicate with any other computer supporting the same standard irrespective of its origin of manufacture. This is known as the *ISO Reference Model for Open Systems Interconnection*. It should be stressed, however, that this model is not concerned with specific applications of computer communication networks but rather with the structuring of the communication software that is needed to provide a reliable, data-transparent communication service, which is independent of any specific manufacturer's equipment or conventions, to support a wide range of different applications.

6.2 THE ISO REFERENCE MODEL

The ISO Reference Model is logically composed of an ordered set of *layers* through which users – application processes – communicate to exchange meaningful messages with other systems. The logical structure of the model is as shown in Fig. 6.2. Essentially, the lowest three layers (1–3) are concerned with the communications protocols associated with the data communications network being used to link the two communicating computers together whilst the upper three layers (5–7) are concerned with the protocols necessary to allow the two (usually) heterogeneous operating systems to interact with each other. The intermediate Transport Layer then masks the upper protocol layers from the detail workings of the lower network-dependent layers.

The function of each layer is formally specified in the form of a protocol which defines the set of rules and conventions which are used by the layer in order to communicate – exchange information – with a similar (*peer*) layer in another (remote) system. Each layer provides a defined set of services to the layer immediately above it and, in turn, uses the services provided by the next lower layer to transport the message units associated with the defined protocol of that layer. Thus the Transport Layer, for example, provides a reliable, network-independent message transport service to the Session Layer above it and uses the services provided by the Network Layer below it to exchange the set of message units associated with the transport protocol. Conceptually, therefore, each layer communicates with a similar peer layer in a remote system according to a defined protocol, but in practice the resulting protocol units of the layer are passed by means of the services provided by the next lower layer.

The *Application Layer* in the Reference Model is concerned with

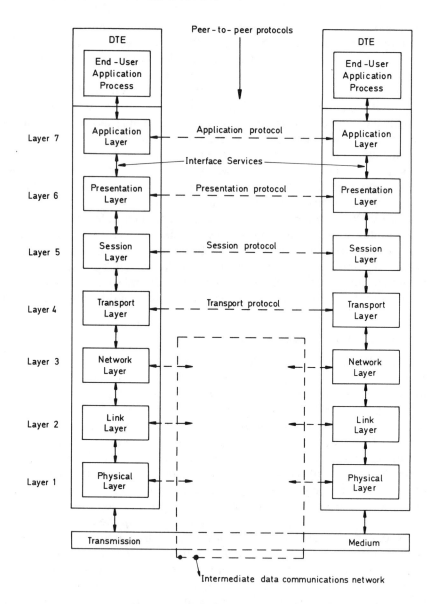

Fig. 6.2 OSI Reference Model

providing a set of *network services* to user application programs (processes). Typically, within an operating system there are a number of different Application Layer processes to support such functions as file transfer, document transfer, electronic mail, and so on. Indeed, a number of standards are currently being developed for these and other types of network service. A user (a user application process in practice) then gains access to these services by issuing a service request primitive which contains all the information necessary for the appropriate Application Layer process to carry out the request; normally, this information is passed in the form of parameters associated with the request primitive. In a small single-user system, only a single network service will be active at a time, whilst in a larger system a possibly large number of different network services may be active concurrently.

The *Presentation Layer* is concerned with the representation of the data being used by the two correspondent Application Layer processes and hence, if necessary, it will perform such functions as data transformation on each message it receives from the Application Layer. For example, if the two communicating computers – application processes within the two operating systems in practice – use different internal character codes such as ASCII and EBCDIC, each message transferred must be converted at each end into the appropriate form before being passed up to the appropriate Application Layer process for further processing. Alternatively, if a network service – document transfer for example – is being used which defines a standard character set, the Presentation Layer would perform the necessary conversions from and to the standard network form if this were different from the internal form used by the computer on which the Application Layer process resides. Another common function is concerned with data security: if the information being communicated is of a confidential nature, the Presentation Layer may perform an *encryption operation* on the contents of each message prior to initiating its transmission through the network layers; similarly, on receipt of each message from the network it would perform the reverse function.

Since the Presentation Layer simply performs a transformation operation on application-specific message units, it is the *Session Layer* that provides the logical user interface with the communications oriented layers. Its function is to establish and manage an open communication path or channel between two communicating application processes – Presentation Layers in practice – for the duration of each network activity. It thus performs an analogous function to the login and logout procedures a user follows at a terminal connected to a conventional multi-access computer system in order to open and subsequently close a user dialogue with the local operating system prior to performing some editing or other processing function. For example, a user at a terminal – through a suitable application process – may wish to perform a transaction with a similar application process in a remote system. At the commencement of the transaction, therefore, the Session Layer would first establish a (logical) communications path (connection) with the remote Session Layer which is then maintained for the duration of the ensuing transaction. It would then manage the subsequent information exchange and, after the transaction is complete, release the established communications path.

Clearly, to establish a communications path between two Session Layers which are resident on two different computers connected through a network, it is necessary for the user application process to provide the necessary addressing information to the local Session Layer to enable it to initiate the connection with the required remote system. The addressing information is normally passed from the application process in the form of parameters associated with the appropriate service request call (primitive) and one of the functions of the Session Layer is to map the addresses passed to it from the Application Layer into a form which is acceptable and meaningful to the lower network layers. Other functions are concerned with controlling the type of information exchange (duplex or half-duplex), and reporting any error conditions (exceptions) that may arise during a session connection to the Application Layer.

The purpose of the *Transport Layer* is to provide a reliable end-to-end service, for the transfer of Session Layer message units, which is independent of the type of data communications facility being used. The Transport Layer thus relieves the Session Layer of any concern with the detailed way in which messages are being transported across the data communications facility. The latter, therefore, can be of many different forms – for example a public switched data network or a private local area data network – but this is transparent to the Session Layer above. For example, with some types of data network, a single session layer entity (message) may be longer than the maximum data unit that can be transmitted across the network. Hence one of the functions of the Transport Layer is to split session layer message units into a number of smaller segments (blocks) for transmission across the data network and, on receipt, to reassemble these segments into meaningful session layer messages. Other functions include the establishment and management of end-to-end (logical) connections for the transfer of session layer messages which are independent of the underlying network type.

The lowest three layers of the Reference Model are network dependent and their detail operation varies therefore from one type of network to another. Two different types of data network will be described in the next two chapters. As will be seen, if the network is a public data network, the Network and Link Layers have only local significance, but if the network is a private local area network they have end-to-end significance. As an example, however, with a public packet-switched data network, the *Network Layer* is responsible for such tasks as establishing and clearing multiple *virtual circuits* across a single physical link between the attached computer (DTE) and the local packet switching exchange, whilst the *Link Layer* is responsible for the reliable transfer of each network layer packet – each possibly related to a different virtual circuit – across the one physical link. The function of the latter thus includes such tasks as link setup and error control. Finally, the *Physical Layer* defines the electrical and mechanical interface with the local data communications terminating equipment.

The remainder of this chapter is concerned only with the function of the higher protocol layers in the Reference Model and the detail operation of the lower, network-dependent layers, for two different types of data network, are discussed in Chapters 7 and 8. It should be stressed that the descriptions which follow are not intended as being complete nor do they adhere strictly to defined standards. Rather, the descriptions are presented in a tutorial form and are intended simply to give the reader an insight into the function of each layer. Indeed, some of the descriptions are only speculative since some of the standards are only in an early stage of development.

6.3 TRANSPORT LAYER

When describing the operation of any protocol layer, it is important from the outset to discriminate between the services provided by the layer, the internal operation (that is the protocol) of the layer, and the services used by the layer. This is important because only then can the function of each layer be defined in the context of the other layers. It also has the effect that a person (programmer) who is implementing just a single protocol layer, need only then have a knowledge of the services the layer is to provide to the layer above, the internal protocol of the layer, and the services which are provided by the layer below to transfer the appropriate items of information associated with the protocol to the similar layer in the remote system; it should not be necessary for the implementor to have any further knowledge of the other layers.

Thus in order to describe the function of the Transport Layer, it is only necessary to consider firstly the defined set of services the Transport Layer is to provide to the Session Layer above it (for the purpose of transporting session layer message units to a peer Session Layer in a remote system); secondly, the internal operation (protocol) of the Transport Layer (this is concerned with such functions as establishing and managing logical connections with a similar peer Transport Layer in a remote system and the error and flow control of transport layer message units across established connections); and thirdly, the services provided by the (lower) Network Layer to transfer these message units to a peer Transport Layer. When describing the functions of each protocol layer, therefore, these three aspects will be treated separately; that is, the services provided by the layer, the internal operation (the protocol) of the layer, and the services used by the layer.

6.3.1 Specification notation

Before defining the set of services provided by the Transport Layer, it is necessary first to describe the notations which are normally used for defining such services. The services provided by a layer are normally specified in the various standards documents by a set of primitive operations each with a set of parameters associated with it. There are four types of primitive which are normally used:

request,
indication,
response,
confirmation.

Each primitive has a direction which is relative to the layer (service provider); the primitive is said to be *from* the user of the layer – the layer above – when the service request is initiated by the user and *to* the user when the primitive is passed from the layer to the user. The *request primitive*, for example, normally comes from the user. This, in turn, may result in a similar request being sent by the layer to the same protocol layer in the remote system – determined by the layer protocol – and the latter may then pass the received request up to the higher layer – normally referred to as the *correspondent user* – in the form of an *indication primitive*. The correspondent user may then reply with a suitable *response primitive* which, typically, will be relayed back to the source system and subsequently passed up to the user in the form of a *confirmation primitive*. This is illustrated diagrammatically in Fig. 6.3.

It can be concluded from the above discussion that there is a logical relationship between the various service primitives and also that these relationships are related in time. The interrelationship of the service primitives associated with a layer are often illustrated, therefore, in the form of a *time sequence diagram* and as an example, part (b) of Fig. 6.3 is a time

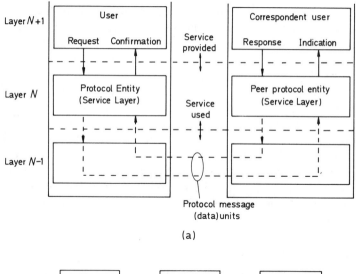

(a)

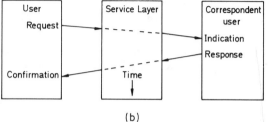

(b)

Fig. 6.3 Interrelationship of service primitives: (a) space representations; (b) time sequence representations

sequence diagram showing the interrelationship of the four primitives just described. It should be apparent from this figure that a time sequence diagram is only an abstract way of representing the logical relationships between the service primitives of a layer and does not indicate how the specified services are provided by the layer. Also, not all services use the full set of primitives; a unidirectional transfer service, for example, uses only a request and an indication primitive and so on.

6.3.2 Transport user services

The services provided by the Transport Layer can be divided into two categories: connection management and data transfer. The connection management services allow a user of the Transport Layer – the Session Layer – to establish and maintain a logical connection to a correspondent transport user in a remote system, whilst the data transfer services provide the means for exchanging data (messages) between the two correspondent users over this connection.

A number of alternative classes of service are normally supported by a single Transport Layer in order to cater for a range of different types of underlying data comunication networks. A simple transport connection, however, can be managed using two basic services: T.CONNECT and T.DISCONNECT; the T prefix indicating it is a transport service. There are four primitives associated with the T.CONNECT service:

T.CONNECT.request,
T.CONNECT.indication,
T.CONNECT.response,
T.CONNECT.confirmation.

The request primitive is first issued by the local transport user to request the Transport Layer to attempt to establish a logical connection with a specified remote transport user; the indication primitive is used to inform the correspondent transport user in the remote system of the connection request; the response primitive is used by the correspondent user to indicate its response to the connection request; and the confirmation primitive informs the initiating transport user of the correspondent user's willingness to accept the connection request.

Similarly, there are two primitives associated with the T.DISCONNECT service which are used to initiate the clearing of a connection: T.DISCONNECT.request and T.DISCONNECT.indication. The issuing of a T.DISCONNECT.request primitive by either the user or the correspondent user results in the clearing of just one half of the connection; that means that to clear the connection completely requires both users to issue a T.DISCONNECT.request primitive.

As was mentioned earlier, there are normally a set of parameters associated with each service request primitive and hence an example of a typical service request primitive may be:

T.CONNECT.request (destination identifier, source identifier, class of
service)

The two identifier parameters are known as *service-access-points* and
specify the identity of both the source and correspondent (destination)
transport user. These identifiers normally contain network-dependent
address information to enable the Transport Layer to inform the Network
Layer to which remote system a network connection is to be made. The
format of the identifier parameters will thus vary and depend on such factors
as the number of simultaneous users of the transport service (access points)
and how they are identified, and the type of underlying network and how the
network addresses are to be given. As an example, a typical request may be:

T.CONNECT.request (05/*xx*/1234, 01/17/5678, 2)

Here the numbers 01/17 and 05/*xx* are intended collectively to indicate
the identity of the transport service user and correspondent transport service
user respectively, 5678 and 1234 the correspondent host system global
network addresses, and 2 the class of network service required. Although the
two numbers making up the identity of each transport user are used
collectively by the appropriate Transport Layer to allow each received
message to be related to a particular transport service access point and
therefore connection, typically they would be interpreted separately by the
higher protocol layers. For example, the Session Layers may use the first
numbers (01 and 05 in the example) to identify the particular application
service process (file transfer, for example) to which the message relates;
similarly, the application processes may then use the second numbers (17 and
xx in the example) as the identity of the local user of that service. It is for this
reason that the identity of the local user in the destination system is shown as
xx as this will normally not be known until it is returned in the
T.CONNECT.confirmation primitive.

A diagrammatic representation of this scheme is shown in Fig. 6.4. In this
example, the calling DTE is assumed to be a multiple user system whilst the
called DTE a single user system and hence the returned local identifier (*xx*)
would be, say, 00. Also, beyond the Session Layer the various identifiers are
shown as local names and hence the identifiers would be mapped from
alphabetic to numeric form by the Session Layer.

Once a connection has been established, the two transport users may then
exchange data across the connection using the two data transfer request
primitives: T.DATA.request and T.DATA.indication. Transport
connections are normally full duplex and hence both the user and the
correspondent user can issue a T.DATA.request primitive to its local
Transport Layer. The associated data will then be transferred across the
logical connection in the appropriate direction and subsequently passed on to
the recipient transport user in the form of a T.DATA.indication primitive.

There are three parameters associated with each of the data transfer
service primitives which specify firstly the identity of both the user and
correspondent user, and secondly the transport-user data associated with the
primitive. This is collectively referred to as a *Transport-Service-Data-Unit* or

TSDU. TSDUs are not normally restricted in length and may vary from one transfer request to another. At the receiving side each TSDU is delivered in a single T.DATA.indication primitive and the Transport Layer protocol ensures that TSDUs are delivered to the recipient user in the same sequence that they are entered by the sending user.

A time sequence diagram illustrating the use of the various service primitives is given in Fig. 6.5. As can be seen, a transport connection is first established using the T.CONNECT service, data are then exchanged over this connection using the T.DATA service, and finally the connection is cleared using the T.DISCONNECT service.

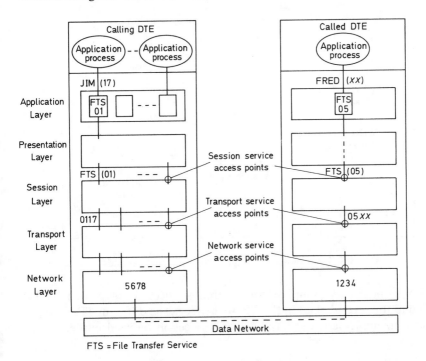

FTS = File Transfer Service

Fig. 6.4 Example address structure

6.3.3 Transport protocol

Two Transport Layers communicate with each other by the two internal *protocol entitites* exchanging *Transport-Protocol-Data-Units* (*TPDUs*). A TPDU may contain transport user data or protocol control information or, in some instances, both. All TPDUs consist of an integral number of octets and the format of the TPDUs used to implement a basic transport protocol are as shown in Fig. 6.6.

The Length Indicator (LI) is the first octet of every TPDU and indicates the number of octets in the header field, excluding the length indication itself and the number of octets in the user data field (if any).

As has been indicated, a number of different classes of transport service are often supported by the one protocol and hence there are a number of

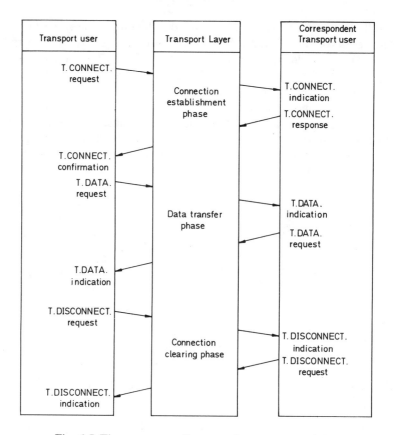

Fig. 6.5 Time sequence diagram of transport services

TPDU types necessary to support the different services. The type of TPDU is specified in the second octet in the TPDU header. The different TPDU types necessary to implement the basic set of services introduced earlier are as follows:

Connection Request (CONREQ),
Connection Confirm (CONCFM),
Disconnect Request (DISCREQ),
Data (DATA),
Data Acknowledgment (ACK).

The use of each TPDU wil be described in relation to the various services previously described. For clarity, the descriptions relate only to a single transport connection although in practice the Transport Layer may have to manage a number of such connections concurrently.

6.3.3.1 Connection establishment phase

Connection establishment begins when a transport user issues a T.CONNECT.request primitive. The local transport protocol entity responds by sending a CONREQ TPDU to its peer transport protocol entity in the remote system. On receipt of this, the latter notifies the designated user in its own system of the connection request by means of a T.CONNECT.indication primitive. Then, providing the correspondent user is prepared to accept the call, it responds by issuing a T.CONNECT. response primitive. Alternatively, if the correspondent user does not wish to accept the call, it issues a T.DISCONNECT.request primitive with the reason for the rejection as a parameter. The peer transport protocol then relays the appropriate response in either a CONCFM TPDU or a DISCREQ TPDU respectively. Finally, this is relayed by the initiating protocol entity to the user by means of the T.CONNECT.confirm primitive or the T.DISCONNECT.indication primitive respectively, the latter containing the reason for the rejection as a parameter.

The parameters contained in the CONREQ and CONCFM TPDUs relay information relating to the connection being established which both transport protocol entities must know in order to manage the established connection. This includes such information as the local identifier of the correspondent user, the class of service required, and the maximum length of subsequent DATA TPDUs; typically, the latter may range from 128 octets to 8192 octets increasing in powers of 2. Once the transport connection has been established data will be accepted by the transport entities for transfer across the established logical connection in either direction.

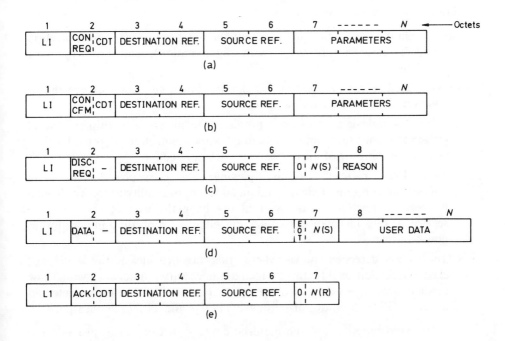

Fig. 6.6 TPDU formats

6.3.3.2 Data transfer phase

A transport user initiates the transfer of data to the correspondent user across a previously established connection using the T.DATA.request primitive. The local transport entity then transfers the user data (TSDU) in one or more DATA TPDUs depending on the amount of user data in the TSDU and the maximum size of TPDU specified for the connection. Each DATA TPDU contains a marker (EOT) which, when set, indicates that this is the last TPDU in a sequence making up a single TSDU. Also, each DATA TPDU contains a send sequence number $N(S)$ which is used both to indicate the order of the TPDU in a sequence and, in conjunction with the ACK TPDU, for acknowledgment and flow control purposes. When the destination transport entity has received – and acknowledged – all the DATA TPDUs making up a TSDU, it then passes the data to the user using the T.DATA.indication primitive.

The acknowledgment and flow control mechanisms used vary for different *classes of service* which in turn are determined by the quality of service provided by the underlying data network being used to transport the TPDUs. With an X.25 public packet-switched network, for example, the integrity and order of transmitted TPDUs is maintained by the Network Layer and hence only minimal acknowledgment and flow control mechanisms are needed in the transport protocol. With other types of network, however, this is not the case and hence more sophisticated mechanisms similar to those described in Chapter 3 must be used. The standards documents specify five different classes of service. These are:

Class 0: **Simple**;   this class provides only the functions needed for connection establishment, data transfer (with segmentation), and protocol error reporting.

Class 1: **Basic error recovery**;   this class is similar to class 0 except that it additionally recovers from network signalled errors.

Class 2: **Multiplexing**;   this class provides the means to multiplex several transport connections onto a single network connection. It provides flow control on the flow of messages over each connection.

Class 3: **Error recovery and multiplexing**;   this class provides the same multiplexing options as class 2 and, in addition, the ability to recover from a network connection failure without involving the user of the transport service. It thus incorporates an acknowledgment procedure in addition to flow control.

Class 4: **Error detection and recovery**;   this class provides all the features of class 3 and additional features which are necessary if a network with a low grade of service is being used – a PSTN for example. The errors detected include: TPDU loss, out-of-sequence TPDUs and TPDU duplication.

To avoid repetition of the material covered in Chapter 3, just selected aspects of the techniques used with the Class 4 protocol will be discussed.

The acknowledgment procedure works as follows: the receiver, on receipt of the next in sequence DATA TPDU or, if the TPDU completes a contiguous sequence of TPDUs, returns an ACK TPDU which contains a receive sequence number, $N(R)$, that positively acknowledges correct receipt of those DATA TPDUs up to and including that with a Send Sequence Number of $N(R) - 1$. If the Network Layer does not ensure that DATA TPDUs always arrive in order, the receiving transport entity uses the sequence numbers contained in each DATA TPDU to reassemble them into the correct order. In such cases, therefore, it is only when a DATA TPDU arrives in sequence or completes a contiguous sequence of outstanding TPDUs that the receiver returns an ACK TPDU indicating their correct receipt. A typical sequence of TPDUs to implement a user data transfer request is shown in Fig. 6.7.

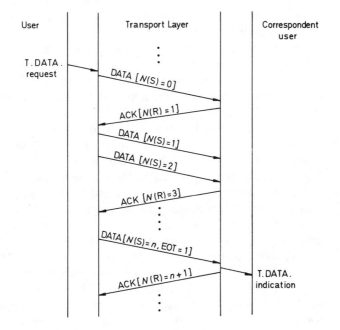

Fig. 6.7 Data transfer

Another factor to consider is that, if the service provided by the Network Layer is of a low quality, it may lose TPDUs without notifying the sender or intended receiver, or it may pass on TPDUs which contain transmission errors. To allow for these possibilities, the Class 4 class of service includes a timeout and retransmission procedure to allow for the possibility of lost TPDUs and also computed checksums and error detection mechanisms to ensure the integrity of each transmitted TPDU.

The protocol mechanism used to implement the timeout and retransmission scheme works as follows: when a transport entity sends a TPDU which requires a response, it sets a timer. Then, if the timer expires before the appropriate response is received, the TPDU is retransmitted and the timer reset. This cycle is repeated for some number of times and, if the appropriate response is still not received, the transport entity assumes communication with its peer has been lost and hence initiates the setting up of a new network connection. The use of timeouts means that duplicates may be generated – TPDU received correctly but acknowledgment lost – and hence if a DATA TPDU is found to be a duplicate of a previously received TPDU – determined by its sequence number – an ACK TPDU is returned but the duplicate is discarded.

Data integrity is accomplished by generating and including a 16-bit checksum as a parameter in the header of each TPDU transmitted. The receiver uses a similar algorithm to compute a checksum for the complete TPDU – including the checksum parameter – and this should be zero if the TPDU does not contain any errors. If the computed checksum is non-zero, the TPDU is discarded but the timeout and retransmission schemes will ensure a new copy of the TPDU is sent.

The objective of a flow control mechanism is to limit the amount of data – DATA TPDUs – transmitted by the sending transport entity to the level which the receiver can accommodate. Clearly, therefore, if the transport entity is only servicing a single user, the appropriate amount of buffer storage required to process the subsequent user TSDUs may be reserved in advance when the transport connection is being established and hence no flow control mechanism need be provided. If the transport entity is servicing multiple users, however, and buffer storage is being reserved on a statistical basis, then a flow control mechanism must be supported by the protocol. This again is determined by the class of service being provided by the transport entity.

When the flow control mechanism has been specified (Classes 2 to 4), the sequence numbers associated with the acknowledgment procedure are also used to implement the flow control strategy. This is based on a *window mechanism*: an initial credit value – number of outstanding (unacknowledged) TPDUs – for each direction of transmission is specified in the CDT field of each CONREQ TPDU and the CONCFM TPDU exchanged during connection establishment. The initial sequence number for each direction of transmission is set to zero when the connection is first established and this becomes the *lower window edge*. The sender can continuously compute the *upper window edge* by adding – modulo the size of the sequence field – the credit value for the connection to the lower window edge which is continuously incremented as ACK TPDUs for outstanding DATA TPDUs are received. The actual number of new DATA TPDUs that can be transmitted by the sender may vary during the lifetime of a connection, however, since this is completely under the control of the receiver. Each ACK TPDU contains, in addition to a receive sequence number, a new credit value which specifies the number of new TPDUs that the receiver is prepared to accept after the one being acknowledged. If this is zero, the sender must clearly cease transmission of DATA TPDUs over the connection. Normally, however, the credit value is used in the situation where the receiver allocates a fixed number of buffers for the connection then, as each TPDU is received, this progressively reduces the number of new TPDUs it is prepared to accept – the upper window edge – as the transfer proceeds and buffers start to be used up. Finally, after all user TSDUs have been transferred in each direction, the connection termination phase is entered.

6.3.3.3 Connection termination phase

Connection termination is initiated by one of the users passing a T.DISCONNECT.request primitive to its local transport entity with the reason for the clearing as a parameter. The local transport entity first sends all outstanding DATA TPDUs to its peer entity and then follows this with a DISCREQ TPDU. This also contains a sequence number as if it were a normal DATA TPDU and hence the recipient transport entity can determine whether any DATA TPDUs are still outstanding for this direction of the connection. Then, when all DATA TPDUs have been received and passed to its local user by the peer transport entity, the latter responds firstly with a normal ACK TPDU back to the sending transport entity, and secondly issues a T.DISCONNECT.indication primitive, with the reason for the closure specified as a parameter, to its local user. This closes the data transfer path in one direction only and the transport user initiating the disconnection must no longer send any TSDUs. It must be prepared to continue to receive data from the correspondent user, however, until the latter initiates the disconnection of the other half of the connection. This it does by issuing a T.DISCONNECT.request primitive to its local transport entity. On receipt of this, all outstanding DATA TPDUs for this direction are first sent and this is followed by another DISCREQ TPDU. Finally, when all DATA TPDUs have been received and passed to its local user by the recipient transport entity, the latter first issues a T.DISCONNECT.indication primitive to the user and then returns a normal ACK TPDU to its peer transport entity. Both sides of the connection are now disconnected. A typical sequence of TPDUs to implement the termination of a connection is shown in Fig. 6.8.

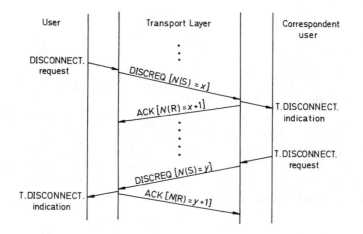

Fig. 6.8 Connection termination

6.3.4 Network services

The Transport Layer requires the Network Layer to provide a set of network services to enable the two communicating transport protocol entities to exchange TPDUs over the particular data network being used. Since both control and data TPDUs are to be treated as transparent network service data units (NSDUs) by the Network Layer, however, the latter can be either connectionless or connection oriented, the only requirement being that the Network Layer provides a set of connection oriented *services* to the Transport Layer. The analogous network services are for network connection establishment, network data transfer, and network disconnection respectively. Each is discussed separately.

6.3.4.1 Network connection establishment

There are four primitives associated with the network connection establishment service: N.CONNECT.request, N.CONNECT.indication, N.CONNECT.response, and N.CONNECT.confirm. Their functions are analogous to those provided at the user interface to the Transport Layer. Each primitive has at least two parameters: the source and destination network addresses. The transport protocol entity, on receipt of the T.CONNECT.request primitive, extracts the network addresses from the parameters associated with the primitive and uses them to establish a network connection between the two specified network entities before it initiates the transfer of any TPDUs. As has been mentioned, the type of network connection established and the quality of service provided by the connection vary for different types of network. It is for this reason that the Transport Layer provides a number of different classes of service and the user specifies the class of service to be used depending on the underlying network type. Also, because of the different classes of service supported, the Transport Layer is said to offer a network-independent message transport service.

6.3.4.2 Data transfer

Once a network connection has been established, transport protocol TPDUs may be sent across the connection. This is accomplished using the N.DATA.request and N.DATA.indication service primitives with the NSDU being passed as a parameter. The latter is used to convey all control and data TPDUs; that is, with the class of service discussed, CONREQ, CONCFM, DISCREQ, DATA and ACK TPDUs.

Notice that no acknowledgment service primitive is provided; the Network Layer endeavours to transmit NSDUs to the appropriate transport entitites free of errors and in the correct sequence according to the quality of service it is capable of providing. If this is not good enough, however, for example lost NSDUs or duplicates may occur, the user specifies a transport service which safeguards against such errors.

6.3.4.3 Network connection termination

The network connection termination service is provided both to terminate an established network connection and to indicate to the network user – the Transport Layer – the refusal of a network connection request. There are two primitives associated with the service: N.CLEAR.request and N.CLEAR.indication. The N.CLEAR.request primitive indicates to the Network Layer that the network connection is to be terminated. It is assumed to have immediate effect and hence the transport protocol must have completed all network transfers before it is issued. The N.CLEAR.indication primitive signals to the network user that either an established network connection has been cleared or that a network connection establishment request has failed, the reason for the clearing or rejection being passed as a parameter associated with the primitive.

A time sequence diagram illustrating a typical exchange of TPDUs across a network connection is shown in Fig. 6.9. It can readily be seen from this figure firstly that each layer provides a well-defined set of services to the layer above, secondly that the layer communicates with its peer layer in the remote system according to the protocol for that layer, and thirdly that the layer uses the defined set of services provided by the next lower layer to transfer the appropriate protocol data units to its peer layer.

6.3.5 Transport protocol specification

As has been stated earlier, it is not the aim of this book to present full specifications of the various protocols in the Reference Model. These can be found in the extensive range of standards documents. Indeed, just to define fully the transport protocol would require a complete book. Rather, the aim here is for the reader to gain a general understanding and insight into the functions and operation of each protocol layer and its interaction with the other layers. The specifications in general, therefore, will be in the form of time sequence diagrams and state transition diagrams or tables together, where appropriate, with some additional descriptive information.

The time sequence diagram shown in Fig. 6.9, coupled with the descriptive information in the preceding sections, should be sufficient for the reader to have gained an insight into the function and operation of the Transport Layer. To help to strengthen this understanding, however, a state transition diagram for the transport protocol described earlier is shown in Fig. 6.10. Essentially, the connection establishment states and transitions form the outer loop in the diagram and the connection clearing states the inner loop. As can be seen, the normal action when data is received either from the user or from the network is to process the data according to the defined protocol and remain in the same state; similarly, when acknowledgments are received from the network. Although this is not shown, however, if a Data TPDU arrives from the network and the sequence number indicates either that the

TPDU is a duplicate or that it falls outside the current flow control window, the normal action is to initiate the connection clearing sequence. Details of this nature can only be defined unambigously with the aid of definitions in the form of program code for each possible event and automaton state as was described in Chapter 3.

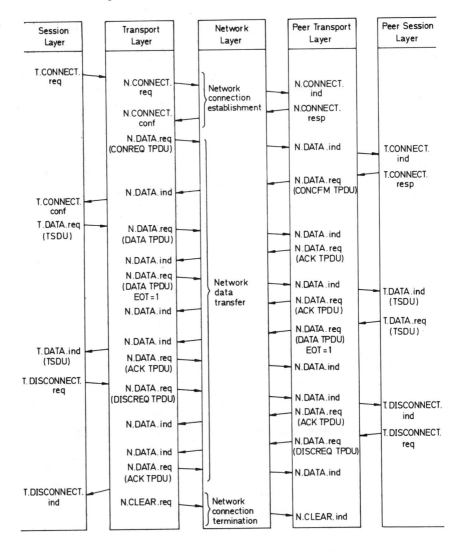

Fig. 6.9 Transport protocol time sequence diagram

6.4 SESSION LAYER

Since the Presentation Layer simply performs a data transformation function on behalf of the Application Layer, the Session Layer effectively forms the logical interface between the Application Layer and the underlying communications-oriented layers. Its function is to build on the basic message transport services provided by the Transport Layer to provide an end-to-end communication path between two application service processes for the duration of each complete application layer activity or transaction. As with the Transport Layer, the operation of the Session Layer will be considered in three parts: the services it provides to the Application Layer (Presentation Layer in practice), the operation of the internal protocol, and the way it uses the services provided by the Transport Layer to transfer session layer protocol data units (SPDUs).

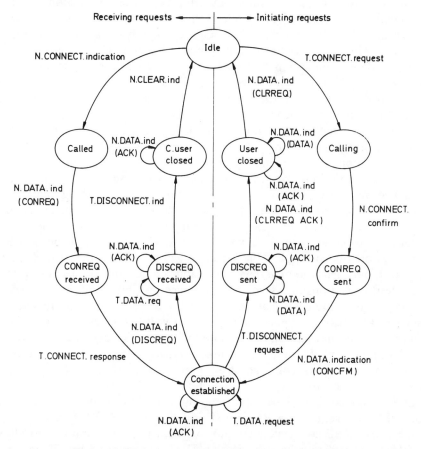

Fig. 6.10 Transport protocol state transition diagram

6.4.1 User services

The basic user services provided by the Session Layer are analogous to those provided by the Transport Layer and hence include primitives for session connection management and session data exchange. The session connection management services allow an application layer process – through the services provided by the Presentation Layer – to establish and maintain an open communications channel with a similar peer application process in a remote system for the duration of a complete activity or transaction. The data exchange services then provide the means for exchanging messages (dialogue units) beween the two communicating application processes over this path.

In addition to these basic services, the Reference Model also defines some additional optional services to be provided by the Session Layer. These include interaction management, session-connection synchronisation and exception reporting.

As with the Transport Layer, the normal data exchange method for transferring session-service-data-units (SSDUs) across an established connection is two-way-simultaneous (duplex). The interaction (token) management service, however, allows the user to define two alternative modes of working: one-way-only (simplex), and two-way-alternate (half-duplex). The session-connection synchronisation service allows two correspondent users optionally to define and identify synchronisation points (checkpoints) and, should the two sides of a connection become unsynchronised, to reset the connection to a defined state. Finally, the exception reporting service is intended to allow the users to be notified of any unrecoverable event occurring; for example, if either user fails to honour the agreed exchange procedure during a session, or the remote Session Layer does not respond over a defined period.

Other suggestions for future extensions to these services include: a sequence numbering scheme for SSDUs, and a so-called stop-go (suspend-resume) service to allow users to inform the Session Layer of impending periods of inactivity over a previously established session connection. The latter may be particularly useful when the next generation of public switched data networks become available since, as will be seen in the next chapter, with such networks the time delay to establish a network connection will be very short – fractions of a second – and hence possibly significant savings in communication line costs may be made if the Session Layer can repeatedly establish and clear transport (and hence network) connections whenever it requires to transmit an SSDU associated with a single session connection.

To implement the basic set of user services requires four primitives to initiate a session connection (S.CONNECT.request, S.CONNECT.indication, S.CONNECT.response, and S.CONNECT.confirmation); four primitives to close a session connection (S.RELEASE.request, S.RELEASE.indication, S.RELEASE.response, and S.RELEASE.confirmation); and two data transfer primitives to allow SSDUs to be exchanged across an established connection (S.DATA.request, and S.DATA.indication). The uses of these primitives are analogous to those provided by the Transport Layer and hence the S.RELEASE.request primitive is analogous to the T.DISCONNECT.request primitive. It is intended therefore to initiate an orderly closure (release) of a previously established session connection. In some instances, however, a session layer user may wish to terminate a connection prematurely; for example, if a user at a terminal aborts a session before completion. Clearly, under such circumstances, it is not necessary for the session layer protocol entity to ensure that all preceding data units have been transferred before the connection is cleared. Hence, to allow users to initiate the premature closing of a session connection, the Session Layer provides the S.U-ABORT service. Either user may initiate the premature closing of a session connection by issuing an S.U-ABORT.request primitive to its local protocol entity. This is then relayed across the connection and passed to the correspondent user in the form of an S.U-ABORT.indication primitive. In addition, there is a third primitive, S.P-ABORT.indication, which may be issued by either of the session protocol entitites to inform the users of a premature closing of a connection as a result of, say, an unrecoverable set of events occurring within the protocol or the underlying transport connection being lost. The reason for the closure is passed in the form of a parameter. Collectively these primitives provide the basic Session Layer user services and these are shown in diagrammatic form in the time sequence diagram of Fig. 6.11.

In addition to the basic set of primitives shown, additional primitives are provided to support the various optional services. In keeping with the aims of the Reference Model, the functions performed by the Session Layer should be independent of the type of end-user application process which initiates the service requests. It is primarily for this reason that most of the optional services are provided. For instance, if the two user processes can support only half-duplex operation, the primitives associated with the interaction management service allow the users to enforce this mode of working across the connection. Some of the additional primitives which are provided are now described.

6.4.1.1 Interaction management

Unless otherwise requested, the normal mode of working between the two users is assumed to be duplex. If half-duplex or simplex operation is required, however, then a control token is used to manage the direction of data transfer across the established connection; essentially, only the session service user possessing the token is allowed to send data across the connection. Hence to allow the two users to manage the exchange of the token, four primitives are provided: S.TOKEN-GIVE.request and S.TOKEN-GIVE.indication, and S.TOKEN-PLEASE.request and S.TOKEN-PLEASE.indication. The first pair allows a user to release the ownership of the token and the second pair to request the ownership of the token. The session layer protocol then implements the transfer of the token from one side of the connection to the other in addition to enforcing the specified type of interaction on the users.

6.4.1.2 Session synchronisation

A single session connection may remain established for a prolonged period of time; for instance, if the connection is being used for the transfer of a number of particularly long data files associated with a file transfer service, the connection may remain established for perhaps an hour or more. Clearly, over this sort of time period, there is always the possibility of the underlying network (and hence transport) connection being lost with the effect that if this should happen towards the end of the session, the complete session activity

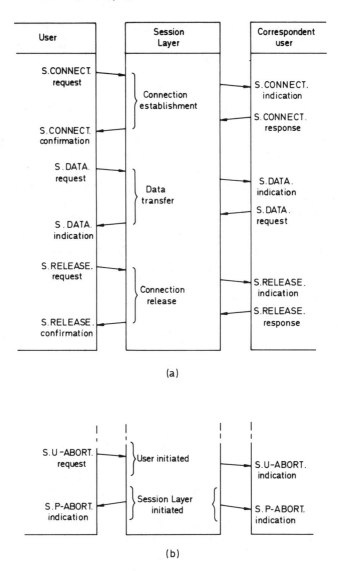

Fig. 6.11 Session layer service primitives: (a) normal closure;
(b) premature/abrupt closure

would have to be repeated even though most transfers had been successfully completed. The primary aim of the session synchronisation service, therefore, is to allow the two users to take appropriate precautionary steps to ensure that, if a transport connection is lost, the complete session activity need not be repeated.

The session synchronisation service allows synchronisation points to be defined during a session connection and subsequently referenced. The synchronisation points may be either minor or major and are identified by means of serial numbers. *Minor synchronisation points* have no implications on the flow of data across a connection but *major synchronisation points* are used to separate so-called *dialogue units*. A synchronisation request primitive, S.SYNC-MINOR or S.SYNC-MAJOR, designates a checkpoint to enable the recipient user to synchronise to the same point in the session. Synchronisation points are identified by serial numbers which are assigned ascending values as the session proceeds. The correspondent user response to a synchronisation request carries the same serial number and signals to the user the arrival at an agreed checkpoint. Any semantics which the users may associate with these checkpoints, however, are transparent to the Session Layer.

Associated with the synchronising primitives is the concept of a dialogue unit; a characteristic of the latter is that all communication within a dialogue unit is guaranteed to be isolated from all communication before and after it. The major synchronisation point service is used to define the beginning and/or end of each dialogue unit. In addition, if required, users may distinguish between different logical pieces of work called *activities*. An activity is started by the use of the S.ACTIVITY-BEGIN service and ended by the use of the S.ACTIVITY-END service.

The relationship between the different session components and synchronisation services are shown in Fig. 6.12. As can be seen, if required, the user application processes may structure a complete session into a number of distinct activities each comprising a number of self-contained dialogue units. The major synchronisation primitives may then be used to ensure the reliable transfer of each dialogue unit within each activity. For example, if the user application process is a file transfer service, a complete session may be concerned with the transfer of a large number of files belonging, say, to

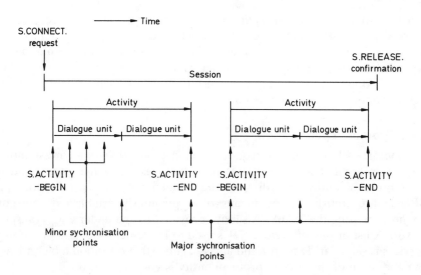

Fig. 6.12 Session composition and synchronisation points

multiple users; an activity, therefore, may be concerned with the transfer of the files belonging to a particular user, and a dialogue unit with a single user file. The minor synchronisation primitives could then be used to, say, make the transfer of each record in a file. In this way, the user could keep a check on the progress made during the transfer of the complete set of files.

Should the user detect that a fault has developed during a session – for example, contact with the remote user is lost – a further service is provided to assist the orderly reestablishment of communication within the current session connection. This is known as the session resynchronisation service and is initiated by either user issuing an S.RESYNCHRONISE.request primitive with the required synchronisation point (serial number) as a parameter. This in turn is passed to the correspondent user as an S.RESYNCHRONISE.indication primitive. The latter then responds with an S.RESYNCHRONISE.response primitive and this is relayed back to the initiator as an S.RESYNCHRONISE.confirmation primitive. This signals to the initiator that a suitable resynchronisation point has been agreed and that communication may continue.

6.4.1.3 Exception reporting

There are two sets of primitives associated with this service. The first (S.P-EXCEPTION-REPORT.indication) enables users to be notified of any unanticipated error situations that may arise within the session protocol entity during a session connection; for example, if a user service cannot be completed owing to a protocol error occuring. The normal action would then be for the two users to be informed by the protocol entity and, typically, they would then attempt to resynchronise to an earlier acknowledged synchronisation point. The second pair of primitives (S.U-EXCEPTION-REPORT.request and S.U-EXCEPTION-REPORT.indication) are provided to allow a user to report an exception condition to a correspondent user. Typically, this may be caused by a temporary loss of memory buffer space or, if the users are implementing their own sequence numbering scheme, an out-of-sequence piece of data. Again, the normal action would be for the two users to try to resynchronise to an agreed synchronisation point before continuing with the session.

6.4.2 Protocol specification

In general, each user service request is mapped directly into a corresponding session-protocol-data-unit (SPDU) and then passed to the correspondent peer protocol entity according to the defined protocol specification. All SPDUs are transferred by means of a previously established transport connection using the T.DATA service provided by the underlying Transport Layer. A list of the different SPDUs used to implement the basic set of user services is shown in Table 6.1 and an associated state transition table showing the operation of the session protocol entity is given in Fig. 6.13.

To implement the various optional services outlined in the previous

Initiating Event (Service Request)	SPDU sent	Comments
S.CONNECT.request (S.CONN.req)	Connect (CONN)	A transport connection is first established and a CONN SPDU sent over this connection. The latter contains parameters defining any optional services required.
S.CONNECT.response (accept)	Accept (ACC)	Signals the acceptance of the session connection request including the specified optional services.
S.CONNECT.response (reject)	Refuse (REF)	Connection request refused with the reason for the refusal returned in a parameter.
S.DATA.request	Data Transfer (DTR)	If half-duplex mode is being used, only the owner of the data token may send a DTR SPDU.
S.RELEASE.request (S.REL.req)	Finish (FIN)	Initiates the orderly release of one half of the connection (assuming full-duplex).
S.RELEASE.response (S.REL.resp)	Disconnect (DISC)	Completes the orderly release of the second half of the connection.
S.U-ABORT.request	Abort (ABT)	Initiates a premature release of the connection as a result of a user condition.

Table 6.1 Service request-to-SPDU mapping

section requires additional SPDU types to those listed in Table 6.1. Also, many more states and conditions are associated with the state transition table. For reasons that were stated earlier, however, it is not the aim of this book to give complete descriptions of each layer and hence, having outlined the function and usage of the various optional services, it is left to those readers who require more detail information to study the various standards documents associated with the Session Layer.

6.4.3 Transport services

The various user services provided by the Transport Layer were described in an earlier section. All Session Protocol-Data-Units (SPDUs) are transferred using the transport data transfer services. Hence, on receipt of a session connection request from the user (S.CONNECT.request), the session protocol entity first ascertains whether an existing transport connection to the required destination is available. If it is, the CONNECT (and subsequent) SPDUs are transferred over this connection using the T.DATA.request primitive. If a suitable connection does not exist, the session protocol entity first initiates the establishment of a transport connection to the peer session entity by passing a T.CONNECT.request primitive to the underlying

Event \ State	Unconnected 1	Wait for ACC SPDU 2	Wait for S.CONN. resp 3	Connected 4	Wait for DISC SPDU 5	Wait for S.REL resp 6	Wait for ABTA SPDU 7	
S.CONN. req	Send S.CONN SPDU 2							Action New state
S.CONN. resp (accept)			Send ACC SPDU 4					Action New state
S.CONN. resp (reject)			Send REF SPDU 1					Action New state
CONN SPDU	S.CONN. ind 3							Action New state
ACC SPDU		S.CONN. conf (accept) 4						Action New state
REF SPDU		S.CONN. conf (reject) 1						Action New state
S.DATA. req				Send DTR SPDU 4				Action New state
DATA SPDU				S.DATA. ind 4				Action New state
S.REL. req				Send FIN SPDU 5		Send DISC SPDU 1		Action New state
FIN SPDU				S.REL. ind 6				Action New state
DISC SPDU					S.REL. conf 1			Action New state
S.ABORT. req		Send ABT SPDU 7		Send ABT SPDU 7	Send ABT SPDU 7			Action New state
ABT. SPDU		S.ABORT. ind Send ABTA 1		S.ABORT. ind Send ABTA 1	S.ABORT. ind Send ABTA 1			Action New state
ABTA SPDU							S.ABORT. ind 1	Action New state

Fig. 6.13 Session protocol state transition table

Transport Layer with the appropriate addressing information as parameters. Then, when a connection has been established, the two peer session protocol entitities start to exchange SPDUs across the connection according to the protocol specification.

In some instances, especially if the session connection is required for a prolonged period of time, it is possible for a transport connection to be lost during the session. Because of the relative independence of each protocol layer, however, the temporary loss of a transport connection may be transparent to the user since the session protocol entity, when it is informed of the disconnection, may initiate the establishment of a new connection. The various optional synchronisation services may then be used to enable the two users to resynchronise should this be necessary. The two alternative session connection to transport connection relationships are shown diagrammatically in Fig. 6.14.

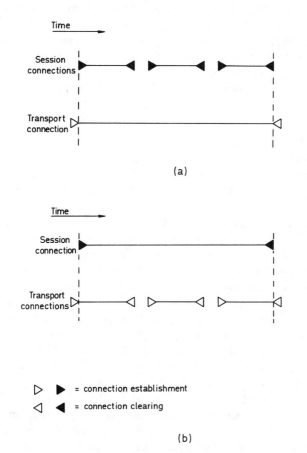

(a)

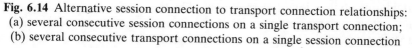

▷ ▶ = connection establishment

◁ ◀ = connection clearing

(b)

Fig. 6.14 Alternative session connection to transport connection relationships:
(a) several consecutive session connections on a single transport connection;
(b) several consecutive transport connections on a single session connection

6.5 PRESENTATION LAYER

The two protocol layers discussed so far, together with the underlying network-dependent layers to be discussed in the next two chapters, are primarily concerned with providing the means for establishing a communications channel between two correspondent application layer processes and for controlling the flow of information across this channel in an orderly and reliable way. The various application layer processes then use this facility to provide end-user processes with a comprehensive set of application services. Very often, however, computers from different manufacturers represent and interpret information in different ways, with the effect that it is not sufficient just to provide the means to allow two application processes to communicate with each other; it is also necessary to ensure that the information being transferred between them is in a form which is meaningful to each recipient process. This is one of the primary functions of the Presentation Layer. Also, in some instances, the information being exchanged by the two application processes may be highly confidential and hence, for security reasons, the Presentation Layer may perform an encryption operation on the information being exchanged across the network. Since a formal definition of the Presentation Layer is not yet available, only a general description of its functions will be presented.

6.5.1 User services

Before any information can be exchanged between two application processes, it is first necessary for both parties to agree on the precise format and structure of the information to be exchanged. For instance, if the data are to be in binary form, such information as the word size associated with the data must be conveyed or, if the data are in the form of character (text) strings, the type of character code used; for example, IA5 or EBCDIC. Also, it must be agreed whether a mapping function is to be performed from one format to another. Similarly, if encryption is to be used, this must be agreed.

The first set of presentation service primitives are concerned with these functions and are collectively referred to as *presentation-image-control primitives*. They allow the two correspondent users to define and agree the format and structure of the data to be exchanged and any transformations that are to be performed on the data. A typical set of primitives is P.I-CONTROL.request, and P.I-CONTROL.confirmation. Two further primitives, P.DATA.request and P.DATA.indication, are then used for the transfer of user (application process) data and a third set, P.CLOSE.request and P.CLOSE.confirmation, to close the presentation connection.

During the transfer of data between two correspondent application processes, there may be three different versions of the data: that used by the originating application process, that used by the recipient application process, and that used during the transfer of the data between the two correspondent presentation entities. The latter is known as the common data syntax and it is of course possible for either of the other two forms to be the same as this. If they are different, however, then the Presentation Layer performs the necessary transformation from the local user form to the common data syntax form. The two basic functions of the Presentation Layer are shown diagrammatically in Fig. 6.15.

There is no single type of common data syntax for all applications and this does in fact vary from one application to another. A number of standard

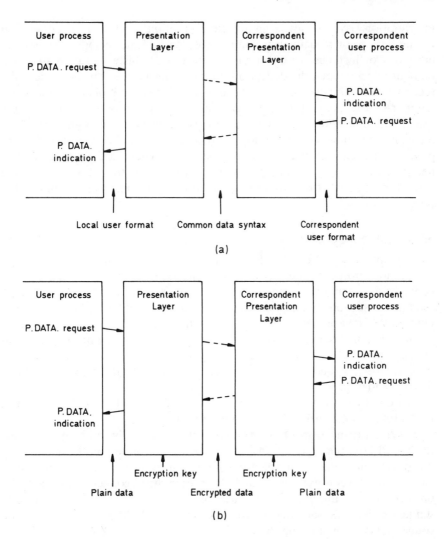

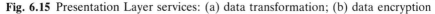

Fig. 6.15 Presentation Layer services: (a) data transformation; (b) data encryption

forms have been defined, however, and these allow two Presentation Layers to freely communicate even though the two correspondent users may be using different data representations. There are standard common data syntax forms for such applications as file transfer, job transfer, electronic mail, document transfer and others. These relate to a standard (virtual) device such as a virtual filestore, a virtual terminal etc. The two correspondent application processes thus communicate as if both are using the same data format and the Presentation Layer performs the necessary transformation function between the local user format and the appropriate common data syntax form.

If data encryption is being performed, the source Presentation Layer performs an encryption (*encipherment*) operation on all data to be sent before forwarding it to its local Session Layer. Similarly, the correspondent

Presentation Layer performs an inverse decryption (*decipherment*) operation on the data prior to delivering the received data to the recipient application process. For instance, if each unit of data to be transmitted is treated as a number which is then divided by another number before it is forwarded, the received data unit will only be meaningful if it is multiplied by the same number before delivery to the recipient application process. In this simple example, the second number (the divisor) is the *encryption key* and only if the recipient Presentation Layer knows and uses the same key will it be able to perform the correct decipherment operation. There are now some well defined data encryption standards available to perform these operations and a brief introduction of one of them is given in Appendix B at the end of the book.

6.5.2 Protocol specification

On receipt of the P.I-CONTROL.request service primitive from the user application process, the presentation protocol entity first extracts the addressing information from the associated parameters and uses these to establish a session connection. All subsequent Presentation-Protocol-Data-Units (PPDUs) are then transferred across this connection using the S.DATA service. The first set of PPDUs exchanged are concerned with presentation-image-control and, after its completion, both protocol entities have agreed the format and structure of the subsequent data and the transformations to be performed (if any).

Each presentation-service-data-unit (PSDU) included in a P.DATA.request primitive is then either passed directly or suitably transformed (if necessary) in a DATA PPDU. Similarly, on receipt of each DATA PPDU, the agreed transformations are performed on the data before it is passed on to the user using a P.DATA.indication primitive. Finally, after all data have been exchanged and the presentation connection closed, the protocol entity initiates the release of the session connection. A time sequence diagram showing a typical exchange of PPDUs over a session connection is shown in Fig. 6.16.

6.6 APPLICATION LAYER

The highest protocol layer in the ISO Reference Model is the Application Layer. It is concerned with the provision of user networking (application) services. Although it is possible for users to define their own application protocols, in order to achieve the goal of open systems interconnection, the provision and adoption of Application Layer standards is all important. Currently, there are no internationally agreed standards for the Application Layer although a number of services such as file transfer, electronic mail, document transfer and others are in various stages of development and standardisation. In order to illustrate the functions of the Application Layer and its interaction with the lower layers, an example based on a file transfer protocol will be described.

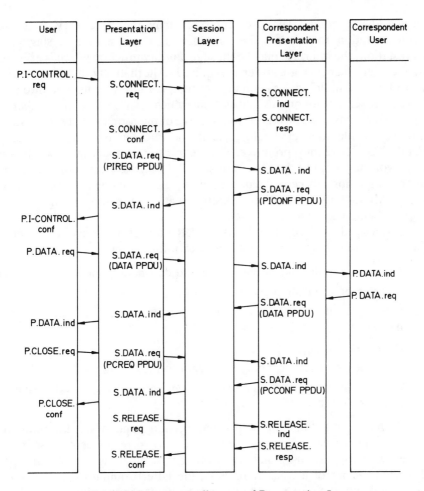

Fig. 6.16 Time sequence diagram of Presentation Layer

Several types of file protocol have been identified: a file transfer protocol is concerned purely with moving a file from one filestore to another, a file access protocol is concerned with the transfer (access) of a specific portion of a file, whilst a file management protocol is concerned with the provision of more extensive facilities such as access to remote file directories and the renaming or deletion of remote files. Since the basic file transfer service is the most frequently used, however, this will be used as an example.

6.6.1 User interface

A file transfer protocol (service) is concerned with the movement of one or more files from one filestore (computer) to another. The two computers involved in a transfer may be quite different; typically, one may be a small single-user workstation containing only a local rudimentary filestore, whilst the other may be a large multi-user system containing a large amount of on-line disc storage. The user interface may therefore vary from one implementation to another. For instance, if the system is a single-user workstation, the interface may be through a utility program which is executed by the user whenever a transfer is required. Alternatively, if the filestore is part of a large multi-access computer system, the interface may be through a separate, semi-autonomous subsystem which can service a number of (queued) requests concurrently. Irrespective of the form of the user interface, however, a file transfer would typically be initiated by a user issuing an F.TRANSFER.request primitive. The file transfer protocol entity would then endeavour to carry out the transfer associated with the request primitive and, upon completion (successfully or otherwise), inform the user by means of an F.TERMINATION.indication primitive with the result of the transfer request being passed as a parameter.

Associated with each F.TRANSFER.request primitive is a set of parameters (attributes) which include such information as:

1. the identity (address) of the source and destination application process;
2. the type of application service protocol;
3. the mode of access (read, write, create, etc.); the username and password;
4. the filename;
5. the data type (text or binary) and data format being used;
6. the type (if any) of optional session-layer services to be used during the transfer.

As has been outlined in the previous section, some of this information – for example the data type – is used by the two correspondent Presentation Layers whilst some is used directly by the remote file transfer protocol entity. Thus, on receipt of a transfer request, the latter examines the parameters associated with the request and responds with either a positive reply (RPOS) if the transfer can go ahead or a negative reply (RNEG) if it is rejecting the transfer request with the reason for the rejection being passed as a parameter – for example invalid password.

6.6.2 File transfer protocol

A typical set of file-transfer-protocol-data-units (FTPDUs) to carry out a file transfer request may be:

Start File Transfer (SFT) this is sent as a result of a user issuing an F.TRANSFER.request primitive;

Reply Positive (RPOS) this is returned if the transfer request can take place;

Reply Negative (RNEG) this is returned if the transfer request cannot be accepted;

Read Request (READREQ) this is used to request data from the correspondent protocol entity;

Data (DATA) this is used to carry data associated with the transfer (read or write);

End File Transfer (EFT) this is sent to signal the end of a transfer;

Termination Acknowledge (EFTACK) this is used to acknowledge receipt of the termination request and results in an F.TERMINATION.indication primitive being passed to the user.

In this set, only two FTPDUs are shown associated with the data transfer phase. In order to exploit the optional services supported by the Session Layer, for example synchronisation, it would be necessary to have additional FTPDUs which, in general, would map directly into session layer service primitives by the Presentation Layer. Assuming this limited set, however, a state transition table showing the operation of the protocol is shown in Fig. 6.17. When in the data transfer phase, data are either transferred directly by the initiating protocol entity (write file) or are received in response to a Read Request FTPDU having been first sent (read file).

6.6.3 Presentation services

A typical set of presentation layer services were outlined earlier in Fig. 6.16. Hence, assuming this set of primitives, on receipt of the F.TRANSFER.request primitive, the local file transfer protocol entity first issues a P.I-CONTROL.request to its local Presentation Layer with the required network addresses, presentation formats, and optional session layer services obtained from the transfer request and passed as parameters. The local Presentation Layer then initiates the establishment of a session connection using the appropriate parameters and then passes the format specification to the correspondent Presentation Layer using this connection. Then, on receipt of the image confirmation primitive, the local file protocol entity sends the SFT FTPDU to the correspondent entity using a P.DATA.request primitive. This is shown in diagrammatic form in the time sequence diagram of Fig. 6.18.

On receipt of the SFT FTPDU, the correspondent file transfer entity responds, again using a P.DATA.request primitive, with either an RPOS or an RNEG FTPDU. Then, assuming the response is positive, the data associated with the transfer is exchanged. Finally, when the complete file transfer has been carried out, the presentation connection is closed and an F.TERMINATION.indication primitive is passed to the local user process with the result of the transfer passed as a parameter.

6.7 IMPLEMENTATION ISSUES

It was stressed in the earlier sections of this chapter that when describing the operation of any communications subsystem which has been structured

State \ Event	Idle 1	Wait for RPOS 2	Data Transfer 3	Wait for EFTACK	
F.TRANSFER. req	Send SFT 2				Action New state
SFT FTPDU	Send RPOS (accept) 3 or Send RNEG (reject) 1				Action New state ———— Action New state
RPOS FTPDU		Send READREQ 3 or Send DATA 3			Action New state ———— Action New state
RNEG FTPDU		F.TERMINATION. ind 1			Action New state
READREQ FTPDU			Send DATA 3		Action New state
DATA FTPDU			Send READREQ 3 or Send EFT 4		Action New state ———— Action New state
EFT FTPDU			Send EFTACK 1		Action New state
EFTACK FTPDU				F.TERMINATION. ind 1	Action New state

Fig. 6.17 File transfer state transition table

according to the ISO Reference Model, it is essential to treat each protocol layer as an autonomous entity which provides a defined set of user services to the layer above it and, in turn, uses the services provided by the layer below it to transport the protocol data units generated by the layer to a similar correspondent layer in a remote system. In the same way, when implementing the various protocol layers in software it is essential to retain the same approach otherwise the benefits gained by the above specification method are, of course, lost.

The way this is achieved in practice varies from one implementation to

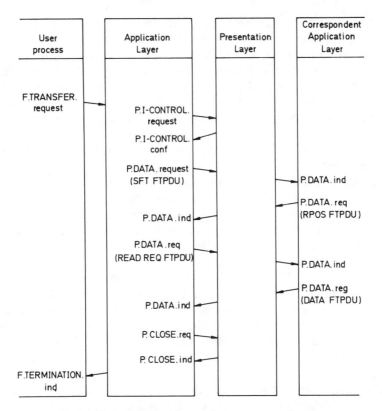

Fig. 6.18 Application Layer time sequence diagram

another; for example, in a large system supporting multi-tasking, each layer would normally be implemented as a separate task module. Alternatively, in a small system supporting, say, a single application program, each layer would be implemented as a separate procedure or small group of procedures. In general, however, this affects only the mechanism which is used to schedule each protocol layer since, irrespective of the type of implementation method being used, in order to achieve the necessary decoupling between each layer, a common approach to passing data between the layers is utilised. The method normally used is based on a set of first-in, first-out (FIFO) queues as shown in part (a) of Fig. 6.19.

Essentially, all items of data – service requests (primitives) – which are passed between layers are contained in a block of memory known as a *message buffer*. Normally, the first element in each buffer is an indication of the service primitive contained within it – CONNECT.request, DATA.indication etc. – and this is then followed by the parameters associated with the primitive. A message – service primitive – is then passed from one layer to another by the initiating layer simply inserting the start address of the message buffer – the *buffer pointer* – at the tail of the appropriate interlayer queue. Then, when a protocol layer is scheduled to run, it simply examines its two input queues – one from the layer above and the other from the layer below – to determine if a message is awaiting processing. If there is, it first reads the entry (buffer pointer) from the head of the appropriate queue and determines the type of service primitive contained within it. It then uses this information – the event type – together with the current present state of the layer, to determine from the event-state table the appropriate action to be performed. Typically, this will result in a suitably formatted message being passed either to the protocol layer above or to the protocol layer below using one of its two output queues. The general structure of each protocol layer is thus as shown in pseudo code form in part (b) of the figure.

The above mechanism is suitable providing there is only a single active service request being processed at one time. In many instances, however, there may be a number of different service requests being processed concurrently. In such cases, either all inter-layer messages are passed using a single set of queues, or there is a separate set of queues associated with each service access point or channel. The problem with the former is that, since there are often conditions associated with the state of a protocol entity (layer) which must be met before a particular action can be carried out (for example the send window associated with a flow control mechanism being closed), it is sometimes necessary to suspend the processing of a message until the inhibiting condition is cleared. Normally, of course, the latter only affects a single channel and hence any other channels that may be active should not be affected.

The management of such issues can in fact become quite complicated and hence, to alleviate this, it is common practice to have a set of queues associated with each access point. Then, if a channel becomes temporarily closed, this is readily controlled simply by suspending the processing of entries in the affected queue until the inhibiting condition is cleared. In this way, the flow of messages through the other channels (queues) is unaffected.

The overall structure of a typical communications subsystem package of the type being considered is thus as shown in Fig. 6.20. For clarity, the

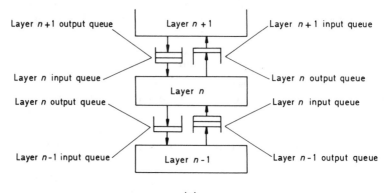

(a)

(continued)

```
task/program  Communications Subsystem;
global  Inter-layer queues + queue handling routines;
        Message buffers;
        .
        .
        .
task/procedure  Layer N−1;
```



```
task/procedure  Layer N;
```

```
local Event-State Table;
      Protocol State variables;

begin  If Input Queue non-empty then
        begin Read first entry from appropriate Input Queue;
              Decode message type (event);
              Consult Event-State Table;
              Perform specified action;
              Update Present State variable; end;

end;
```

```
        .
        .
        .
```

(b)

Fig. 6.19 Inter-layer communication and basic layer structure: (a) inter-layer
communication mechanism; (b) program structure

Application and Presentation Layers are shown closely coupled together
although in practice the layered structure would be maintained. Typically,
there is a separate protocol entity for each application service – electronic
mail, remote file access etc. – and these then share the services provided by
the Session Layer. It should be stressed that the effect of multiple channels at
each layer only involves the provision of a relatively small amount of

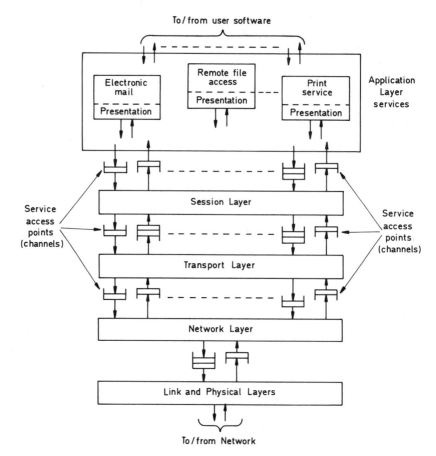

Fig. 6.20 Overall software structure

additional memory; firstly, for the state variables for each channel – present state, sequence numbers etc. – and secondly, for the increase in the number of message buffers that will be required. Other data structures such as the event-state table array are essentially constants and hence only one copy per layer is required.

Another issue relating to the implementation of the communication subsystem is the way the complete software package is interfaced to the host operating system. It may be concluded from the earlier descriptions of the various protocol layers that the processing overheads associated with their implementation are not insignificant. Hence, if just a single processing element was used to perform both the communications processing and the normal processing functions of the system, the amount of processing time available to perform the latter would be reduced considerably, especially during periods of high network activity.

The approach normally adopted, therefore, is to use an additional processing element to perform most of the communications processing functions. Typically, this is located on a single printed-circuit board which plugs into the internal bus – the internal interconnection mechanism – of the host system. The board also contains an amount of program memory for the communications software, additional memory for protocol state information and message buffers, and the circuitry that is required to perform the physical interface to the communications network which is being used. As has been mentioned, the latter may be a public data network or a local area data network, the only differences being the type of interface circuitry required and, as will be seen in the next two chapters, slightly different network protocol software.

Clearly, if the complete communications subsystem was implemented on the additional communications processor board, then the software interface to the various network services would be at the application services level. Although at first sight this may appear attractive, the problem with this approach is that many application layer services require access to the host file system for their implementation – electronic mail, file transfer etc. – and hence, since the latter is normally an integral part of the host operating system, an additional software interface would also be required between the communications software and the host file system.

The approach normally adopted, therefore, is to implement only up to the Session Layer on the communications processor board and then to have the various application/presentation layer entities as an integral part of the I/O control section of the host operating system. Typically, access to the various application layer services is then through a defined set of operating system calls analogous to normal file or I/O calls. The Application/ Presentation Layers then use the services provided by the Session Layer as appropriate.

Problems

6.1 What is the aim of the ISO Reference Model for open systems interconnection?

Produce a sketch showing the constituent protocol layers which make up the Reference Model and outline the function of each layer. Briefly describe the user services associated with each layer and how the detail operation of the underlying network is transparent to the higher protocol layers.

6.2 a) Use a time sequence diagram to illustrate a typical set of user services for the Transport Layer in the ISO Reference Model and describe their function.

b) Define a typical set of Transport Protocol Data Units (TPDUs) to implement these services and hence derive a time sequence diagram showing a typical sequence of TPDUs exchanged to implement the defined services.

c) Define an example set of network service primitives provided by the Network Layer and hence derive a time sequence diagram showing how the previously defined TPDUs associated with the Transport Layer protocol are transferred using these services.

6.3 a) What is meant by a finite state machine or automaton?

b) Use the connection establishment phase of the Transport Layer protocol to illustrate how the operation of a protocol may be defined using:

   i) a state transition diagram,
   ii) a state transition table,
   iii) a structured program.

6.4 a) Define a basic set of user service primitives associated with the Session Layer and use a time sequence diagram to illustrate their interrelationships. Outline the function of each service.

b) Describe the purpose of the following additional services provided by the Session Layer and the primitives associated with them:

   i) interaction management,
   ii) session synchronisation,
   iii) exception reporting.

6.5 a) Explain the meaning of the following terms in connection with the Presentation Layer in the ISO Reference Model:

   i) presentation-image-control,
   ii) common data syntax.

b) Define a typical set of user service primitives associated with the Presentation Layer and hence sketch a time sequence diagram showing how these are implemented by the Presentation Layer using the services provided by the Session Layer.

6.6 a) Explain the function of the Application Layer in the ISO Reference Model for open systems interconnection and list some typical examples.

b) Assume you are to define an application layer process for the access of files from a remote file system.

   i) Define a suitable set of user service primitives.
   ii) Define a corresponding set of file-transfer-protocol-data-units (FTPDUs) suitable for implementing these services.
   iii) Sketch a time sequence diagram to illustrate how the application layer protocol entity implements the service primitives using the defined FTPDUs and the services provided by a typical Presentation Layer.

Chapter 7 **Public Data Networks**

Objectives:
When you have completed studying the material in this chapter you should:

- know the different types of public data network;

- understand the difference between a circuit-switched and a packet-switched network and the relative advantages and disadvantages of each type;

- be able to describe the structure of the X.25 protocol as used in packet-switched data networks and the operation of the Packet (Network) Layer in the context of the ISO Reference Model;

- be able to describe the function of a PAD and the various protocols associated with its use and operation;

- be able to explain how a call is established and cleared using the X.21 protocol and a circuit-switched data network.

7.1 INTRODUCTION

In Chapter 4 the use of the public switched telephone network (PSTN) for the transmission of data was considered. Indeed, prior to the advent of public data networks, this was the only method available for the transmission of data between user equipment belonging to different establishments. As was indicated, however, a switched connection made through the PSTN currently supports only a modest – typically less than 4800 bps – user data rate. Also, because telephone calls are charged on a time and distance basis, the cost of a typical transaction involving data can be very expensive owing to the often long distances involved and slow response times, especially when a human user is involved.

It was for these reasons that many large organisations established their own proprietary nationwide private data networks. Typically, these used dedicated lines leased from the telephone authorities – the PTTs in Europe, for example – to interconnect a number of privately owned switching nodes or exchanges. Clearly, although offering the user security, flexibility and ultimate control, networks of this type involve high investment costs in purchased and leased equipment. Such networks are therefore generally owned by large organisations such as the major clearing banks who can both afford the initial capital outlay and also generate sufficient traffic to justify this level of investment.

At the time of introduction of the many private data networks, the PTT authorities would only lease lines to an organisation to enable it to build its own private data network; that is, the PTTs would not supply lines to allow such networks to be connected together. The demand and subsequent establishment of public data networks stemmed, therefore, from the ever increasing demands from users of these private networks for facilities to enable them to communicate with each other.

7.2 PDN CHARACTERISTICS

A *public data network* or *PDN* is a network established and operated by a national network administration authority specifically for the transmission of data. It can be concluded from the previous section that a primary requirement for a PDN from the outset was to facilitate the interworking of equipment from a number of different manufacturers. Hence a first requirement was to establish agreed standards for the access and use of these networks. After much discussion and experimentation firstly at national and later at international level, a set of internationally agreed standards were accepted by the International Telegraph and Telephone Consultative Committee (*CCITT*) for use with a range of public data networks. These standards are known as the *X-Series Recommendations* and include standards for user data signalling rates and also user interfaces with such networks.

There are two main types of PDN: *Packet-Switched Data Networks* (*PSDNs*) and *Circuit-Switched Data Networks* (*CSDNs*) and different standards have been defined for each type. Also, since the PSTN is still widely used for the transmission of data, standards have also been established for interfacing to this type of network. In general, with each of these networks the standards refer to the lowest three layers of the ISO Reference Model and the functions of each of these layers is as shown in Fig. 7.1. It should be remembered that the type of characteristics of the network-dependent layers in the ISO Reference Model are made transparent to the higher protocol layers by the Transport Layer which offers the higher layers a network-independent message transport service. This chapter is concerned with the different types of PDN and the various interface protocols which have been defined for use with each type.

7.2.1 Circuit and packet switching

Before describing the various interface standards associated with PDNs, it is necessary to first outline the differences between the two types of switching used in these networks. Each connection established through a *circuit-switched network* results in a specific physical communications channel being set up through the network from the calling to the called subscriber equipment which is then used exclusively by the two subscribers for the

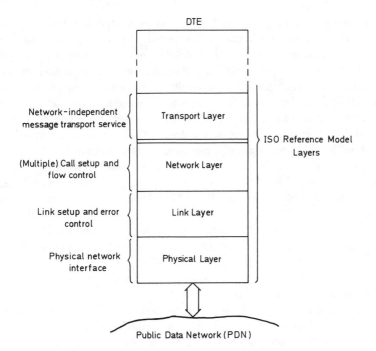

Fig. 7.1 Network-dependent protocol layers in PDNs

duration of that call. An example of a circuit-switched network is the PSTN and indeed all connections established using the PSTN are of the circuit-switched type.

In the context of data transmission, a feature of a circuit-switched connection is that it effectively provides a fixed data rate channel and hence both subscribers must operate at this rate. Also, before any data can be transmitted over such a connection, it is necessary to first set up or establish the connection through the network. Currently, the time required to set up a call through the PSTN is relatively long (tens of seconds) owing to the type of equipment used in each exchange. Normally, therefore, when used for data, a connection is first established and this is then kept open for the duration of the transaction. The introduction of new computer-controlled switching exchanges, however, coupled with the adoption of digital transmission throughout the network, will mean that the setup time of a connection through the PSTN will be much shorter (tens of milliseconds). Also, the extension of digital transmission right back to the subscriber's equipment will mean that a high bit rate (typically 64 kbps or higher) switched transmission path will be available at each subscriber outlet. It will then be possible to use this facility for data without the necessity of using modems. The resulting digital PSTN can then also be regarded as a public CSDN or, since such networks can support both digitised voice and data, *Integrated Services Digital Networks* or *ISDNs*.

Although the connection setup time associated with an all digital circuit-switched network is relatively fast, the resulting connection still only provides a fixed data-rate path and hence both subscribers must transmit and receive at this rate. In contrast, with a *packet-switched network*, because of its internal mode of operation, it is possible for two communicating subscribers (DTEs) to operate at different data rates since the rate at which data are passed at the two interfaces to the network is separately regulated by each subscriber's equipment. Also, with a packet-switched network, no physical connections are established through the network. Instead, all data to be transmitted are first assembled into one or more message units called *packets* by the source DTE which include both the source and the required destination DTE network addresses. These are then passed bit serially by the source DTE to its local *packet-switching exchange* (*PSE*). The latter, on receipt of each packet, first stores the packet and then inspects the required destination address contained within it. Each PSE contains a *routing directory* which specifies the outgoing link(s) – transmission path(s) – to be used for each network address. On receipt of a packet, therefore, the PSE forwards the packet on the appropriate link at the maximum available bit rate. This mode of working is often referred to therefore as *packet store-and-forward*.

Similarly, as each packet is received (and stored) at each intermediate PSE along the route taken, it is forwarded on the appropriate link interspersed with other packets being forwarded on that link. Then, at the appropriate destination PSE – determined from the destination address within the packet – the packet is finally passed to the destination DTE.

This procedure is shown in diagrammatic form in Fig. 7.2. As can be seen, since packets from different sources are interspersed on the various network links with packets from other sources, each overall transaction occupies only a (random) portion of the available bandwidth on each link. In the limit, this will vary from zero when the user is not transmitting any data to the full bandwidth if it is transmitting packets continuously.

It can also be deduced from the figure that it is possible for a number of packets to arrive simultaneously at a PSE on different incoming links and for each to require forwarding on the same outgoing link. Clearly, therefore, if a number of particularly long packets are waiting to be transmitted on the same link, other packets may experience unpredictably long delays. Consequently, to avoid this happening and hence ensure the network has a reliably fast *response time* – that is, the time delay between the first bit of a packet entering the network and the last bit leaving the network – there is a maximum length allowed for each packet. It is for this reason that when a packet-switched network is being used, a message as used by the Transport Layer within the DTE may first have to be divided by the source transport protocol entity into a number of smaller packet units before transmission and, in turn, reassembled into a single transport message by the correspondent protocol entity at the destination DTE. This is, of course, transparent to the Transport Layer user.

Another difference between a CSDN and a PSDN is that with a CSDN there is no error or flow control applied by the network on the transmitted

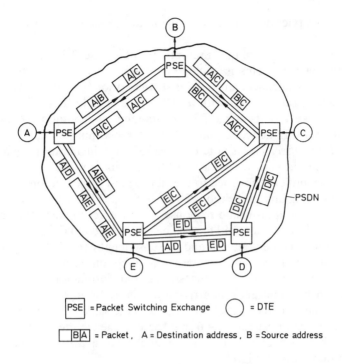

PSE = Packet Switching Exchange   ◯ = DTE

▢BA = Packet,   A = Destination address,   B = Source address

Fig. 7.2 Packet-switching schematic

data and hence this must be performed by the user. With a PSDN, however, sophisticated error and flow control procedures are applied on each link by the network PSEs and hence the class of service provided by a PSDN is normally much higher than that provided by a CSDN.

It can be concluded from the above that circuit and packet switching offer the user two different types of serivce. Hence, even with the advent of all-digital networks, both types of service will still be supported and it will then be up to the user to select the particular service to be used.

7.2.2 Datagrams and virtual circuits

With a PSDN, two types of service are normally supported: *Datagram* and *Virtual Call* (*Circuit*). To explain the difference between the two types of service the analogy between sending a message by means of a letter and by means of a telephone call is often used. In the first case the letter containing the message is treated as a self-contained entity by the postal authorities and its delivery is independent of any other letters. In the case of a telephone call, however, before the message can be sent a communications path must first be established through the network.

The Datagram service is analogous to sending a message by means of a letter since each packet entering the network is treated as a separate, self-contained entity with no relationship to other packets. Each packet is simply received and forwarded in the way just outlined and hence the

Datagram service is primarily used for the transfer of short, single-packet messages.

If a message contains multiple packets, the Virtual Call service is normally selected. This is analogous to sending a message by means of a telephone call since when using this service, prior to sending any information (data packets) associated with a call, the source DTE sends a special call request packet to its local PSE containing, in addition to the required destination DTE network address, a reference number called the *Logical Channel Identifier*. This is noted by the PSE and the packet is then forwarded through the network as before. At the destination PSE, a second Logical Channel Identifier is assigned to the call request packet before it is forwarded on the outgoing link to the required destination DTE. Then, assuming the call is accepted, an appropriate response packet is returned to the calling DTE and a virtual call is then said to exist between the two DTEs. The information transfer phase is then entered and all subsequent data packets relating to this call are assigned the same reference numbers on each interface link to the network. In this way, both the source and destination DTEs can readily distinguish between packets arriving on the same link which may relate to different calls. Hence packets belonging to the same call can be passed to the user – the Transport Layer – in the same sequence they were entered. The relationship between a logical channel and a virtual circuit is shown diagrammatically in Fig. 7.3.

It should be noted that, although a virtual circuit may appear to the user as being similar to a connection established through a circuit-switched network, a virtual circuit, as the name implies, is purely conceptual.

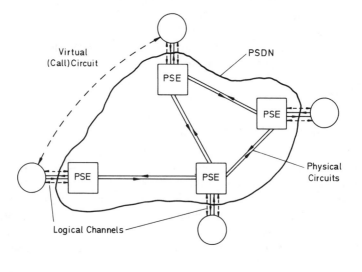

Fig. 7.3 Logical Channels and Virtual Calls

Moreover, since with the Virtual Circuit service the PSDN is able to apply additional error and flow control procedures at the packet level as well as those used at the link level, the class of service supported by a Virtual Cicuit is very high; that is, the probability of all the packets relating to a particular call being delivered free of errors and in the correct sequence without duplicates is very high.

Normally, with the Virtual Circuit service, after all data relating to a call have been exchanged, the virtual circuit is cleared and the appropriate Logical Channel Identifiers released. If a user requires to communicate with another user very frequently, however, to avoid the necessity of having to set up a new virtual circuit for each individual call, it is possible for the virtual circuit to be left permanently established. This is then known as a *Permanent Virtual Circuit* and, although the user must pay for this facility, the cost of each call is based only on the quantity of data transferred. As has been mentioned, with a circuit-switched network, charges are normally made based on a distance and call duration basis.

7.3 PACKET-SWITCHED DATA NETWORKS

The internationally agreed network access protocol which has been defined to interface a DTE to a PSDN is X.25. X.25 is in fact a set of protocols and the various protocol layers which make up X.25 are shown in Fig. 7.4. As can be seen, in contrast to the Transport Layer, the three protocols making up X.25 have only local significance.

At the lowest layer, the X.21 interface standard is used to define the physical interface between the DTE and the PTT supplied local *data circuit terminating equipment* which is normally referred to as the DCTE or simply DCE. The Link Layer protocol used with X.25 is a version of HDLC known as LAPB and its function is to provide the Packet Layer with an error-free packet transport facility over the physical link between the DTE and its local PSE. Finally, the Packet Layer is concerned with the reliable transfer of transport layer protocol data units and with the multiplexing of one or more transport layer service access points (virtual calls) onto the single physical link controlled by the Link Layer. The message units and interactions between the various layers are shown in Fig. 7.5. Each layer will now be considered separately.

7.3.1 The physical interface

The physical interface between the DTE and the local PTT supplied DCE is defined in recommendation *X.21*. The DCE plays an analogous role to a synchronous modem since its function is to provide a full-duplex, bit-serial, synchronous transmission path between the DTE and the local PSE. As will be seen in the next section, X.21 is in fact the same interface as that to be used with an all-digital circuit-switched network. Before all-digital networks become widely available, however, a second standard known as *X.21 bis* has been defined for use with existing (analogue) networks. This is in turn a

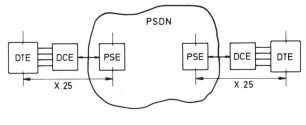

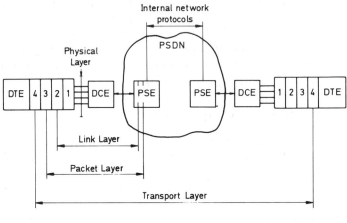

Fig. 7.4 The X.25 network access protocol: (a) applicability; (b) protocol components

subset of RS-232C/V.24 and hence existing user equipment can be readily interfaced using this standard. The various interchange circuits associated with X.21 and X.21 (bis) are defined in recommendation X.24. They are shown in Fig. 7.6 and the use of each line will be described in more detail in the next section when CSDNs are discussed.

7.3.2 Link Layer

The aim of the *Link Layer* – often referred to as *Level 2* because of its position in the ISO Reference Model – is to provide the Packet Layer with a reliable – error-free and no duplicates – packet transport facility across the physical link between the DTE and the local PSE. The Link Layer has no knowledge of the logical channel to which a packet may belong since this is only known by the Packet Layer. The error and flow control procedures used by the Link Layer apply, therefore, to all packets irrespective of the virtual circuits to which they belong.

The frame structure and error and flow control procedures used by the Link Layer are based on the High-Level Data Link Control (HDLC)

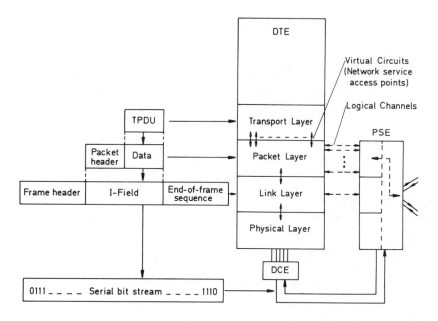

Fig. 7.5 X.25 message units and layer interactions

protocol. Since the basic operation of HDLC was described in a previous chapter, it will not be repeated here. It uses the Asynchronous Balanced Mode (ABM) of operation which is also referred to as LAPB in the CCITT X.25 standards documents. This stands for Link Access Procedure version B since it superseded the earlier version A link access procedure.

Using ABM, both the DTE and PSE operate asynchronously and hence both can initiate the transmission of commands and responses at any time. Also, since the protocol only controls the flow of information frames across a point-to-point link – that is, across the link between the DTE and its local PSE – the address field in each frame is not used to convey network-wide address information; this is carried in the I-field since network addressing is handled by the Packet Layer. Instead, the address field contains either the DTE or DCE (PSE) address: if the frame is a command frame the address specifies the recipient's address, if the frame is a response frame the address specifies the sender's address. This is shown in diagrammatic form in Fig. 7.7.

7.3.3 Packet Layer

In the context of the ISO Reference Model, the Packet Layer is the same as the Network Layer. Also, because of its position in the Reference Model, the Packet Layer is often referred to simply as Level 3. The Transport Layer thus uses the services provided by the Packet Layer to enable it to exchange Transport Protocol Data Units (TPDUs) with one or more remote Transport Layers.

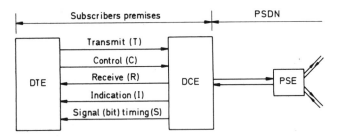

Fig. 7.6 X.21 Physical Layer interface circuits

7.3.3.1 User services

In the ISO standards documents, three user services are supported by the Network Layer:

> N.CONNECT.request/indication/response/confirmation,
> N.DATA.request/indication,
> N.CLEAR.request/indication.

There are parameters associated with each service primitive. It should be stressed, however, that the Network (Packet) Layer itself need not necessarily operate in a connection oriented mode – that is, using virtual circuits – it may operate using datagrams, for example. The only requirement is that the Packet Layer adheres to the defined user interface.

As can be seen from Fig. 7.5, the Transport Layer may have a number of network connections (calls) set up at one time, each call being associated with a particular network service access point. The Packet Layer thus performs a multiplexing function: all connections – Virtual Circuits (VCs) and Permanent Virtual Circuits (PVCs) ; are multiplexed onto the single data link controlled by the Link Layer. The flow of packets over each virtual circuit is then separately controlled by the Packet Layer protcol.

7.3.3.2 Protocol specification

Two Packet Layer protocol entities communicate with each other to implement the above user services by exchanging Packet-Protocol-Data-Units (PPDUs). Each PPDU may contain either user (Transport Layer) data, protocol control information or, in some instances, both. The different PPDU types used to implement the user services listed earlier are shown in Fig. 7.8. The use of each PPDU and its relationship with the various service requests will now be described.

Virtual call establishment and clearing

A time sequence diagram illustrating the various phases of a virtual call is shown in Fig. 7.9. A virtual circuit is established (set up) as a result of the user issuing an N.CONNECT.request primitive at a user service access point. The request has parameters associated with it which include the network address of the called DTE and also a limited amount of user data. The source protocol entity first selects the next free Logical Channel Identifier (LCI) and creates a

Packet (PPDU) types		Protocol usage
DTE → DCE	DCE → DTE	
Call Request	Incoming Call	Call setup
Call Accepted	Call Confirmation	
Clear Request	Clear Indication	Call clearing
DTE Clear Confirmation	DCE Clear Confirmation	
DTE Data	DCE Data	Data transfer
DTE RR	DCE RR	Flow control
DTE RNR	DCE RNR	
DTE REJ		
Reset Request	Reset Indication	
DTE Reset Confirmation	DCE Reset Confirmation	
Restart Request	Restart Indication	Restart
DTE Restart Confirmation	DCE Restart Confirmation	

Fig. 7.7 Packet (PPDU) types and their usage

Call Request packet (PPDU) containing the calling and called DTE addresses and the selected LCI. The packet is then passed to the Link Layer for forwarding to its local PSE.

On receipt of the packet, the local PSE notes the LCI selected and forwards the packet, according to the internal protocol of the network, to the appropriate destination PSE. The latter then selects the next free LCI for use on the link to the called DTE, writes this into the packet and changes the packet type into an Incoming Call packet. The latter is then forwarded to the called DTE where it is converted by the correspondent packet protocol entity into an N.CONNECT.indication primitive and passed to the correspondent user.

Assuming the correspondent user is prepared to accept the call, it responds with an N.CONNECT.response primitive which, in turn, is converted by the packet protocol entity into a Call Accepted packet. The latter is assigned the same LCI as the one that was used in the corresponding Incoming Call packet. The Call Accepted packet is then forwarded to the called DTE's local PSE. The reserved logical channel on this link then enters the data transfer phase. Similarly, the source PSE, on receipt of the Call

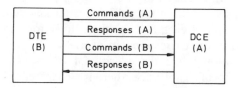

Fig. 7.8 Link layer addresses

Accepted packet, inserts the previously reserved LCI for use on this part of the circuit into the packet and sets the logical channel into the data transfer state. It then converts the packet into a Call Connected packet and forwards this to the calling DTE. Finally, on receipt of this packet, the calling packet protocol entity passes on an N.CONNECT.confirmation primitive to the user and enters the data transfer state.

If the correspondent user does not wish, or is not able, to accept an incoming call, it responds to the N.CONNECT.indication primitive with an N.CLEAR.request primitive. This results in the called packet protocol entity returning a Clear Request packet to its local PSE. The latter first releases the previously reserved LCI and then returns a Clear Confirmation packet to the called DTE. It then sends a Clear Request packet to the source PSE which, in turn, passes the packet to the packet protocol entity in the calling DTE as a Clear Indication. The DTE first releases the reserved LCI and then passes an N.CLEAR.indication primitive to the user. It then returns a Clear Confirmation packet to its local PSE to complete the clearance of the virtual circuit. Similarly, either the user or the correspondent user can initiate the clearing of a call at any time by issuing an N.CLEAR.request primitive at the corresponding user interface.

Data transfer
After a virtual call (network connection) has been established, both the user and correspondent user may initiate the transfer of data independently of one another by issuing an N.DATA.request primitive at its network interface with the data to be transferred as a parameter. As has been mentioned, the maximum length of each Data packet in a packet-switched network is limited, typically to 128 octets of data, to ensure a reliably fast response time. Hence, if a user wishes to transfer a message containing more than this number of octets, the message must first be divided into an appropriate number of data packets and each packet sent separately. In order for the recipient user to know when each message is complete, therefore, each Data packet sent through the network contains a single bit in its header known as the *More-data bit* which is set whenever further Data packets are required to complete a user-level (that is, Transport Layer) message.

Although the Transport Layer normally initiates the transfer of its own protocol control messages (TPDUs) – to one or more peer Transport Layers – using an N.DATA.request primitive with the TPDU as a data parameter, the X.25 Packet Layer also allows the user to specify whether the associated parameter contains user-level control or data information. The type of the information is then embedded into the resulting Data packet by the Packet Layer which sets a special bit in the packet header known as the *Qualifier* or *Q bit*. Then, on receipt of each Data packet, this information is passed with the associated data to the correspondent user.

In addition, although the three protocol layers associated with X.25 normally have only local significance, there is also a facility provided to allow acknowledgment information at the Packet Level to have end-to-end

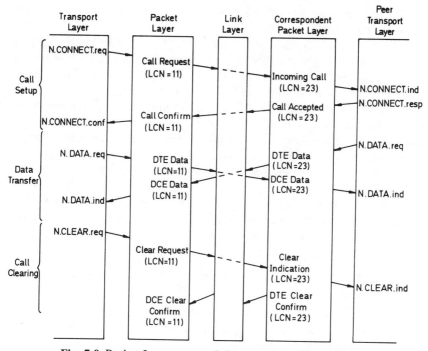

Fig. 7.9 Packet Layer protocol time sequence diagram

significance. This again is implemented by means of a special bit in each packet header known as the *Delivery Confirmation* or *D bit*. The D-bit in the header of a data packet is set to 1 if the source DTE requires an end-to-end confirmation (acknowledgment) of correct receipt by the remote peer Packet Layer. As will be seen in the next section, this information is carried in the header of a packet flowing in the reverse direction.

Flow control
All Packet Layer packets are transferred from a DTE to its local PSE using the services provided by the Link Layer. The use of HDLC at the Link Layer means that the basic packet transport facility supported is relatively reliable and hence the emphasis at the Packet Layer is on flow control rather than error control. The flow control algorithm is based on a *window mechanism* similar to that which was first introduced in Chapter 3. The flow of packets is controlled separately for each logical channel and for each direction of a call; that is, the flow of data packets relating to each call from DTE to PSE is controlled separately from the flow of packets from PSE to DTE.

To implement the window mechanism, all data packets contain a *Send Sequence Number*, $P(S)$, and a *Receive Sequence Number*, $P(R)$. The sequence numbers are normally incremented modulo 8 and hence they cycle repeatedly from 0 through to 7. The $P(R)$ contained in each data packet relates to the flow of data packets in the reverse direction. Alternatively, if there are no data packets awaiting transmission in the reverse direction, the

$P(R)$ may be sent by the receiver in a special *Receiver-Ready* (*RR*) *supervisory packet*.

The first data packet in each direction (DTE to PSE and PSE to DTE) of a logical channel is given a $P(S)$ of 0 and each subsequent packet in the same direction carries the previous $P(S)$ incremented by 1. The number of packets relating to the same call that may be sent in each direction before a response is received is then limited by the agreed *window size*, K, for the channel which, for reasons described in Chapter 3, has a maximum value of 7 if 8 unique sequence numbers are being used. Thus, once the sender has initiated the transfer of a number of data packets up to the window size, it must then cease transmitting further packets until it receives a Data Packet or a Receiver-Ready supervisory packet containing a $P(R)$ which indicates the willingness of the receiver to accept further packets on this channel.

To implement this scheme, the DTE and PSE each maintain three variables for each active logical channel (and hence virtual circuit):

$V(S)$ this is known as the *Send Sequence Variable* and indicates the $P(S)$ which will be assigned to the next data packet *sent* on this logical channel;

$V(R)$ this is known as the *Receive Sequence Variable* and indicates the $P(S)$ of the next in-sequence data packet which is expected to be *received* on this logical channel;

$L(W)$ this is known as the *Lower Window Variable* (Edge) and is used to determine when the flow of data packets should be stopped.

All three variables are set to zero when the virtual circuit is first set up or subsequently reset (see later). Then, as each Data packet is prepared for sending, it is assigned a Send Sequence Number, $P(S)$, equal to the current $V(S)$ and the latter is then incremented (modulo 8). Similarly, on receipt of each Data packet or Receiver-Ready flow control packet, the Receive Sequence Number, $P(R)$, contained within it is used to update $L(W)$. The sender can continue sending Data packets until either, the window size is reached – that is, until the incremented $V(S)$ reaches $L(W) + K$ – or, a Data or a Receiver-Ready packet is received containing a $P(R)$ which advances the current $L(W)$. Further Data packets may then be sent until the window limit is again reached. A typical packet sequence illustrating this procedure for a window size of 3 is given in part (a) of Fig. 7.10. For clarity, just a single logical channel is assumed and only a unidirectional flow of Data packets is shown.

The use of a window mechanism to control the flow of Data packets means that the maximum number of packet buffers required to handle each call is readily determined. In practice, however, the total number of buffers provided to cater for all the calls which may be currently active is often less than the maximum number required. A facility is provided in the protocol, therefore, to allow the DTE (or PSE) to temporarily suspend the flow of Data packets associated with a specific call (virtual circuit). This is achieved by the receiver, instead of returning a Receiver-Ready packet, returning a *Receiver-*

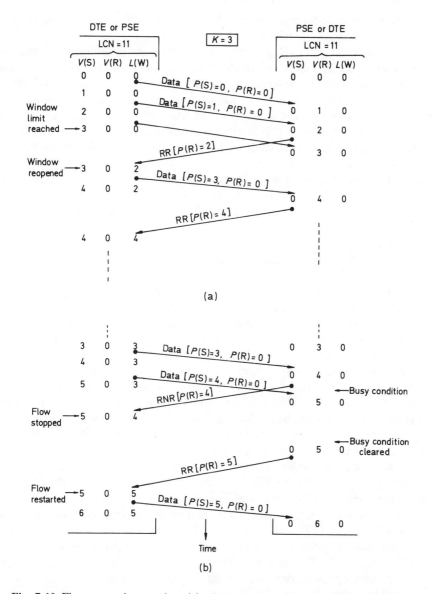

Fig. 7.10 Flow control examples: (a) windows operation; (b) RNR operation

Not-Ready (*RNR*) packet for this logical channel. Each RNR packet contains a $P(R)$ which defines the new $L(W)$ for this channel but, on receipt of an RNR, the sender must cease transmission of further packets until the receiver is ready to continue receiving Data packets on this channel. This is normally achieved by the receiver returning an RR packet. A typical packet sequence illustrating the use of the RNR packet is shown in part (b) of Fig. 7.10. It can be deduced from this that the RNR packet cannot stop the flow of packets immediately since there may be packets already in transit on the link. Any packets received in this way must be accepted, however, because of the lack of any error control associated with the Packet Layer.

Although the two mechanisms just described are provided to control the flow of Data packets over each logical channel, provision is also made in the protocol for a DTE to send a single high priority Data packet to a correspondent DTE which is independent of the normal flow control procedures. Such a packet is known as an *Interrupt packet* and, since it is not affected by the normal flow control mechanisms, an Interrupt packet may be received out of sequence from other Data packets over this circuit. On receipt of an Interrupt packet, the receiving DTE – Packet Layer – must return an *Interrupt Confirmation* packet since there can be only one outstanding unacknowledged Interrupt packet per virtual circuit at any time. This then allows a further such packet to be sent should this be required.

Error recovery

The main error recovery mechanisms associated with the Packet Layer are the Reset and Restart procedures. The Reset procedure is used only during the data transfer phase and affects just a single virtual call (circuit). The Restart procedure, however, affects all virtual calls currently in progress.

A *Reset Request packet* is sent by either DTE if it receives a Data packet which is outside the current window limit. This indicates the two DTEs have become unsynchronised and hence the flow of Data packets must be restarted. A typical packet sequence associated with the Reset procedure is shown in part (a) of Fig. 7.11. Any Data packets associated with the affected virtual circuit are discarded by the Packet Layer and the user is informed the network connection has been cleared. The reason for the clearing is passed as a parameter and it is then up to the user – the Transport Layer in practice – to recover from any possible loss of data.

The Restart procedure is used to simultaneously clear all virtual circuits currently in progress at a DTE. It is used when the DTE and PSE become unsynchronised at a level which affects all currently active calls; for example, an Incoming Call with a logical channel number which is currently in use is received from the PSE. A typical packet sequence associated with the Restart procedure and the effect on a number of active virtual circuits is shown in part (b) of Fig. 7.11. The figure only shows the possible effect at a single correspondent packet layer, but clearly a number of other DTEs may also be affected in a similar way.

7.3.4 Terminal access

The preceding sections relating to the X.25 network access protocol have assumed that the DTE to be connected to the network has sufficient intelligence – processing capability – to be able to implement the various protocol layers just described. In general this is true, certainly if the DTE is a computer, for example. In some instances, however, the DTE may not operate in a packet mode nor have sufficient processing capability to implement a protocol like X.25. Hence, to interface this type of DTE to the

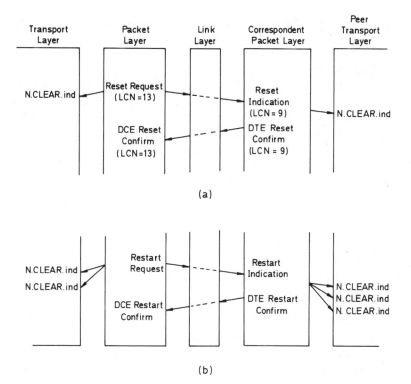

Fig. 7.11 Error recovery procedures: (a) reset; (b) restart

network it then becomes necessary to provide an additional piece of equipment to implement the various protocol layers on its behalf and to provide a much simpler user-level interface to the DTE. An example of a DTE in this category is a simple asynchronous character-mode terminal like a visual display unit (VDU); this normally has only a limited level of intelligence with a simple RS-232C/V.24 character interface.

To meet this type of requirement, the user may, of course, choose to provide the additional equipment himself to perform the necessary assembly of character strings from the terminal into network packets and vice versa himself. Alternatively, because this is not an uncommon requirement, the various PSDN authorities also offer users with an alternative network access protocol which is intended for use with asynchronous character-mode terminals. This is known as X.28 and the additional equipment necessary to provide this type of interface is known as a *Packet Assembler-Disassembler* or *PAD*. Since the latter is provided by the PSDN authority, it is normally located with the local packet-switching exchange and a single PAD is then used to support a number of character-mode DTEs. A schematic diagram showing the function and location of a PAD together with the additional protocols which have been defined for use with it is given in Fig. 7.12. As can be seen, protocol X.3 defines the operation and facilities that are provided by the PAD and X.29 defines the interface between the PAD and a remote packet-mode DTE. Selected aspects of this mode of working will now be considered.

7.3.4.1 The PAD and X.3

Essentially, the function of a PAD is to assemble the individual characters entered by a user at a character-mode asynchronous terminal into meaningful packets which are suitable for transmission through an X.25 PSDN. Similarly, on receipt of such packets, the PAD disassembles them and passes the individual characters contained within them to the terminal a single character at a time. The PAD, therefore, must perform all the X.25 protocol functions on behalf of the terminal such as call establishment, flow control etc. and in general make the packet mode of working of the network transparent to the user.

The function and facilities of a PAD are defined in recommendation X.3. In addition to the basic functions just outlined, because character-mode terminals vary widely in their operation and characteristics, each terminal connected to a PAD has a number of parameters associated with it. These are normally set from the terminal or, alternatively, from the remote packet-mode DTE which is being accessed. They relate to such features as:

1. whether local echo checking is required;
2. selection of *packet terminating* (*data forwarding*) characters – these allow the user of the terminal to signal to the PAD that the transmission of a (partly complete) packet should be initiated;
3. specification of alternative control characters such as line feed and carriage return.

In order to facilitate the use of the PAD, all the parameters associated with a terminal have a default value and hence only those parameters which differ from these need be changed. The initial parameter settings are determined by the *standard profile* selected for use with the terminal. There are a number of alternative standard profiles which have been defined for use with the more popular types of terminal. Both the standard profile to be used and any changes to be made from this are normally selected and entered at logging-on time. The procedure to do this is as defined in recommendation X.28.

7.3.4.2 Recommendation X.28

This recommendation specifies the protocol to be used between an asynchronous character-mode terminal and the PAD. It contains the procedures to be followed to:

1. access the PAD;
2. set the terminal parameters to the required values;
3. establish a virtual call to a destination packet-mode DTE;
4. control the exchange of user's data between the terminal and the PAD;
5. clear an established call.

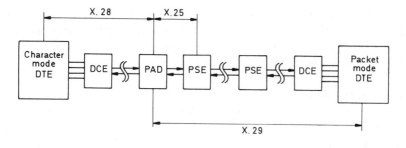

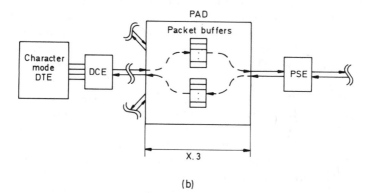

Fig. 7.12 The PAD and its interface protocols: (a) interface protocols;
(b) internal protocol

Access to the PAD may take several forms. It may be via a switched connection setup using the PSTN or it may be over a leased line. Clearly, if the PSTN uses analogue transmission, then modems must be used at each end of the link. Alternatively, where digital data services are provided by the network, a direct digital path can be either set up or leased and hence a conventional RS-232C/V.24 interface may be used.

Once the terminal has gained access to the PAD, the terminal sends a *service request* character sequence. Firstly, this enables the PAD to determine the data rate being used by the terminal, and secondly it enables the terminal to select an initial standard profile. Procedures are then defined to allow the terminal user to read the parameters associated with the profile and, if required, to change them to other values. The PAD is then ready to establish a virtual call through the PSDN to a remote packet-mode DTE.

To establish a virtual call, the user first indicates to the PAD the address of the required packet-mode terminal. The PAD then follows the virtual call establishment procedure outlined earlier. Once the call has been established, the PAD then enters the data transfer phase.

When in the data transfer phase, the PAD performs the necessary packet assembly and disassembly functions. During the assembly process, the PAD will initiate the transfer of a packet either when the user enters an agreed packet termination control character or after an agreed time-out period. Finally, after all information has been exchanged, the user may request the PAD to initiate the clearing of the call.

7.3.4.3 Recommendation X.29

This recommendation specifies the interaction between the PAD and the remote packet-mode DTE. The basic procedures associated with X.29 for call establishment and data transfer are essentially the same as those used in X.25. Additional procedures are also defined in the recommendation, however, which reflect the presence of the PAD between the terminal and remote packet-mode DTE. For instance, during the call establishment phase, the PAD uses the first four octets of the optional user data field in a Call Request packet as a so-called *Protocol Identifier* field. This has been done to allow different types of calling subscriber (terminal) to be identified so that the called packet-mode DTE can utilise alternative protocols should this be necessary.

Similarly in the reverse direction, when in the data transfer phase the packet-mode DTE is able to communicate with the PAD directly using the Qualifier (Q) bit in the header of each Data packet. When the Q bit is set, this indicates the remaining information in the packet is intended for use by the PAD and should not therefore be disassembled and passed to the user terminal. This procedure allows, for example, the remote packet-mode DTE to read and, if necessary, set the current values of the parameters associated with the calling terminal.

7.4 CIRCUIT-SWITCHED DATA NETWORKS

The various protocols associated with the lowest three network-dependent layers in the ISO Model for use with a circuit-switched data network (CSDN), are as shown in Fig. 7.13. The operational characteristics of the physical interface to a circuit-switched network are defined in recommendation X.21. The aim is to provide the user with a full-duplex synchronous data transmission path which is available for the duration of the call. The various interchange circuits associated with X.21 were shown in Fig. 7.6 and hence the remainder of this section will concentrate on the operation of the X.21 interface.

7.4.1 The X.21 interface

With a circuit-switched network, once a call has been established, a physical communications path exists between the calling and called DTEs. The X.21 interface protocol is concerned, therefore, only with the setup and clearing operations associated with each call. The control of the ensuing data transfer is then the responsibility of the Link Layer which, because of the operation of a circuit-switched network, operates on an end-to-end basis. This is shown in diagrammatic form in Fig. 7.14.

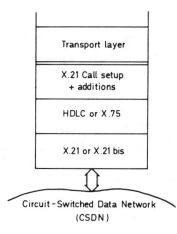

Fig. 7.13 CSDN network-dependent protocols

A typical interchange sequence to first set up a call, perform an exchange of data, and then clear the call using the various interchange circuits associated with X.21 is shown in Fig. 7.15. Part (a) shows the interchange sequence across the calling DTE/DCE interface and part (b) the interchange sequence across the called DTE/DCE interface. Initially, the Transmit (T) circuit from both the calling and called DTE are both at logical 1, indicating that they are both ready to either initiate a call or receive a call. Similarly, the Receive (R) circuit from each DCE is also at logical 1 indicating their availability.

The calling DTE first indicates it wishes to make a call by setting its Control (C) circuit from the Off to the On state and simultaneously setting its Transmit circuit to the logical 0 state – part (a). When the DCE is ready to accept the call, it responds by transmitting an SYN synchronising character on the Receive (R) circuit followed by a series of '+' IA5 (ASCII) characters. On receipt of the '+' characters the calling DTE proceeds by transmitting a

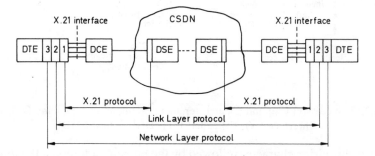

DSE = Digital Switching Exchange

Fig. 7.14 Applicability of the network protocols with a CSDN

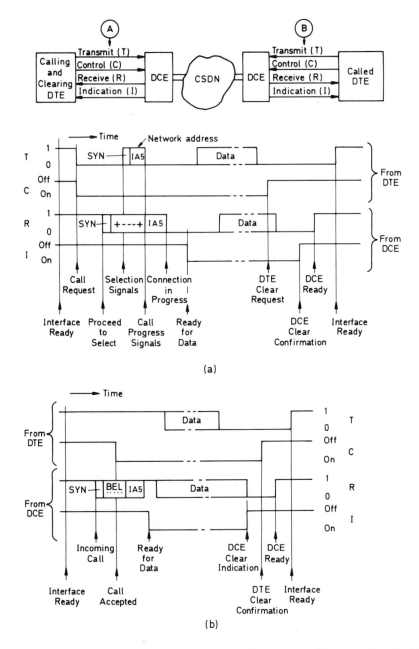

Fig. 7.15 Successful Call and Clear Interchange sequences: (a) calling DTE/DCE
Interface (A); (b) called DTE/DCE Interface (B)

SYN synchronising character followed by the network address of the required
destination DTE, again in the form of IA5 characters each with a single parity
bit. The DTE then enters a wait state and the DCE responds by transmitting
idle (call progress) characters whilst it attempts to set up the call.

When the call request reaches the required destination DCE, the latter informs the called DTE by first transmitting a SYN synchronising character folllowed by a series of BEL characters – part (b). The called DTE then accepts the call by setting its Control circuit from Off to On and the DCE, in turn, passes other call setup information in the form of a series of IA5 characters on the Receive circuit; this information includes reverse charging and other similar imformation. Finally, the call setup phase is completed by both the calling and called DCEs setting their Indication (I) control circuits to indicate a circuit has been set up and the network is ready for data.

After the connection has been established, a data-transparent, full-duplex communications path is available to both the calling and called DTEs for the transfer of Link Layer data. (Typically this involves the exchange of frames according to the HDLC protocol.) Each DTE initiates the transmission of a data frame on its Transmit circuit. This is then sent through the network and passed to the recipient DTE on the incoming Receive circuit from its local DCE. Finally, after one of the DTEs has finished transmitting all its data, it initiates the clearing of the call (circuit) by switching its Control circuit Off (DTE Clear Request) – part (a). As can be seen, however, since the circuit is full-duplex, the clearing DTE must be prepared to accept further data on the incoming Receive circuit.

The Clear Request signal is passed through the network to the remote DCE and the latter then informs its local DTE by setting the Indication control circuit to the Off state (DCE Clear Indication) – part (b). The local DTE then responds by setting its Control circuit to the Off state (DTE Clear Confirmation). This is then passed through the network to the clearing DCE which informs the DTE by setting its Indication circuit Off (DCE Clear Confirmation) – part (a). Finally, both sides of the connection return to the Interface Ready State.

7.4.2 X.21 bis

The X.21 interface protocol is intended for use with an all-digital CSDN. Before such networks become fully available, therefore, and to ease the transition from existing RS-232C/V.24-based equipment to the newer equipment needed with X.21, an alternative interface protocol has been defined known as X.21 bis, the bis indicating it is the alternative protocol. This is the same interface as that already used with a synchronous modem – that is, one which supplies a bit-timing clock signal – since it must perform the necessary conversions from digital-to-analogue form for transmitting data through the network and from analogue-to-digital form on receipt of data from the network.

7.4.3 Link and Network Layers

As was indicated in Figure 7.14, both the Link Layer and Network Layer protocols with a circuit-switched network are end-to-end protocols. With an all-digital network, since a full-duplex circuit is set up, the Link Layer protocol can be the same as that used in X.25: that is, HDLC with LAPB. With the older analogue access circuits and networks, however, only a two-wire, half-duplex circuit is set up and hence a derivative of HDLC as defined in recommendation X.75 must be used. The link setup procedure with X.75 is also a derivative of LAPB and is known as LAPX. This again is intended for the setup of a logical data link over a half-duplex physical circuit.

If no flow control functions are being supported, the Network Layer (level 3) with a CSDN can be relatively simple since each network service primitive – N.CONNECT/DATA/CLEAR – issued by the Transport Layer can be mapped directly into a similar request to the intermediate Link Layer. The Transport Layer would then perform its own flow control functions. Alternatively, to ease interworking with other types of network, it is possible to have a Network Layer similar to that used with X.25. If this is done, however, the various logical channel identifiers discussed in the previous section would have an end-to-end significance rather than local significance as with an X.25 packet-switched network. Also each call would, of course, be a separate circuit with a CSDN.

Problems

7.1 a) Describe the differences between a circuit-switched data network and a packet-switched data network. Clearly identify the effects on the users of these networks.

   b) Explain what is understood by the following techniques used in packet-switched data networks:

   i) datagram,
   ii) virtual call (circuit),
   iii) logical channel.

7.2 Sketch diagrams to illustrate the applicability and components of the X.25 network access protocol and write explanatory notes describing the function of each component.

7.3 a) Define the set of user service primitives associated with the Packet (Network) Layer of the X.25 protocol.

   Explain the use of the following additional facilities:

   i) More-data,
   ii) Qualifier,
   iii) Delivery Confirmation.

   b) Tabulate the main protocol data units (packet types) used by the Packet Layer protocol to perform the following operations:

   i) establish a virtual call (circuit),
   ii) exchange a message unit over this circuit,
   iii) clear the call.

   Sketch a time sequence diagram to illustrate the sequence in which the protocol data units are exchanged to implement these operations.

7.4 a) Describe the flow control method used by the Packet Layer protocol in X.25 and list the Packet Layer protocol data units (packet types) which are used to implement it.

b) Sketch diagrams to illustrate how the flow of data packets relating to a single logical channel is controlled by:

i) the window mechanism,
ii) the use of additional supervisory packets.

Include in your diagrams the state of the Send and Receive Variables, $V(S)$ and $V(R)$, and the window variable, $L(W)$, at both sides of the logical channel as each data packet is transmitted.

7.5 Discriminate between the Reset and Restart error recovery procedures used in the Packet Layer of X.25 and explain their operation.

7.6 a) Describe the function of a Packet Assembler-Disassembler (PAD) as used in X.25-based networks and identify on a diagram the various protocols which have been defined for use with it.

b) Outline the essential features of the following protocols which are used with PADs:

i) X.3,
ii) X.28,
iii) X.29.

7.7 a) Outline the function of the three lowest network- dependent protocol layers used with a circuit-switched data network.

b) Sketch a diagram showing the various interchange circuits associated with X.21 and outline their function.

c) With the aid of a time sequence diagram, describe the operation of the X.21 interface protocol. Clearly show the transitions on each interchange circuit at both the calling DTE/DCE interface and also the called DTE/DCE interface. Identify on your diagram the call setup, data transfer, and call clearing phases.

Chapter 8 **Local Area Data Networks**

Objectives:

When you have completed studying the material in this chapter you should:

- know the different topologies and transmission media commonly used in local area networks (LANs);

- know the difference between baseband and broadband working;

- be able to describe the alternative medium access control methods used in LANs;

- be able to describe the major components and mode of operation of a CSMA/CD Bus network;

- be able to describe the major components and mode of operation of a Token Ring network;

- be able to describe selected aspects of the operation of a Token Bus network;

- appreciate the function of the various network-dependent protocols used with LANs and be able to describe the services and operation of the Logical Link Control (LLC) protocol layer;

- understand the function of a Gateway and describe how two DTEs connected to two separate LANs may communicate through an intermediate public data network.

8.1 INTRODUCTION

Local area data networks, normally referred to simply as *local area networks* or *LANs*, are concerned with the interconnection of distributed communities of computer-based data terminal equipments whose physical separation is confined to a single building or localised group of buildings. For example, a LAN may be used to interconnect a community of computer-based workstations distributed around a block of offices within a building. Alternatively, it may be used to interconnect various computer-based items of equipment distributed around a factory or hospital complex. Since all the equipment is located within a single organisation, however, LANs are normally installed and maintained by the organisation and hence they are also referred to as *Private Data Networks*.

The main difference between a communications path established using a LAN and a connection made through a public data network is that with a LAN, because of the relatively short distances between the various items of interconnected equipment, much higher data transmission rates are normally available. In the context of the ISO Reference Model for open systems interconnection, however, this difference manifests itself only at the lower network-dependent layers and hence, as was indicated in Chapter 6, the higher protocol layers in the Reference Model are in fact the same for both types of network. This chapter, therefore, is primarily concerned with a description of the different types of LAN and the function and operation of the associated network-dependent protocol layers.

8.2 LAN CHARACTERISTICS

Before describing the structure and operation of different types of LAN, it is helpful to first outline some of the basic techniques which are used with LANs and which are different from those used with other types of network. These are concerned with:

network topology,
transmission medium,
network (medium) access control methods.

Each will be considered separately.

8.2.1 Topology

Most wide area networks – PSTN, PDN etc. – use a *mesh* (sometimes referred to as a *network*) *topology*. With LANs, however, the limited physical separation of the subscriber DTEs means simpler topologies may be used. The three topologies in common use are Star, Bus, and Ring. These are shown in diagrammatic form in Fig. 8.1.

Perhaps the best example of a LAN based on a *Star topology* is the digital *Private Automatic Branch Exchange* (*PABX*). A connection established through a traditional analogue PABX is in many ways similar to a connection made through an analogue PSTN insomuch that all paths through the network are designed to carry limited-bandwidth analogue speech. To use such a facility to carry data, therefore, requires modems as discussed in Chapter 4. The more modern types of PABX, however, utilise digital switching techniques within the exchange and for this reason they are also referred to as *Private Digital Exchanges* (*PDX*). Moreover, the availability of inexpensive integrated circuits to perform the necessary analogue-to-digital and digital-to-analogue conversion functions means that it is rapidly becoming common practice to extend the digital mode of working right back to the subscriber outlets. This means that a switched 64 kbps path – the digitising rate normally used for digital voice – is then available at each

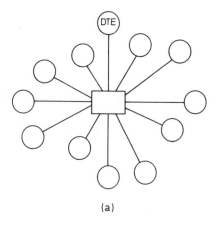

(a)

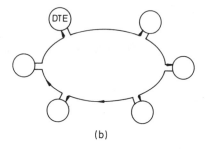

(b)

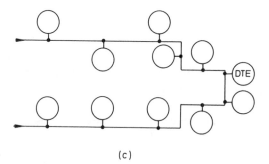

(c)

Fig. 8.1 LAN topologies: (a) star; (b) ring; (c) bus

subscriber outlet which can therefore be used for both voice and data.

The main use of a PDX, however, is likely to be to provide a switched communications path between a localised community of integrated voice and data terminals (workstations) for the exchange of such information as electronic mail, electronic documents etc. in addition, of course, to normal voice communications. Also, the use of digital techniques within the PDX will mean the latter can also be used to provide such services as voice store-and-forward – that is, a subscriber may leave (store) a voice message for another subscriber for later retrieval (forwarding) – and teleconferencing – multiple subscribers taking part in a single call.

The preferred topologies of LANs designed specifically to function as a data communications subnetwork for the interconnection of local communities of computer-based equipment are Bus (Linear) and Ring. In practice, Bus networks are normally extended into an interconnected set of buses and the resulting topology therefore resembles an unrooted tree structure. Typically, with a *Bus topology*, the single network cable is routed through those locations (offices for example) which have a DTE to be connected to the network and a physical connection (tap) is then made to the cable to allow the user DTE to gain access to the network services supported. Appropriate medium access control circuitry and algorithms are then used to share the use of the available transmission bandwidth between the attached community of DTEs.

With a *Ring topology* the network cable passes from one DTE to another until all the DTEs are interconnected in the form of a loop or ring. A feature of a Ring topology is that there is a direct point-to-point link between each neighbouring DTE which is unidirectional in operation. Appropriate medium access control algorithms then ensure the use of the ring is shared between the community of users. The data transmission rates used with both Ring and Bus topologies – typically from 1 to 10 Mbps – means that they are best suited for interconnecting local communities of computer-based items of equipment; for example, intelligent workstations in an office environment or intelligent controllers around a process plant.

8.2.2 Transmission media

Shielded twisted-pair, coaxial cable, and optical fibre are the three main types of transmission medium used for LANs. One of the main advantages of both twisted-pair and coaxial cable is that it is straightforward to make a physical connection (tap) to the cable. This is necessary with a bus topology, for example, and hence bus networks mainly use these types of transmission media.

Optical fibre cable, as was mentioned in Chapter 4, is best suited to those applications which demand either high levels of immunity to electromagnetic interference or very high data rates. Also, it is not easy to make a number of physical taps to a single optical fibre cable. Optical fibre is best suited, therefore, for point-to-point communications as used with a ring network for example.

The form of the electrical interface with the different types of transmission media were discussed in Chapter 4. Coaxial cable, when used for a LAN, however, is operated using either *baseband* techniques, as were described in Chapter 4, or *broadband*. With the latter, instead of transmitting information onto the cable in the form of, say, two voltage levels corresponding to the bit stream being transmitted (baseband), the total available bandwidth (frequency range) of the cable is divided into a number of smaller *subfrequency bands* or *channels*. Each subfrequency band is then used, with the aid of a pair of special modems, to provide a separate data communications channel. This style of working is known as *frequency division multiplexing* and, since the frequencies used are in the radio frequency band, the modems are known as radio frequency or simply *r.f. modems*. This approach is known as broadband working and the same principle is currently in widespread use in the *Community Antenna Television* (*CATV*) industry to multiplex a number of TV channels onto a single coaxial cable.

A schematic of a typical CATV system is shown in part (a) of Fig. 8.2. Each TV channel is allocated a particular frequency band, typically of 6 MHz bandwidth. Each received video signal (from the various aerials) is then used to modulate a *carrier frequency* in the selected *frequency band*. The modulated carrier signals are then transmitted over the cable network and are thus available at each subscriber outlet. The subscriber then selects a particular TV channel by tuning to the appropriate frequency band.

In a similar way it is possible to derive a range of data transmission channels from a single cable by allocating each channel a portion of the total bandwidth, the amount of bandwidth for each channel being determined by the required data rate. For data communication, however, a two-way (duplex) capability is normally required. This may be achieved in one of two ways: either the transmit and receive paths are assigned two different frequency bands on the same cable – *single-cable system* – or two separate cables are used, one for the transmit path and the other for the receive path – *dual-cable system*. A schematic of each type of system is shown in parts (i) and (ii) of Fig. 8.2(b). The main difference between the two systems is that a dual-cable system requires twice the amount of cable and cable taps to install. Nevertheless, with a dual-cable system the total cable bandwidth – typically 5 to 440 MHz – is available in each direction. Moreover, the headend equipment is simply an amplifier, whereas with a single-cable system a frequency translator is required to translate the incoming frequency signals associated with the various receive paths to the corresponding outgoing frequencies used for the transmit paths.

The selected frequency band in the reverse direction is first modulated – using an r.f. modem – using the data to be transmitted and this signal is fed onto the cable using a special *directional coupler* or *tap*. The latter is designed so that most of the transmitted signal flows in the reverse direction to the cable *Headend* (*HE*). Another special device known as a *frequency translator* is then used which converts (translates) the signals received on the different receive frequency bands to a corresponding set of forward frequency bands. The transmitted modulated signal is thus remodulated by the headend and the r.f. modem associated with the receiving DTE tuned to receive the matching remodulated signal frequency band. The transmitted data are then demodulated from the received signal by the receiving modem and passed on to the attached DTE.

It may be deduced from this that a single pair of frequencies provides just a simplex (unidirectional) data path between the two DTEs and hence to support duplex communication, two separate pairs of frequencies must be

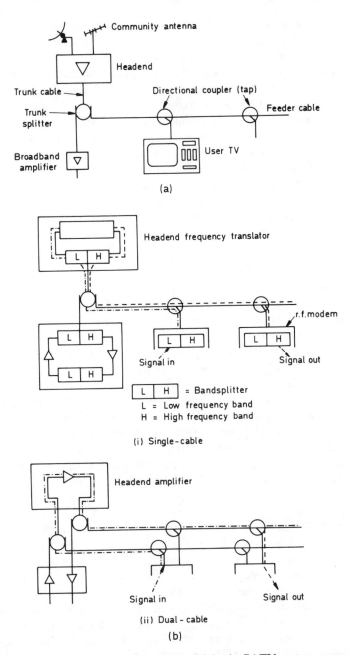

Fig. 8.2 Broadband coaxial cable systems: (a) basic CATV system components; (b) broadband data network alternatives

used. Nevertheless, a 9.6 kbps simplex data channel requires only in the order of 20 kHz of the total available bandwidth and hence a pair of 6 MHz subfrequency bands, for example, can be used to provide 300 such channels or 150 full-duplex channels. Higher data rate channels then require progressively more of the available bandwidth; for example, two 6 MHz bands for a 5 Mbps full-duplex channel or four 6 MHz bands for a 10 Mbps full-duplex channel.

The price to pay for deriving this multiplicity of different data channels from a single cable is the relatively high cost of each pair of r.f. modems. An added advantage of a broadband coaxial cable, however, is that it can be used over longer distances than a baseband cable. The primary use of broadband coaxial cable, therefore, tends to be as a flexible transmission medium for use in establishments comprising multiple buildings, especially when the physical separation of the buildings is quite large (up to tens of kilometres, for example). When used in this way, other services such as closed-circuit television and voice can be readily integrated onto the same cable as that being used for data and hence broadband is a viable alternative to baseband for networks which must provide a range of services.

8.2.3 Medium access control methods

When a communications path is established between two DTEs through a star network, the central controlling element – a PDX for example – ensures that the transmission path between the two DTEs is reserved for the duration of the call. With both a ring and a bus topology, however, there is only a single logical transmission path linking all the items of equipment together and hence a discipline must be imposed on all the items connected to the network to ensure that the transmission medium is accessed and used in a fair way. The two techniques which have been adopted for use in the various standards documents are *Carrier-Sense-Multiple-Access with Collision Detection* (CSMA/CD) for use with Bus network topologies, and *Control Token* for use with either Bus or Ring networks. Both will now be described. In addition, an access method based on a *Slotted Ring* is also in widespread use in the UK with Ring networks and hence this will also be described.

8.2.3.1 CSMA/CD

The CSMA/CD access method is used solely with Bus networks. With this type of network topology, all DTEs are connected directly to the same cable and hence the latter is used for transmitting all data between any pair of DTEs. The cable is said to operate, therefore, in a *multiple access* (*MA*) *mode*. All data are transmitted by the sending DTE first encapsulating the data in a frame with the required destination DTE address at the head of the frame. The frame is then transmitted (*broadcast*) on the cable. All DTEs connected to the cable detect whenever a frame is being transmitted and, when the required destination DTE detects that the frame currently being transmitted has its own address at the head of the frame, it continues reading the data contained within the frame and responds according to the defined link protocol. The source DTE address is also included as part of the frame header and hence the recipient DTE can direct its response to the originating DTE.

With this style of operation, it is clearly possible for two DTEs to attempt to transmit a frame over the cable at the same time, with the effect that the data from each source is corrupted. To reduce the possibility of this before transmitting a frame, the source DTE first *listens* to the cable to detect if a frame is currently being transmitted and, if it is – that is, a *carrier* signal is *sensed* (CS) – the DTE *defers* its transmission until the passing frame has been transmitted. Even so, two DTEs wishing to transmit a frame may determine that there is no activity (transmission) currently taking place on the bus at the same instant of time and hence both start to transmit their frames simultaneously. A *collision* is then said to occur since the contents of both frames will collide and hence be corrupted.

To allow for this possibility, as a DTE transmits the contents of a frame onto the cable, it simultaneously monitors the data signal actually present on the cable and, if the transmitted and monitored signals are different, a collision is assumed to have occurred – *Collision Detected* (CD). To ensure that the other DTE(s) involved in the collision is (are) aware that a collision has occurred, when a DTE detects a collision, it first *enforces* the collision by continuing to send a random bit pattern for a short period known as the *Jam Sequence*. The two (or more) DTEs involved then wait for a further short random time interval before trying to retransmit the affected frames again. It can be concluded from this that access to a CSMA/CD Bus is probabilistic and clearly depends on the network (cable) loading. It should be stressed, however, that since the bit rate used on the cable is very high (up to 10 Mbps) the network loading tends to be low. Also, since the transmission of a frame is initiated only if the cable is inactive, the probability of a collision occurring is in practice quite low.

8.2.3.2 Control token
Another way of controlling access to a shared transmission medium is by the use of a *control (permission) token*. The control token is passed from one DTE to another according to a defined set of rules understood by all DTEs connected to the medium. A DTE may only transmit a frame when it is in possession of the token and, after it has transmitted the frame, it passes the token on to allow another DTE to access the transmission medium. The sequence of operation is as follows:

1. a logical ring is first established, which links all the DTEs connected to the physical medium, and a single control token is created;
2. the token is passed from DTE to DTE around the logical ring until it is received by a DTE waiting to send a frame(s);
3. the waiting DTE then sends the waiting frame(s) using the physical medium and then passes the control token to the next DTE in the logical ring.

Monitoring functions within the active DTEs connected to the physical medium provide a basis for initialisation and recovery of both the connection of the logical ring and from the loss of the token. Although the monitoring functions are normally replicated among all the DTEs on the medium, only one DTE at a time carries the responsibility for recovery and re-initialisation.

The physical medium need not necessarily be a ring topology; a token may also be used to control access to a Bus network for example. The establishment of a logical ring on the two types of network is shown in parts (a) and (b) of Fig. 8.3.

With a physical ring, part (a), the logical structure of the token-passing ring is the same as the structure of the physical ring with the order of the token-passing the same as the physical ordering of the connected DTEs. With a Bus network, however, part (b), the ordering of the logical ring need not necessarily be the same as the physical ordering of the DTEs on the cable. Moreover, with a token access method on a Bus network, all DTEs need not necessarily be connected in the logical ring; for example, DTE H is not part of the logical ring shown in part (b) of Fig. 8.3. This means that DTE H can only operate in a receive mode since it will never own the control token. Another feature of the token access method is that it is possible to associate a priority with the token thereby allowing higher-priority frames to be transmitted first. This and other aspects will be expanded upon in later sections.

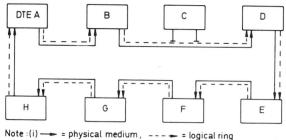

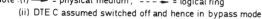

Note : (i) ——▶ = physical medium, ‑ ‑ ‑ ▶ = logical ring
(ii) DTE C assumed switched off and hence in bypass mode

(a)

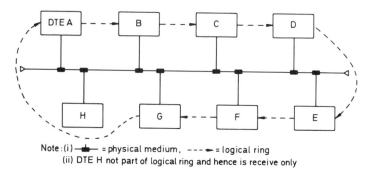

Note : (i) ——▲— = physical medium, ‑ ‑ ‑ ▶ = logical ring
(ii) DTE H not part of logical ring and hence is receive only

(b)

Fig. 8.3 Control token medium access control: (a) Token Ring; (b) Token Bus

8.2.3.3 Slotted ring

Slotted Rings are used solely for controlling the access to a Ring network. With this approach, the ring is first initialised to contain a fixed number of binary digits by a special node in the ring known as a *Monitor*. This stream of bits continuously circulates around the ring from one DTE to another; then, as each bit is received by a DTE, the DTE interface examines (reads) the bit and passes (repeats) it on to the next DTE in the ring and so on. The Monitor ensures that there is always a constant number of bits circulating in the ring irrespective of the number of DTEs making up the ring. The complete ring is arranged to contain a fixed number of slots, each made up of a set number of bits and capable of carrying a single, fixed-size frame of information. The format of a frame slot is shown in Fig. 8.4.

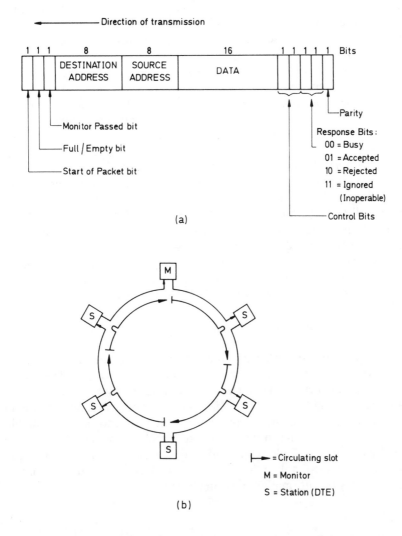

(a)

(b)

Circulating slot

M = Monitor

S = Station (DTE)

Fig. 8.4 Slotted Ring principles: (a) bit definitions of each slot; (b) outline topology

Initially, all the slots are marked empty by the Monitor setting the *Full/Empty Bit* at the head of each slot to the empty state. Then, when a DTE wishes to transmit a frame, it first waits until an empty slot is detected. It then marks the slot as full and proceeds to insert the frame contents into the slot with both the required destination DTE address and the source DTE address at the head of the frame and the *Response Bits* at the tail of the frame both set to 1. The slot containing the frame then circulates around the physical ring from one DTE to another. Each DTE in the ring examines the destination address at the head of any slot marked full and, if it detects its own address and assuming it is willing to accept the frame, it reads the frame contents from the slot whilst at the same time repeating the unmodified frame contents around the ring. In addition, after reading the frame contents, it modifies the pair of Response Bits at the tail of the slot to indicate that it has read the frame contents or, alternatively, if the addressed DTE is either busy or inoperable, the Response Bits are marked accordingly or left unchanged (inoperable).

The source DTE, after initiating the transmission of a frame, waits until the frame has circulated the ring by counting the (fixed number) of slots which are repeated at the ring interface. Then, on receipt of the first bit of the slot used to transmit the frame, it marks the slot as empty once again and waits to read the Response Bits from the tail of the slot to determine what action to take next.

The *Monitor Passed Bit* is used by the Monitor to detect if a DTE fails to release a slot after it has transmitted a frame. The Monitor Passed Bit is reset by the source DTE as it transmits a frame onto the ring. The Monitor then subsequently sets the Monitor Passed Bit in each full slot as it is repeated at its ring interface. Hence, if the Monitor detects that the Monitor Passed Bit is set when it repeats a full slot, it assumes the source DTE has failed to mark the slot as empty and hence resets the Full/Empty Bit at the head of the slot. The two Control bits at the tail of each slot are provided for use by the higher protocol software layers within each DTE and have no meaning at the medium access level.

It should be noted that, with a slotted ring medium access method, each DTE can only have a single frame in transit on the ring at a time, and also that it must release the slot used for transmitting a frame before trying to send another frame. In this way access to the ring is fair and shared between the various interconnected DTEs. The main disadvantages of a Slotted Ring are firstly a special (and hence vulnerable) Monitor node is required to maintain the basic ring structure, and secondly since each slot can carry only 16 bits of useful information, the transmission of each complete link-level frame normally requires multiple slots. With a Token Ring, of course, once a DTE receives the control token it may transmit a complete frame containing multiple bytes of information as a single unit.

8.3 LAN NETWORKS

The two dominant types of LAN which have been developed specifically for interconnecting localised communities of computer-based equipment are Bus and Ring. Currently, there are many different varieties of both types, although many of these do not adhere to the emerging international standards for LANs. The three types in the standards documents are: CSMA/CD Bus, Token Ring and Token Bus, and hence the descriptions which follow will be constrained to these three types.

8.3.1 CSMA/CD bus

Perhaps the best example of a CSMA/CD Bus network is *Ethernet* which is a 10 Mbps baseband coaxial cable network. Other bit rates and cable media are however supported in the standards documents. A typical CSMA/CD Bus network is shown in part (a) of Fig. 8.5 and a schematic diagram showing the various components necessary to connect a DTE to this type of network is given in part (b).

The integrated *Tap and Transceiver Unit* (also known as the *Medium Access Unit*) includes a Tap, which makes a non-intrusive physical connection to the coaxial cable, and this is closely coupled to the Transceiver itself. The Transceiver contains the necessary electronics to:

1. send and receive data onto and from the cable;
2. detect occurrences of collisions on the cable medium;
3. provide electrical isolation between the coaxial cable and the cable interface electronics;
4. protect the cable from any malfunctions in either the transceiver or the attached DTE.

The latter function is often referred to as *Jabber Control* since without the appropriate protection electronics, if a fault develops, it is possible for a faulty transceiver (or DTE) to transmit continuously random data onto the cable medium (jabber) and hence inhibit or corrupt all other transmissions. The Jabber Control essentially isolates the transmit data path from the cable if certain defined limits are violated: for example, all frames transmitted on the cable have a defined maximum length and, if this is exceeded, the Jabber Control inhibits further output data from reaching the cable.

The Transceiver Unit is connected to its host DTE by means of a shielded cable containing five sets of twisted-pair wires: one for carrying power to the Transceiver from the DTE, two for data (one send and one receive), and two for control purposes (one to allow the Transceiver to signal a collision to the DTE and the other for the DTE to initiate the isolation of the transmit data path from the cable). The four signal pairs are differentially driven, which means that the host DTE may be up to 50 m from the Transceiver and hence from the cable tapping point.

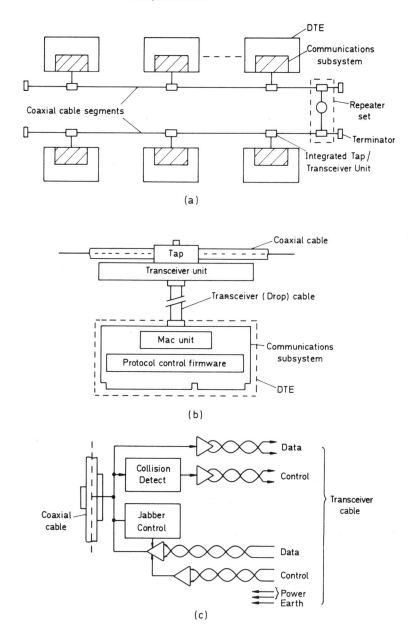

Fig. 8.5 CSMA/CD Bus network components: (a) cable layout; (b) DTE interface; (c) transceiver schematic

The Communications Controller Card contains a Medium Access Control (MAC) Unit (which is responsible for such functions as the encapsulation and de-encapsulation of frames for transmission/reception on the cable, error detection and the implementation of the medium access control algorithm) and a separate microprocessor which implements both the network-dependent protocols (to be described in a later section) and also the higher-level protocols described earlier in Chapter 6. In this way, the complete Communications Subsystem is normally self-contained on a single printed circuit card which slots into the host system bus and provides a defined set of network (application) services to the host software.

8.3.1.1 Frame format and operational parameters

The format of a frame and the operational parameters of a typical CSMA/CD Bus network are shown in Fig. 8.6. The meaning and use of the various parameters will be described as the operation of the MAC Unit is presented.

Each frame transmitted on the cable has eight fields: the Preamble, a Start-of-Frame Delimiter (SFD), the Destination and Source network

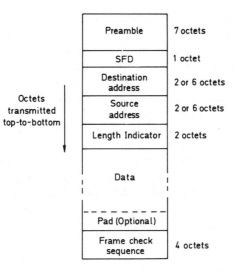

(a)

Cable medium	50Ω coaxial cable
Bit rate	10 Mbps (Manchester encoded)
Slot time	512 bit times
Inter-frame gap	9.6 μs
Attempt limit	16
Backoff limit	10
Jam size	32 bits
Maximum frame size	1518 octets
Minimum frame size	512 bits

(b)

Fig. 8.6 CSMA/CD Bus characteristics: (a) frame format; (b) operational parameters

addresses, a Length Indicator, the Data field, an optional Padding (null-data) field, and a Frame Check Sequence (FCS). All are of fixed length except the data and associated padding fields.

The *Preamble* field is sent at the head of all frames and its function is to allow the receiving electronics in each MAC unit to reliably achieve bit synchronisation before the actual frame contents are received. The preamble pattern is a sequence of seven octets each equal to the binary pattern 10101010. All frames are transmitted on the cable using Manchester encoding and hence, as was described in Chapter 2, the Preamble results in a periodic waveform being received by the receiver electronics. The *Start-of-Frame Delimiter* is a single octet comprising 10101011. This immediately follows the Preamble and signals to the receiver the start of a valid frame.

The Destination and Source network addresses specify the identity of both the intended destination DTE(s) and the originating DTE respectively. Each address field may be either 16 or 48 bits but for any particular LAN installation the size used must be the same for all DTEs. The first bit in the destination address field specifies whether the address is an *Individual Address* or a *Group Address*. If the former is specified, the transmitted frame is intended for a single destination DTE; if the latter is specified, the frame is intended either for a logically related group of DTEs (*Group Address*) or for all other DTEs connected to the network (*Broadcast* or *Global Address*). In the latter case, the address field is set to all binary 1s.

The *Length Indicator* is a two octet field whose value indicates the number of octets in the *Data* field. If this value is less than the minimum number required for a valid frame – Minimum Frame Size – a sequence of octets is added known as *padding*. Finally, the FCS field contains a 4-octet (32-bit) cyclic redundancy check value which is used for error detection purposes.

8.3.1.2 Frame transmission

When a frame is to be transmitted, the frame contents are first encapsulated by the MAC Unit into the format shown. To avoid contention with other transmissions on the medium, the medium access control section of the MAC Unit first monitors the carrier sense signal and, if necessary, defers to any passing frame. Then, after a short additional time delay (known as the *Inter-Frame Gap*) to allow the passing frame to be received and processed by the addressed DTE(s), transmission of the frame is initiated. The Manchester encoded bit stream is first sent to the Transceiver Unit via the interconnecting cable and the latter converts this into the appropriate format for transmission on the cable.

As the bit stream is being transmitted on the cable, the transceiver electronics simultaneously monitors the cable signal to detect if a collision occurs. Then, assuming a collision is not detected, the complete frame is transmitted and, after the FCS field has been sent, the MAC Unit awaits the arrival of a new frame either from the cable or from the controlling microprocessor. If a collision is detected, the transceiver electronics immediately turns on the Collision Detect signal. This, in turn, is detected by the MAC Unit which first enforces the collision by transmitting the *Jam Sequence* to ensure that the collision is detected by all other DTEs involved in the collision. Then, after the Jam Sequence has been sent, the MAC Unit terminates the transmission of the frame and schedules a retransmission attempt after a short randomly selected time interval.

In the event of a collision, retransmission of the frame is attempted up to a defined maximum number of tries known as the *Attempt Limit*. Since repeated collisions indicates a busy medium, however, the MAC Unit attempts to adjust to the medium load by progressively increasing the time delay between repeated retransmission attempts. The scheduling of retransmissions is controlled by a process called *truncated binary exponential backoff* which works as follows: when transmission of the Jam Sequence is complete and assuming the Attempt Limit has not been reached, the MAC Unit delays (backsoff) a random integral number of *Slot Times* before attempting to retransmit the affected frame. A given DTE can experience a collision during the initial part of its transmission – the *Collision Window* – which is effectively twice the time interval for the first bit of the Preamble to propagate to all parts of the cable medium (network). The Slot Time is thus the worst-case time delay a DTE must wait before it can reliably know a collision has occurred. It is defined as:

Slot Time = 2 (Transmission Path Delay) + Safety Margin

where *Transmission Path Delay* is the worst-case signal propagation delay going from any transmitter to any receiver on the cable network. This includes, therefore, any delays experienced in repeaters. The Slot Time is then double this delay (to allow for the corrupted signal to propagate back to the transmitting DTE) plus a safety margin. The Slot Time used is made equal to this figure rounded up to be a multiple number of octets at the bit-rate used. As an example, for a 10 Mbps baseband coaxial cable network with a maximum of 2.5 km between any transmitter and any receiver, this is equal to 512 bit times or 64 octets. The number of Slot Times before the Nth retransmission attempt is then chosen as a uniformly distributed random integer, R, in the range $0 \leqslant R \leqslant 2^K$, where $K = $ Min $(N,$ Backoff Limit$)$.

8.3.1.3 Frame reception

At each active DTE connected to the cable, the receiving electronics within the MAC Unit first detects the presence of an incoming signal from the Transceiver and switches on the Carrier Sense signal to inhibit any new transmissions from this DTE. The incoming Preamble is then used to achieve bit synchronisation and, after synchronisation has been achieved, the Manchester encoded data stream translated back into normal binary form. The incoming bit stream is then processed.

First, the remaining preamble bits are discarded together with the Start-of-Frame Delimiter when this is detected. The Destination Address field is then processed to determine whether the frame should be received by this DTE. If so, the frame contents comprising the Destination and Source Addresses and the Data field are loaded into a frame buffer to await further processing. The received FCS field is then compared with that computed by the MAC Unit during reception of the frame and, if they are equal, the start address of the buffer containing the received frame is passed to the next higher protocol layer – in the form of a service primitive – for further processing. Also, other validation checks are made on the frame before initiating further processing. These include checks to ensure that the frame contains an integral number of octets and that it is neither too short nor too long. Then, if any of these checks fail, the frame is discarded and an error report made to the Network Management Section.

Initially, the transmitted bit stream resulting from a collision will be received by each active DTE in the same way as a valid frame. After the colliding DTEs have detected the collision and transmitted the Jam Sequence, however, they will cease transmission. Fragmentary frames received in this way will therefore violate the *Minimum Frame Size* limit and hence be discarded by the receiving DTEs. Also, the adoption of a *Maximum Frame Size* means that the length of the frame buffers used for transmission and reception purposes can be quantified. The FCS field is a 32-bit sequence generated using a polynomial code and a generator polynomial of degree 32.

8.3.2 Token ring

A typical Token Ring network is shown in part (a) of Fig. 8.7 and a schematic diagram showing the various components necessary to connect a DTE to the cable medium is given in parts (b) and (c). The (trunk) cable medium is typically screened twisted-pair which, since each segment around the ring forms a point-to-point link, is differentially driven at a bit rate of between 1 and 4 Mbps.

8.3.2.1 Ring interface

The *Trunk Coupling Unit* (*TCU*) forms the physical interface with the cable medium. It contains a set of relays and additional electronics to drive and receive signals from the cable. The relays are so arranged that whenever the DTE is switched off, the TCU is in the *bypass state* and a continuous transmission path through the TCU is maintained. The insertion of a DTE into the ring is controlled by the Medium Access Control (MAC) Unit on the Communications Controller card within the DTE. The MAC Unit initiates the insertion of the DTE by activating both pairs of relays in the TCU and, as can be seen in part (c) of Fig. 8.7, when inserted, this causes all received signals to be routed through the MAC Unit. The receive/transmit electronics in the latter then either simply reads and relays (repeats) the received signal to the transmit side if this DTE is not the originator of the frame, or removes the received signal from the ring if it initiated the transmission.

The use of two pairs of relays connected in this way means that the MAC Unit can detect certain open-circuit and short-circuit faults in either the transmit or receive pair of signal wires. Also, in the bypass state, the MAC Unit can

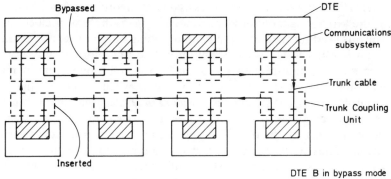

(a)

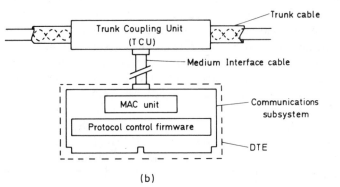

(b)

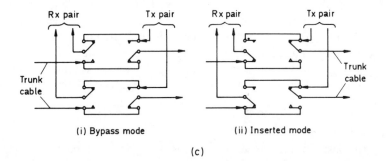

(i) Bypass mode   (ii) Inserted mode

(c)

Fig. 8.7 Token Ring network components: (a) ring configuration; (b) DTE interface; (c) TCU schematic

conduct self-test functions since any data output on the transmit pair are looped back on the receive pair. The DTE is connected to the TCU by means of a shielded cable containing two twisted-pair wires: one for transmission and the other for reception.

The MAC Unit is responsible for such functions as frame encapsulation and de-encapsulation, FCS generation and error detection, and the implementation of the medium access control algorithm. Also, when the DTE is the active ring monitor (see later), it supplies the master clock for the ring which is used for data encoding and decoding purposes; each circulating bit stream is Manchester encoded by the active ring monitor and all other DTEs on the ring then frequency and phase lock to this bit stream by means of a phase-locked-loop (PLL) circuit. In addition, when the DTE is the active ring monitor, it ensures the ring has a *minimum latency time*; that is, the time – measured in bit times at the ring data transmission rate – for a signal to propagate once around the ring. The ring latency time thus includes the signal propagation delay through the ring transmission medium plus the sum of the progagation delays through each MAC Unit. Hence, in order for the control token to circulate continuously around the ring when none of the DTEs requires to use the ring – that is, all DTEs are simply in the repeat mode – the ring must have a minimum latency time of at least the number of bits in the token sequence to ensure the token is not corrupted.

•   As will be defined later, the token is 24 bits in length and hence to allow for this, when a DTE is the active ring monitor, its MAC Unit provides a fixed 24-bit buffer which effectively becomes part of the ring to ensure its correct operation under all conditions. Although the mean data signalling rate around the ring is controlled by a single master clock in the active monitor, the use of a separate phase-locked-loop circuit in each MAC Unit means that the actual signalling rate may vary slightly around the ring. The worst case variation is when the maximum number of DTEs (250) are all active which is equivalent to plus or minus 3 bits. Unless the latency of the ring remains constant, however, bits will be either corrupted as the latency of the ring decreases, or additional bits added as the latency increases. In order to maintain a constant ring latency, therefore, an additional *elastic* (*variable*) *buffer* with a length of 6 bits is added to the fixed 24-bit buffer. The resulting 30-bit buffer is first initialised to 27 bits then, if the received signal at the master MAC Unit is faster than the master oscillator, the buffer is expanded by a single bit. Alternatively, if the received signal is slower, the buffer is reduced by a single bit. In this way the ring always comprises sufficient bits to allow the token to circulate continuously around the ring in the quiescent (idle) state.

8.3.2.2 Frame formats

There are two basic formats used in Token Rings: one for the control token and the other for normal frames. The control token is the means by which the right to transmit (as opposed to the normal process of repeating) is passed from one DTE to another, whereas a normal frame is used by a DTE to send either data or medium access control information around the ring. The format of the two types of frame is given in Fig. 8.8 together with the bit sequence used for each field.

The *Start Delimiter* (*SD*) and *End Delimiter* (*ED*) fields are special bit sequences used to achieve data transparency. They exploit the symbol

(a)

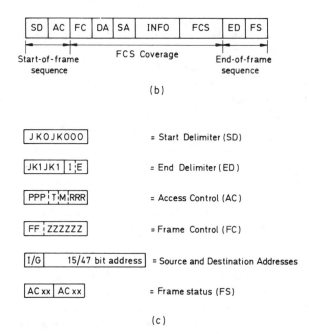

Fig. 8.8 Token Ring frame formats and field descriptions: (a) token format;
(b) frame format; (c) field descriptions

encoding method used on the cable medium: all information bits transmitted
on the medium are Manchester encoded except for selected bits in the SD and
ED fields. The J and K symbols depart from the normal encoding rules and
instead are constant levels for the complete bit cell period; the J symbol has
the same polarity as the preceding symbol whereas a K symbol is the opposite
polarity to the preceding symbol. In this way the receiver can reliably detect
the start and end of each transmitted token or frame irrespective of its
contents or length. It should be noted that only the first six symbols – JK1JK1
– are used to indicate a valid end of frame and the other two bits, I and E,
have other functions:

1. in a token, both the I and E bits are zero;
2. in a normal frame, the I bit is used to indicate whether the frame is the
   first (or an intermediate) frame in a sequence (I=1) or is the last (or only)
   frame (I=0);

3. the E bit is used for error detection purposes: it is set to 0 by the originating DTE but, if any DTE detects an error whilst receiving or repeating the frame (FCS error, for example) it sets the E bit to 1 to signal to the originating DTE an error has been detected.

The *Access Control (AC)* field comprises the Priority Bits, the Token and Monitor Bits, and the Reservation Bits. As the name implies, it is used to control access to the ring. When it is part of the token, the *Priority Bits* (P) indicate the priority of the token and hence those frames a DTE may transmit on receipt of the token; the *Token Bit* (T) is used to discriminate between a token and an ordinary frame (a 0 indicates a token and a 1 a frame); the *Monitor Bit* (M) is used by the active monitor to prevent a frame from circulating around the ring continuously; and the *Reservation Bits* (R) allow DTEs holding high priority frames to request (in either repeated frames or tokens) that the next token to be issued should be of the requisite priority.

The *Frame Control* (*FC*) field defines the type of the frame – medium access control or information – and also certain control functions: if the *Frame Type Bits* (F) indicate a MAC frame, all DTEs on the ring interpret and, if necessary, act on the *Control Bits* (Z); if it is an I-frame, the Control Bits are only interpreted by those DTEs identified in the Destination Address field.

The *Destination Address* (*DA*) and *Source Address* (*SA*) fields can be either 16 bits or 48 bits in length but for any specific LAN are the same for all DTEs. The Destination Address field identifies the DTE(s) for which the frame is intended. The first bit of the field indicates whether the address is an *Individual Address* (0) or a *Group Address* (1); individual addresses identify a specific DTE on the ring whilst group addresses are used to send a frame to multiple destination DTEs. The Source Address is always an individual address and identifies the DTE originating the frame. In addition, a Destination Address consisting of all 1s is known as a *Broadcast Address* and denotes that the frame is intended for all DTEs on the ring.

The *Information* (*INFO*) field is used to carry either user data or additional control information when included in a MAC frame. Although there is no maximum length specified for the information field, in practice it is limited by the maximum time a DTE is allowed to transmit a frame when holding the control token. A typical maximum length is 132 octets.

The *Frame Check Sequence* (*FCS*) field is a 32-bit CRC. Finally, the *Frame Status* (*FS*) field is made up of two fields: the *Address Recognised Bits* (A) and the *Frame Copied Bits* (C). Both the A and C bits are set to 0 by the DTE originating the frame. If the frame is recognised by one or more DTEs on the ring, the DTE(s) sets the A bits to 1; also, if it copies the frame, it sets the C bits to 1. In this way the originating DTE can determine if the addressed DTE(s) is non-existent or switched off, is active but did not copy the frame, or is active and copied the frame.

8.3.2.3 Frame transmission

On receipt of a service request to transmit a piece of data (which includes the priority of the data as a parameter), the data are first encapsulated by the MAC Unit into the standard format shown earlier in Fig. 8.8. The MAC Unit then awaits the reception of a token with a priority less than or equal to the priority of the assembled frame. Clearly, in a system which employs multiple priorities, a procedure must be followed to ensure that all DTEs have an opportunity to transmit frames in the correct order of priority. This works as follows.

After formatting a frame and prior to receiving an appropriate token – that is, one with a priority less than or equal to the priority of the waiting frame – each time a frame or a token with a higher priority is repeated at the ring interface, the MAC Unit reads the value of the Reservation Bits contained within the AC field. If this is higher than the priority of the waiting frame, the Reservation Bits are simply repeated unchanged. If it is lower, however, the MAC Unit replaces the current value with the priority of the waiting frame. Then, assuming there are no other higher priority frames awaiting transmission on the ring, when the token is passed on by the current owner (user), the waiting MAC Unit, on receipt of the token, detects that the priority of the token is equal to the priority of the frame it has waiting to be transmitted. It therefore accepts the token by changing the Token Bit in the AC field to 1 prior to repeating this bit which effectively converts the token to a start-of-frame sequence for a normal frame. The MAC Unit then stops repeating the incoming signal and follows the converted start-of-frame sequence with the preformatted frame contents. Also, whilst the frame contents are being transmitted, the FCS is computed and subsequently appended after the frame contents before transmitting the end-of-frame sequence.

After starting to transmit the waiting frame(s) (it is possible to send more than one frame providing, firstly, that the priority of the other waiting frame(s) is (are) greater than or equal to the priority of the token, and secondly that the total time taken to transmit the other frame(s) is within a defined limit known as the *Token Holding Time*) the MAC Unit stops repeating, thus removing the transmitted frame(s) from the ring, and notes the state of the A and C bits in the Frame Status field at the tail of the frame(s) to determine if the frame(s) has (have) been copied or ignored. It then generates a new token and forwards this on the ring to allow another waiting DTE to gain access to the ring.

8.3.2.4 Frame reception

The MAC Unit within each active DTE on the ring, in addition to repeating the incoming signal (bit) stream, detects the start of each frame by recognising the special start-of-frame bit sequence. It then determines whether the frame should simply be repeated or copied: if the Frame Type bits indicate the frame is a MAC frame (see later section on Ring Management), the frame is copied and the Control Bits are interpreted and, if necessary, acted upon; if the frame is a normal data carrying frame and the Destination Address matches with either the DTE's individual address or relevant group address, the frame contents are copied into a frame buffer and passed on for further processing. In either case the A and C bits in the Frame Status field at the tail of the frame are set accordingly.

8.3.2.5 Priority operation

The priority assigned to the token by a MAC Unit after it has completed transmitting any waiting frame(s) is determined according to a mechanism which endeavours firstly to ensure that frames with a higher priority than the current ring service priority are always transmitted on the ring first, and secondly all DTEs holding frames with the same priority have equal access rights to the ring. This is accomplished by a combination of the use of the Priority and Reservation Bits in the AC field of each frame coupled with a mechanism which ensures that a DTE which raises the service priority level of the ring returns the ring to its original level after the higher priority frames have been transmitted.

To implement this scheme, each MAC Unit maintains two sets of values: the first comprises three variables P_m, P_r and R_r. P_m specifies the highest priority value contained within any of the frames currently waiting transmission at this DTE whilst P_r and R_r are known as *Priority Registers* and contain, respectively, the priority and reservation values which were contained within the AC field of the most recently repeated token or frame. The second set of values comprises two stacks known as the S_r and S_x stacks which are used as follows.

All frames transmitted by a DTE when it receives a usable token are assigned a priority value in the AC control field equal to the present ring service priority P_r and a reservation value of zero. After all waiting frames – at or greater than the current ring priority – have been transmitted or until the transmission of another frame would not be completed before the Token Holding Time expires, the MAC Unit generates a new token with:

$P = P_r$ and $R = $ the greater of R_r and P_m,
   if the DTE does not have any more waiting frames to transmit which have a priority (as contained in register P_m) equal to or greater than the current ring service priority (as contained in register P_r) or does not have a reservation request (as contained in register R_r) greater than the current priority;

$P = $ the greater of R_r and P_m and $R = 0$,
   if the DTE has another waiting frame(s) with a priority (as contained in P_m) greater than the current priority P_r, or if the current contents of R_r are greater than the current priority.

Since in the latter case the DTE effectively raises the service priority level of the ring, it becomes what is known as a *stacking station* (DTE) and, as such, stores the value of the old ring service priority (P_r) on stack S_r and the new ring service priority (P) on stack S_x. These values are saved since it is the responsibility of a DTE which becomes a stacking station to subsequently lower the ring service priority level when there are no further frames ready to transmit – at any point on the ring – with a priority equal to or greater than the stacked S_x. Also, a stack is used rather than a single register because a stacking station may need to raise the service priority of the ring more than once before the service priority is returned to a lower priority level. The different values assigned to the P and R bits of the token and the actions performed on the two stacks are summarised in part (a) of Fig. 8.9.

Having become a stacking station, the MAC Unit claims every token

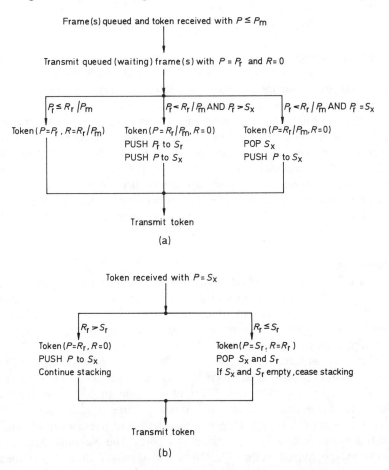

Fig. 8.9 Token generation and stack modification: (a) token generation [*Note*: $S_x=0$ if stack empty]; (b) stack modification

which it receives which has a priority equal to the stacked S_x in order to examine the value in the R bits of the Access Control field of the token to determine if the service priority of the ring should be raised, maintained, or lowered. The new token is then transmitted with:

$P = R_r$ and $R = 0$,

if the value contained in the R bits – the current contents of register R_r – is greater than S_r. The new ring service priority – P – is stacked (PUSHed) onto S_x and the DTE continues its role as a stacking station.

$P = S_r$ and $R = R_r$ (unchanged),

if the value contained in the R bits is less than or equal to S_r. Both values currently on the top of stacks S_x and S_r are POPped from the stack and, if both stacks are then empty, the DTE discontinues its role as a Stacking Station.

The above two operations are summarised in part (b) of Fig. 8.9.

8.3.2.6 Ring management

The preceding sections were primarily concerned with the transmission of frames and tokens during normal operation of the ring. Before this can take place, however, the ring must first be set up. Also, if a DTE wishes to join an already operational ring, it is necessary for the DTE to first go through an initialisation procedure to ensure that it does not interfere with the correct functioning of the already established ring. In addition, during normal operation, it is necessary for each active DTE on the ring to monitor continuously its correct operation and, if a fault develops, to take corrective action to try to re-establish a correctly functioning ring. Collectively, these functions are known as *Ring Management* and selected aspects of this will now be described.

Initialisation

When a DTE is first switched on (or after it has been reset) and wishes to become part of the ring, an initialisation sequence is entered firstly, to ensure that no other DTEs present in the ring are using the same address and secondly, to inform its immediate downstream neighbour that it has (re)entered the ring.

This starts with the transmission of a *Duplicate Address Test (DAT) MAC frame* by the DTE with the A bits in the Frame Status field set to 0. On receipt of a DAT frame, each active DTE in the ring inspects the Destination Address field contained within it and, if it determines it is the same as its own address, sets the A bits to 1. Hence, if the DAT frame returns to its originator with the A bits set to 1, the originator informs the Network Manager and returns to the bypass state. The Network Manager then determines if it should retry to become inserted into the ring. Alternatively, if on return of the DAT frame the A bits are still set to 0, the DTE continues the initialisation sequence by transmitting a *Standby Monitor Present (SMP) MAC frame*.

A DTE which receives an SMP frame with the A and C bits set to 0 regards the frame as having originated from its immediate upstream neighbour and hence records the Source Address contained within the frame as the *Upstream Neighbours Address (UNA)*. This is required for fault detection and monitoring functions as will be described later. The initialisation phase is then complete.

Standby monitor

Upon completion of the intialisation function, the DTE can start to transmit and receive normal frames and tokens. In addition, the DTE enters the *Standby Monitor state* to monitor continuously the correct operation of the ring. It does this by monitoring the passage of tokens and special *Active Monitor Present (AMP) MAC frames* – which are periodically transmitted by the current active monitor – as they are repeated at the ring interface. Then, if tokens or AMP frames are not periodically detected, the standby monitor times out (it maintains two timers for this function) and enters the Claim Token State.

When in the Claim Token state, the DTE continuously transmits *Claim Token (CT) MAC frames* and also inspects the Source Address in any CT frames it receives. Each CT frame transmitted contains, in addition to the Source Address of the originating DTE, the latter's stored Upstream Neighbours Address (UNA). Consequently, if a CT frame is received with a Source Address which matches its own address and a UNA which matches its own stored UNA, the CT frame has successfully circulated around the ring and hence the DTE becomes the new active ring monitor. Alternatively, if a CT frame is received with a Source Address greater than its own address, this means that another DTE has made an earlier bid to become the new monitor and hence the DTE effectively relinquishes its bid by returning to the Standby Monitor state.

Active monitor

If the DTE is successful in its bid to become the new active monitor – there is only one active monitor in the ring at any point in time – the DTE first inserts its latency buffer into the ring and enables its own clock. It then initiates the transmission of a *Purge (PRG) MAC frame* to ensure that there are no other tokens or frames on the ring before it initiates the transmission of a new token. Then, when the DTE receives a PRG frame containing a Source Address equal to its own address, this indicates the ring has been successfully purged. The DTE – that is, the active monitor – then initiates the neighbour notification process by broadcasting an Active Monitor Present (AMP) MAC frame. It then follows this with the transmission of a new control token after a short time delay.

The DTE immediately downstream of the monitor detects the A bits in the AMP frame are 0 and hence reads the Upstream Neighbours Address (UNA) from within the frame and updates its existing UNA variable. It then sets the A and C bits to 1 and repeats the frame. Subsequent DTEs around the ring detect the A bits are non-zero and hence just record the passage of the AMP frame by resetting the AMP timer.

In addition, the DTE immediately downstream from the monitor, after repeating the AMP frame, continues the neighbour notification process by broadcasting a similar Standby Monitor Present (SMP) frame. The next DTE downstream then, in turn, detects the A bits set to 0 in this frame, updates its UNA variable, sets the A and C bits to 1 and repeats the frame. It then continues the process by broadcasting a new SMP frame with the A bits again set to 0. This procedure is carried out by each DTE around the ring and is subsequently re-initiated by the monitor transmitting a new AMP frame at regular intervals. In this way, each active DTE in the ring can detect such failures as a DTE jabbering (continuously sending tokens for example): the absence of AMP frames flowing around the ring will mean that the AMP timer in all the other DTEs will expire, thus initiating the transmission of Claim Token frames followed, if the fault is still present, by entering a failure diagnostic procedure known as Beaconing. This is now described.

Beaconing

If a serious failure arises in the ring – for example, a broken cable – each DTE on the ring is informed that the token-passing protocol has been suspended (until the affected failure domain has been located and subsequently repaired) by means of a procedure known as *Beaconing*. The failure domain consists of:

1. the DTE reporting the failure – the *Beaconing Station*,
2. the DTE upstream of the Beaconing Station,
3. the ring medium between them.

As an example, Fig. 8.10 illustrates a failure domain assuming a break has occurred in the ring medium between DTEs F and G. In this example, G would be the Beaconing Station and F its upstream neighbour. Normally the Beaconing state is entered if the timers associated with the AMP or token passing procedures expire. When in this state, *Beacon (BCN) supervisory frames* are continuously transmitted until either a Beacon frame is received or a timer expires. If the latter occurs, the Network Manager is notified and transmissions cease. Alternatively, if a Beacon frame is received by a DTE with a source address equal to its own address, the failure is assumed to have cleared and the DTE enters the Claim Token state or, if a Beacon frame is received with a source address different from the DTE address, the DTE enters the Standby Monitor state.

It can be concluded from the previous paragraphs that the medium access control procedures used with a Token Ring network are quite complicated, certainly compared with a CSMA/BUS, for example. It should be remembered, however, that most of the procedures described are implemented in special controller integrated circuits within the MAC Unit and hence their operation is transparent to the user. Moreover, many of the ring management procedures which have been described are only invoked

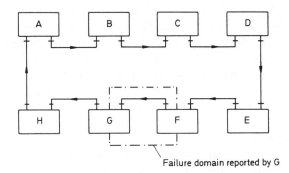

Fig. 8.10 An example failure domain

when faults develop and hence the overheads associated with them are, on the whole, modest.

8.3.3 Token bus

The third type of LAN supported in the IEEE standards documents is the Token Bus network. Under normal (error-free) conditions, the operation of this type of network is similar to a Token Ring network. Because of the differences in the two medium access methods, however (broadcast for bus, sequential for ring) the various procedures used for handling the management of the logical ring, such as initialisation and lost token, are inevitably different. To avoid repetition, therefore, this section will concentrate mainly on the management procedures associated with Token Bus networks.

Before describing the various ring management procedures, it is perhaps helpful to restate two basic properties of bus networks. Firstly, with a bus network all DTEs are connected directly to the transmission medium and hence, when a DTE transmits (broadcasts) a frame on the medium, it is received (or heard) by all active DTEs in the network; secondly, there is a maximum time a DTE need wait for a response to a transmitted frame before it can assume that either the transmitted frame was corrupted or the specified destination DTE is inoperable. This time is known as the *Slot Time* (not the same as that used with a CSMA/CD bus) and can be defined as:

Slot Time = 2 (transmission path delay + processing delay)

where *transmission path delay* is the worst-case transmission propagation delay going from any transmitter to any receiver in the network and *processing delay* the maximum time for the MAC Unit within a DTE to process a received frame and generate an appropriate response. A safety margin is then added and the Slot Time value is then expressed in bit times rounded up to a multiple number of octets.

Under normal operation, the token is passed from one DTE in the logical ring to another using a short token frame. Each DTE need only know, therefore, the address of the next (downstream neighbour or successor) DTE in the logical ring. If a DTE fails to accept the token, however, the sending DTE uses a series of recovery procedures to find a new successor which get progressively more drastic if it fails to evoke a response from a neighbouring DTE. Other procedures are concerned with establishing the ring initially – initialisation – and maintaining the correct operation of the ring as DTEs enter and leave the ring. Although it is possible to prioritise the token as with a Token Ring, only a single priority ring will be considered initially.

8.3.3.1 Token passing

On receipt of a valid token frame, a DTE may transmit any frames it has waiting. It then passes the token to its known successor. After sending the token, the DTE listens to any subsequent activity on the bus to make sure its successor is active and has received the token. If it hears a valid frame being transmitted, it assumes all is well and its successor received the token correctly. If it does not hear a valid frame being transmitted after the Slot Time interval, however, it must take corrective action.

If the DTE after sending the token hears a noise burst or frame with an incorrect FCS, it continues to listen for up to four more slot times. Then, if nothing more is heard, the DTE assumes the token itself was corrupted during transmission and hence repeats the token transmission. Alternatively, if a valid frame is heard during the delay of four slot times, it again assumes its successor has the token. Also, if a second noise burst is heard during this interval, the DTE treats this as a valid frame being transmitted by its successor and hence assumes the token has been passed.

If after following the above procedure the sending DTE does not hear a valid response after the delay of four slot times, it repeats the token-passing operation and performs the same monitoring as before. Then, if the successor does not respond to the second token frame, the DTE assumes its successor has failed and hence proceeds to establish a new successor. The sender first broadcasts a *Who Follows Me* frame with its current successor's address in the data field of the frame. On receipt of this type of frame, all DTEs compare the address in the data field of the frame with its own *predecessor address*; that is, the address of the DTE that normally sends it the token. Then, the DTE whose predecessor is the same as the successor contained within the frame, responds by sending its own address in a *Set Successor* frame. The DTE holding the token has thus established a new successor and in so doing has bridged around the failed DTE.

If the sending DTE does not receive a response to a Who Follows Me frame, it repeats the frame a second time. If there is still no response, the DTE takes more drastic action by sending a *Solicit Successor* frame with its own address in the destination address field. This effectively asks any DTE in the network to respond to it and hence, if there are any operational DTEs which hear the frame, they respond and the logical ring is re-established using the *Response Window* procedure discussed next. Alternatively, if no response is received, the DTE assumes that a catastrophe has occurred; for example, all other DTEs have failed, the medium has broken, or the DTE's own receiver section has failed (and hence cannot hear the response(s) from other DTEs to its own requests). Under such conditions, the DTE becomes silent but continues to listen for another DTE's transmissions.

8.3.3.2 Response window

This procedure is followed at random time intervals to allow new DTEs to enter an operational logical ring. The Response Window is in fact a length of time which a DTE needs to wait for a response after transmitting a frame, and hence is the same as the network Slot Time. Each Solicit Successor frame transmitted by a DTE specifies a source and a destination address, and the frame is responded to by a DTE which wishes to enter the ring and has an address between the two addresses specified. Each DTE sends a Solicit Successor frame at random intervals whenever it is the owner of the token.

When a DTE sends a Solicit Successor frame, it is said to have opened a *response window* since, after sending a Solicit Successor frame, the sending DTE waits for a response within the Response Window period. Then, if a DTE whose address lies within the range specified in the Solicit Successor frame is waiting to enter the ring, it responds by sending a request to the sender of the frame to become its new successor in the logical ring. If the sender hears the response – called a *Set Successor* frame – it allows the new DTE to enter the ring by making it its new successor and, in turn, passes it the token. Clearly, the address range specified may contain multiple DTEs all waiting to enter the ring and hence the response frames returned by each DTE will be corrupted. If this happens, the soliciting DTE must then try to identify a single responder. This is accomplished by the soliciting DTE entering an arbitration procedure which works as follows.

Having ascertained that more than one DTE in the specified address range is waiting to enter the ring, the soliciting DTE starts to sequence through the possible DTEs by sending each a *Resolve Contention* frame until it receives a positive reply. In addition, the DTEs which had responded to the earlier Solicit Successor frame and which did not subsequently receive the token, each choose a value in the range 0 to 3 and listen for any further activity on the bus for this number of slot times. Then, if a DTE hears a transmission during its selected time, it delays its request and waits for another opportunity to become part of the ring; that is, when the next response window is opened. Alternatively, if it does not hear a transmission during its selected time, it continues to wait for the possible receipt of a Resolve Contention frame. In this way, the worst-case delay the soliciting DTE need spend resolving the contention is limited.

8.3.3.3 Initialisation

The initialisation procedure is in fact built on top of the Response Window procedure just described to allow a new DTE to enter an operational ring. Each DTE in the network monitors all transmissions on the bus and, whenever a transmission is heard, it resets a timer – known as the *inactivity timer* – to a preset value. At initialisation, since there is no token circulating –

or if the token is lost during normal operation – the inactivity timer will expire and, if this happens, the DTE enters the initialisation phase and sends a *Claim Token* frame. Clearly, as before, a number of DTEs may try to send a Claim Token frame simultaneously and hence the following procedure is followed to ensure that only a single token is generated.

Each potential initialiser sends a Claim Token frame with an information field length that is a multiple number of Slot Times. The multiple chosen is either 0, 2, 4 or 6, the number chosen being derived from the first two bits in the DTE's network address. After sending its particular Claim Token frame, the DTE first waits a further Slot Time and then listens to the medium. If it hears a transmission while listening, it knows another DTE(s) has sent a longer Claim Token frame and the DTE simply eliminates itself from trying to become the first owner of the token. If a transmission is not heard, however, the DTE repeats the above process using the next two bits from its address field. Again, if no transmission is detected it uses the next pair of bits and so on until all address bits have been used. Then, if the medium is still quiet, the DTE has successfully become the first owner of the token. The unique owner of the token then continues the initialisation process by using the Response Window procedure already described to allow the other waiting DTEs to enter the logical ring.

Although a DTE may remove itself from the logical ring at any time by simply not responding when the token is passed to it, a cleaner method is for the DTE to first wait until it receives the token and then to send a Set Successor frame to its predecessor – that is, the DTE it got the token from – with the address of its own successor in the information field. The DTE then sends the token to its own successor as usual in the knowledge that it is no longer part of the (logical) ring.

8.3.3.4 Priority operation

As with a Token Ring network, it is also possible to implement a priority mechanism with a Token Bus network. The access method used with a Token Bus, however, distinguishes only four levels of priority called *access classes*. These are named 0, 2, 4 and 6 with 6 being the highest priority. Not all DTEs in the ring need use the priority mechanism, however, and in these cases the DTEs treat all frames as having the highest priority.

Transmission of waiting frames with the highest priority is controlled to ensure that the available ring capacity (bandwidth) is shared between all DTEs. On receipt of the token, a DTE may send any waiting high priority frames up to a maximum governed by a time interval known as the *high priority token-hold time*. Then, when this time expires, it must pass on the token to its successor. Thus, when a DTE receives the token, it first sends any high priority frames it has waiting; then assuming the DTE is using the priority mechanism and providing the token-hold time has not expired, the DTE begins to transmit any waiting lower priority frames using the following control algorithm.

Each DTE in the logical ring keeps a timer which indicates the time which has expired since the DTE *last received* the token. This is held in a variable known as the *token rotation timer* or *TRT*. Then, when the DTE next receives the token, it first transmits any waiting high priority frames – thus increasing the TRT value – and it then computes the difference between a fixed time known as the *target token rotation time* and its current TRT. If the difference is positive, the DTE can send any waiting lower priority frames until the target token rotation time is reached; if the difference is zero or negative, the DTE cannot send any lower priority frames on this pass of the token. Each DTE using the priority mechanism maintains a separate token rotation timer for the three lowest priority access classes and transmits waiting frames working from higher to lower access class until the target token rotation time is reached.

To illustrate the operation of this mechanism, consider the example shown in Fig. 8.11. For clarity, the example assumes only two access classes, the highest and one lower class. Also, all frames transmitted are assumed to be of a fixed length and hence the various times are directly proportional to the number of frames. The example assumes DTEs 9 and 1 each send only high priority frames each time they receive the token and DTEs 7 and 5 send only lower priority frames whenever possible. Note that the logical ring is built such that the physical DTE addresses are in descending numerical order. Also, the target token rotation time (TTRT) for the lower priority frames is fixed at a value equivalent to 8 frames. The values in the left-hand column under each DTE labelled TRT are the token rotation times measured by that DTE for the previous rotation of the token. The values in the right-hand column labelled XMIT are the number of frames transmitted by the DTE each time it receives the token. Each row represents one rotation of the token.

All transmissions are assumed to begin after a period of inactivity and hence after the token has been rotating as rapidly as possible. The TRT in DTE 9 is therefore shown as zero to begin with. This assumes that the token passing and propagation delays are negligible compared with the time taken to transmit a normal frame. Also, it is assumed that the high priority token-hold time is such that a DTE can send up to three high priority frames on receipt of the token.

During the first rotation of the token, DTE 9 receives the token and sends its maximum of three high priority frames before passing on the token. When DTE 7 receives the token from DTE 9, therefore, its TRT will have incremented to 3 since three frames have been transmitted since it last received the token. This means that DTE 7 can therefore transmit five (TTRT−TRT) lower priority frames before passing on the token. On receipt of the token, the TRT held by DTE 5 will now be 8 since a total of eight frames have been transmitted since it last received the token. It cannot therefore transmit any lower priority frames on this pass of the token. DTE 1 then transmits three high priority frames unconstrained by its computed TRT.

During the second rotation of the token, both DTE 9 and DTE 1 send three high priority frames unaffected by their computed TRT as before but

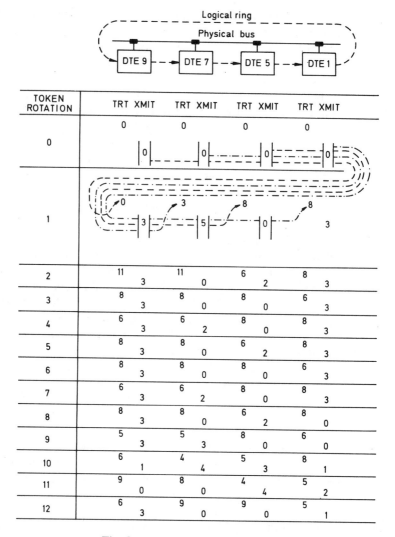

TOKEN ROTATION	DTE 9		DTE 7		DTE 5		DTE 1	
	TRT	XMIT	TRT	XMIT	TRT	XMIT	TRT	XMIT
	0		0		0		0	
0		0		0		0		0
1		3		5		0		3
2	11	3	11	0	6	2	8	3
3	8	3	8	0	8	0	6	3
4	6	3	6	2	8	0	8	3
5	8	3	8	0	6	2	8	3
6	8	3	8	0	8	0	6	3
7	6	3	6	2	8	0	8	3
8	8	3	8	0	6	2	8	0
9	5	3	5	3	8	0	6	0
10	6	1	4	4	5	3	8	1
11	9	0	8	0	4	4	5	2
12	6	3	9	0	9	0	5	1

Fig. 8.11 Prioritorised ring example

this time DTE 7 is blocked from transmitting any lower priority frames (since its computed TRT exceeds 8 on receipt of the token) and DTE 5 is able to transmit two lower priority frames (TTRT − TRT = 2).

During the third rotation of the token, again both DTE 9 and DTE 1 each send three high priority frames but this time both DTE 7 and DTE 5 are blocked from sending any lower priority frames since both their computed TRTs have reached the TTRT limit (8).

During the fourth rotation of the token, a similar situation prevails as in the second rotation but notice this time that the computed TRTs are such that DTE 7 has an opportunity to send two lower priority frames instead of DTE 5 which this time cannot send any frames. Similarly, during the fifth rotation of the token DTE 5 is able to transmit two lower priority frames but DTE 7 is inhibited from sending any lower priority frames. The cycle then repeats itself and it can readily be deduced that, over any three rotations, DTEs 9 and 1 use 18/22nds (82 percent) of the available capacity and DTEs 7 and 5 share the remaining 4/22nds (18 percent) equally.

During the eighth rotation of the token, it is assumed that DTE 1 temporarily runs out of high priority frames to transmit and hence DTEs 7 and 5 are able to transmit more of their waiting lower priority frames. Similarly, during the tenth rotation DTE 9 runs out of high priority frames and so on.

Although this of necessity is a simple example, it nevertheless shows how the priority mechanism allows firstly high priority frames to be transmitted relatively unconstrained, and secondly lower priority frames to be transmitted in a fair manner whenever there is spare capacity available.

8.4 LAN PROTOCOLS

The various protocol standards for local area networks – which deal with the Physical and Link Layers in the context of the ISO Reference Model – are those defined in IEEE Standard 802. This standard defines a family of protocols, each relating to a particular type of medium access control method. The various IEEE Standards and their relationship to the ISO Reference Model are shown in Fig. 8.12.

The three Medium Access Control (MAC) Standards together with their associated physical media specifications are contained in the following IEEE Standards documents:

IEEE 802.3   CSMA/CD Bus,
IEEE 802.4   Token Bus,
IEEE 802.5   Token Ring.

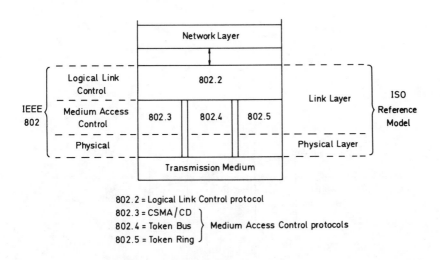

802.2 = Logical Link Control protocol
802.3 = CSMA/CD ⎫
802.4 = Token Bus ⎬ Medium Access Control protocols
802.5 = Token Ring ⎭

Fig. 8.12 IEEE 802 protocol set

The descriptions which have been presented so far in this chapter have been concerned with the MAC Control and Physical Layers of these three standards. Although each is different in its internal operation, however, they all present a standard set of services to the Logical Link Control (LLC) Layer and the latter is intended therefore to be used in conjunction with any of the underlying MAC Standards. In general, as has been mentioned earlier, the various MAC Control and Physical Layers are normally implemented in firmware in special purpose integrated circuits. This section, therefore, will concentrate only on the LLC Layer and simply define the interface between the LLC and MAC Layers. It should be noted that with a LAN the LLC and MAC Layers are peer (end-to-end) protocols since there are no intermediate switching nodes within the network itself similar, for example, to a packet-switching exchange in a public packet-switched data network.

8.4.1 Logical link control layer

The description of the LLC Layer will be presented in the form used with the higher protocol layers described in Chapter 6; that is, first the user (Network Layer) services provided by the layer will be described, then the operation of LLC protocol entity itself, and finally the services used by the LLC layer to transfer LLC protocol data units to a peer LLC layer. In general, the primitives used in the IEEE Standards are similar to those used in the ISO Standards except that with the IEEE Standards there are no response primitives. This means that when a confirmation primitive is associated with the user service, it is generated either by the local protocol entity directly or by the remote peer protocol entity; that is, it is not generated as a result of a response primitive being received at the remote user interface. The two alternatives are shown in parts (a) and (b) of Fig. 8.13.

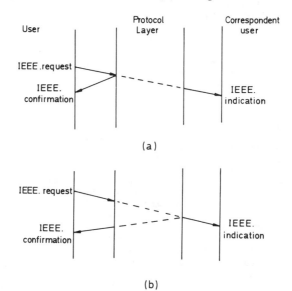

Fig. 8.13 IEEE service primitives: (a) local confirmation; (b) remote confirmation

In the case of part (a), the confirmation primitive simply indicates to the user whether the local protocol entity was successful (or unsuccessful) in sending the associated request to the remote peer protocol entity; that is, it does not imply that the latter received it correctly. Similarly, in the case of part (b), the confirmation primitive indicates that the remote peer protocol entity successfully passed the associated indication primitive to the correspondent user; that is, it has not been generated as a result of a response from the correspondent user as is the case in the ISO documents.

8.4.1.1 User services

Two types of user service are provided by the LLC layer: an *unacknowledged connectionless service* and a set of *connection oriented services*. The unacknowledged connectionless service provides the user with the means of initiating the transfer of service data units with a minimum of protocol overheads. Typically, this service is used when such functions as error recovery and sequencing are being provided in a higher protocol layer and hence need not be replicated in the LLC layer. Alternatively, the connection oriented services provide the user with the means to first establish a link-level logical connection before initiating the transfer of any service data units and, should it be required, to then implement error recovery and sequencing of the flow of these units across an established connection.

The various primitives associated with the two sets of services are shown in diagrammatic form in the time sequence diagram of Fig. 8.14. Each of the primitives illustrated has parameters associated with it. These include a specification of the source (local) and destination (remote) addresses and other parameters where appropriate. The source and destination addresses are present in all primitives. They specify, at a minimum, the physical addresses to be used on the network medium, and hence the destination address can be either an individual or a group address. Normally, however, both addresses are a concatenation of the addresses as used on the physical medium and the local service access point identifier (LLC-SAP).

With the unacknowledged connectionless service, on receipt of a data transfer request primitive (L.DATA.request), the LLC protocol entity makes a best attempt to send the accompanying data using the MAC sublayer; there is no confirmation that the transfer was successful or indeed unsuccessful.

With the connection oriented service, however, the receipt of each error-free data unit is acknowledged by the remote LLC entity and this is then converted by the local entity into a L.DATA.CONNECT.confirm primitive and passed to the user.

The RESET and FLOWCONTROL service primitives are provided to allow the user – the Network Layer – to control the flow of service data units across an established connection. The RESET service has an abortive action since it results in any unacknowledged data being discarded. It is used, therefore, only if the Network Layer protocol entity loses track of the sequence of data units being transferred.

The two flowcontrol primitives have only local significance. Thus the

L.FLOWCONTROL.request primitive specifies the amount of data the user is prepared to accept from its local LLC protocol entity and the L.FLOWCONTROL.indication primitive the amount of data the LLC protocol entity is prepared to accept from the user; both related to a specific connection. If the amount is specified as zero, then the flow of data is stopped; if the amount is infinite, no flowcontrol is to be applied on the connection. The amount of data allowed is dynamically updated by each request.

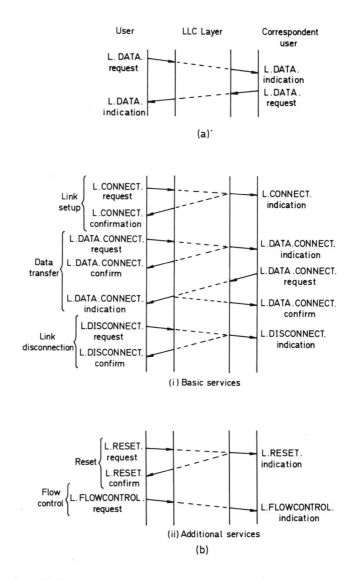

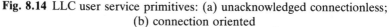

Fig. 8.14 LLC user service primitives: (a) unacknowledged connectionless; (b) connection oriented

8.4.1.2 Protocol operation

The format of each LLC Protocol Data Unit (LLC-PDU) is shown in part (a) of Fig. 8.15. The source and destination address fields both refer to the LLC service access point only, they do not contain the addresses to be used on the network medium. Also, there is no FCS field. Essentially, the complete LLC-PDU is passed to the MAC layer – as a service data unit – in the form of a primitive which includes the LLC-PDU and the address to be used on the network medium as parameters. It is thus the MAC layer which handles the network addressing and error detection functions. If is for this reason that, in the context of the ISO Reference Model, the Link Layer is equivalent to a combination of the LLC layer and a portion of the MAC layer.

The control field in each LLC-PDU is a single octet and defines the type of the PDU and, where appropriate, send and receive sequence numbers for error and sequence control purposes. The use of the various bits in this field are shown in more detail in part (b) of Fig. 8.15.

The LLC protocol entity supports two types of operation: Type 1 to support the unacknowledged connectionless service and Type 2 to support the connection oriented service. Type 2 is in practice very similar to HDLC

Octets   1   1   1   M

Destination address	Source address	Control	Information

(a)

Bits   1   2   3   4   5   6   7   8

0	$N(S)$			P/F	$N(R)$			Information frames
1	0	S		P/F	$N(R)$			Supervisory frames
1	1	M		P/F	M			Unnumbered frames

$N(S)$, $N(R)$ = Send, Receive Sequence Numbers

S = Supervisory function definition

M = Modifier function definition

P/F = Poll/Final bit

(b)

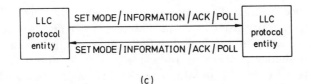

(c)

Fig. 8.15 Aspects of LLC protocol: (a) LLC-PDU format; (b) control field bit definitions; (c) data link control functions (Type 2)

except that the framing and error detection functions are provided by the MAC layer.

The data link control functions for Type 2 operation are shown in schematic form in part (c) of Fig. 8.15. A description of HDLC was presented in Chapter 5 and hence this will not be repeated here. The major difference between the LLC protocol and HDLC is the provision of the unacknowledged connectionless (Type 1) service. The set of commands and responses supported in Type 1 are:

Commands	*Responses*
UI	–
XID	XID
TEST	TEST

The *UI command PDU* is used to send a block of data (information) to one or more LLCs. Since there is no acknowledgment or sequence control associated with Type 1 operation, however, the UI PDU does not contain an $N(S)$ or $N(R)$ field. Also, there is no response to a UI PDU.

The *Exchange Identification* (*XID*) and *TEST command PDUs* are optional although if they are sent, the recipient LLC(s) is (are) obliged to respond. The uses of these commands are not fully defined but include:

1. The XID command PDU used with a group address is used to determine the current membership of the group; each member of the group responds to the command by returning an XID response PDU addressed specifically to the originating LLC entity.

2. An LLC entity may use an XID command PDU with a broadcast (global) destination address to announce its presence on the network medium.

3. The TEST comand PDU is used to provide a loopback test facility on each LLC to LLC transmission path.

8.4.1.3 MAC services

Irrespective of the mode of operation of the underlying MAC layer – CSMA/CD, Token Ring, Token Bus – a standard set of user services are defined for use by the LLC layer to transfer LLC protocol data units to a correspondent layer. The user service primitives supported are:

MA.DATA.request,
MA.DATA.indication,
MA.DATA.confirmation.

A time sequence diagram illustrating their use is shown in Fig. 8.16.

Each service primitive has parameters associated with it. The MA.DATA.request primitive includes: the required destination address (this may be an individual, group or broadcast address), a service data unit (containing the LLC-PDU), and the required class of service associated with the PDU. The latter is used with Token Ring and Token Bus networks, for example, when a prioritised medium access control protocol is being used.

The MA.DATA.confirmation primitive includes a parameter which

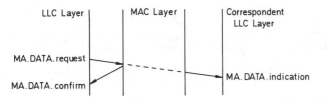

Fig. 8.16 MAC user services

specifies the success or failure of the associated MA.DATA.request primitive. As can be seen from the figure, however, the confirmation primitive is not generated as a result of a response from the remote LLC layer but rather by the local MAC entity; if the parameter is successful, this simply indicates that the MAC protocol entity (layer) was successful in transmitting the service data unit onto the network medium; if unsuccessful, the parameter indicates why the transmission attempt failed. As an example, if the network is a CSMA/CD Bus, 'excessive collisions' may be a typical failure parameter.

8.4.2 Network layer

It should be remembered that the primary aim of the ISO Reference Model is to achieve true open systems interconnection so that pieces of equipment from different manufacturers can freely communicate with each other, irrespective of whether the physical communications path is through a public wide area network or a private local area network. As was indicated in Chapter 6, however, in the context of the ISO Reference Model the Transport Layer is the first true end-to-end (peer) protocol layer and its aim is to shield the higher protocol layers from the different types of underlying network. Providing the LAN is only being used to provide a communications facility between a localised community of equipments, therefore, the Network Layer can contain only a minimum protocol entity supporting, for example, a basic datagram service. The main requirement of the Network Layer would then be to provide a standard set of user services to the Transport Layer above it and to transform these requests into the standard LLC form.

In many instances, however, and certainly in the context of true open systems interconnection, a DTE connected to one LAN, in addition to requiring to communicate with other DTEs on the same LAN, may also require to communicate with a DTE which is connected to another LAN which is geographically situated in a different part of the country. Clearly, to meet this type of requirement it is necessary to provide some form of link between the two (or more) LANs and a suitable public data network. Essentially, the approach is to connect a device known as a Gateway to each LAN which, as the name implies, provides a communications path between the LAN and the public data network. This is shown in diagrammatic form in Fig. 8.17.

The basic function of a Gateway is to form a bridge or relay to enable the

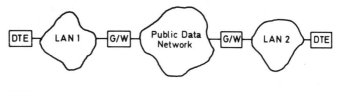

G/W = Gateway

(a)

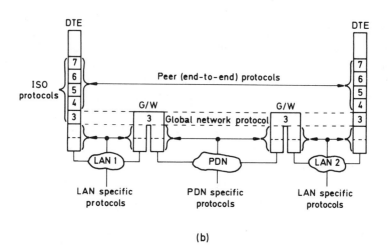

(b)

Fig. 8.17 Internetworking schematic: (a) Gateway schematic; (b) protocol hierarchy

lower network-dependent protocol layers in a DTE connected to one LAN to establish a connection with a remote DTE through the intermediate public data network. There are a number of alternative ways of achieving this and one approach is as shown in part (b) of the figure. With this approach, the Network Layer in each DTE is able to establish a connection with any other DTE whether it is connected locally to its own LAN or to another LAN through an intermediate public data network. The network addressing information would then have to be arranged in a hierarchical form analogous to that used in the switched telephone network, for example.

8.5 PERFORMANCE ISSUES

In general, the user of a LAN is concerned only with three things: firstly, has his or her system – office workstation for example – got the necessary hardware to allow the system to be physically connected to the network; secondly, does the system have the appropriate software to allow the services supported by the network – electronic mail, file archiving etc. – to be accessed; and thirdly, is the access time to these services within acceptable limits. Providing these conditions are met, the user is not concerned with the type of underlying LAN which is being used to access these services.

Moreover, as can be concluded from the previous section and the earlier discussions in Chapter 6, the overall end-to-end (Application Layer-to-Application Layer) performance of any computer communication network is likely to be dominated by the delays experienced in the higher protocol layers rather than any small variations that may be caused by the different LAN topologies and MAC methods. Nevertheless, since the different types of LAN clearly have varying operational characteristics, it is important, certainly for the network designer, to have a knowledge of these characteristics in order that he or she can determine whether a particular LAN design will meet the expectations of the users under, for example, various offered load conditions.

Although some detail comparison figures for the three types of LAN considered – CSMA/CD Bus, Token Ring, and Token Bus – have been published by the IEEE, the aim of this section is simply to outline how some informative estimates of overall network performance can be made by applying some basic requirements analysis and it is left to the reader to refer to the references at the end of the book for more detail analysis.

Assume, for example, that a LAN is to be installed to provide a range of network-wide services for a defined number of user workstations. The first estimate the network designer must make is the frequency with which each user will generate a network service request and also the likely length (in bits) of the messages which are exchanged to implement each request. Then, from these estimates, coupled with an estimation of the additional messages which will be required to implement the overheads associated with the various protocol layers, it is possible to derive an estimate of the aggregate mean offered load to the network. The latter can then be used to define the minimum cable bandwidth (network capacity) that is required to ensure that any delays introduced at the network interface will be within acceptable limits.

For example, assume that a network to support up to 100 workstations is to be installed and that it is anticipated that each user will generate a network transaction once every five minutes. It is estimated that each transaction will involve, on average, the exchange of six 1000-bit data frames. Also, the additional frames associated with the overheads of the intermediate protocol layers are estimated to be, say, twelve 500-bit frames. A simple calculation then shows that this is equivalent to a mean offered load per user of 40 bits per second. Clearly, therefore, even allowing for up to, say, 10 or more users being active concurrently, the total mean offered load will be in the order of 400 bits per second which is of course only a small fraction of the bandwidth of the cables used in the three types of network considered. This means that irrespective of the type of LAN which is selected, the delays introduced by the network will, on average, be very small.

In general, it is good design practice to ensure that the capacity (bandwidth) of an installed LAN is more than adequate to handle the aggregate mean offered load of its users. Conversely, it is bad practice to try to operate a network near its total capacity since, under these conditions, predictably long delays at the network interface are inevitable with the effect that the end-to-end response time will rapidly rise above the maximum level which is acceptable to its users. This is especially the case with a CSMA/CD protocol since, because it is a contention protocol, its performance under heavy offered loads is relatively unstable: as the offered load increases to the point at which the network utilisation starts to become a significant proportion of its maximum capacity, so the probability of collisions will also increase. This has the effect that in some instances, even with a backoff mechanism, some frames will fail to be transmitted. Of course with heavy offered loads this is also the case with a token-based protocol since, as the transmission medium approaches saturation, only high priority frames will be transmitted and lower priority frames will be queued indefinitely.

It should be stressed that, even with a small mean offered load and a cable bandwidth of, say, 10 Mbps, the maximum end-to-end data transfer rate associated with a particular user transaction is likely to be nearer to tens of kilobits (rather than megabits) because of the processing delays associated with the higher protocol layers. Providing the aggregate mean offered load remains only a modest fraction of the cable bandwidth, however, many user transactions at this rate can be in progress concurrently.

Problems

8.1 a) List the three main types of network topology currently in widespread use for local area networks (LANs) and explain their major differences.

b) What is understood by broadband working in the context of a coaxial cable LAN? Sketch a typical broadband LAN showing the main networking components required and explain their function. Describe the overall operation of such a network and how multiple data transmission services are derived from a single cable.

8.2 a) Describe the principle of operation of the following medium access control methods as used in LANs:

    i) CSMA/CD,
    ii) Control Token,
    iii) Slotted Ring.

b) Explain the meaning of the following terms associated with a CSMA/CD Bus network:

    i) slot time,
    ii) jam sequence,
    iii) random backoff.

8.3 a) Describe the principle of operation of the Control Token medium access control method and, with the aid of diagrams explain how it may be used with both a Bus and a Ring network topology.

b) Define the structure and contents of a typical frame as used in a Slotted Ring. Describe the meaning of each field within a frame and the operation of the associated ring protocol. Clearly explain how access to the ring is shared between the stations (DTEs) making up the ring.

8.4 Produce a sketch showing the components necessary to attach a DTE (station) to a CSMA/CD Bus network. Give an outline of the function of each component in the context of the overall operation of such a network.

Define the structure and contents of each frame transmitted and the meaning of each field.

8.5 a) Produce a schematic diagram showing the components necessary to attach a DTE (station) to a Token Ring network and give an outline of the function of each component. Include sufficient detail to show how a DTE, once attached to the network, may operate in either the Inserted or Bypassed mode.

b) Explain what is understood by the following terms as used in Token Ring networks:

   i) Minimum Latency Time,
   ii) Token-Holding Time,
   iii) Modified Manchester encoding.

8.6 Describe the operation of the priority control scheme used with Token Ring networks to control the order of transmission of frames of varying priority onto the ring. Include in your description the function of:

   i) the Priority and Reservation Bits contained within each frame;
   ii) the Priority Registers and Stacks held in each station;
   iii) a Stacking Station.

8.7 State the aims of the following ring management procedures used with a Token Ring network and explain their operation:

   i) Initialisation,
   ii) Standby Monitor,
   iii) Active Monitor,
   iv) Beaconing.

8.8 Define the meaning of the term Slot Time as used with a Token Bus network and explain the token-passing procedure used with such networks during both normal and abnormal operation. Include in your descriptions references to the procedures followed:

   i) to bridge around a faulty DTE;
   ii) to allow new DTEs to enter an operational logical ring;
   iii) to create a new token when a ring is first established.

8.9 Explain the function of the following variables held by each DTE to control the order of transmission of frames which have varying priority on a Token Bus network:

    i) high priority token-hold-time,

    ii) token rotation timer,

    iii) target token rotation time.

Produce a sketch, with an accompanying description, of an example which illustrates how the token rotation timer varies as frames are transmitted and the token rotates around the ring. Assume just two priority levels and deduce, from your example, the percentage of the available transmission capacity used by each level.

8.10 a) Outline the function of the Logical Link Control (LLC) and Medium Access Control (MAC) protocol layers as defined in the IEEE 802 standards documents and indicate their relationship with the lower protocol layers in the ISO Reference Model.

    Define a typical set of user service primitives for both the LLC and MAC layers and produce a time sequence diagram to illustrate how each LLC primitive is implemented using the defined MAC services.

    b) Explain the function of a Gateway and hence outline how two DTEs, each connected to a different local area network, can communicate with one another through an intermediate network using two such devices.

Appendix A **Forward Error Control**

With an ARQ error control scheme, additional check digits are appended to each transmitted message to enable the receiver to detect, assuming certain types of error, when an error is present in a received message and, should an error be detected, additional control procedures are then used to request another copy of the message to be sent. With Forward Error Control (FEC), however, sufficient additional check digits are added to each transmitted message to enable the receiver not only to detect the presence of one or more errors in a received message but also to locate the position of the error(s). Then, since the message is in a binary form, correction is achieved simply by inverting the identified erroneous bit(s).

A comprehensive description of the subject of coding theory is beyond the scope of this book and hence the aim here is simply to give the reader a brief introduction to the subject. A list of references is given at the end of the book, however, to allow those who have an interest in this field to gain a more extensive coverage.

The term used in coding theory to describe the combined message unit comprising the useful data bits and the additional check bits is *codeword*. Also, the minimum number of bit positions in which two valid codewords differ is known as the *Hamming distance* of the code. As an example, consider a coding scheme which has seven data bits and a single parity bit per codeword. Assuming even parity is being used, consecutive codewords in this scheme will be:

```
0000000 0
0000001 1
0000010 1
0000011 0
etc.
```

It can be deduced from this list that such a scheme has a Hamming distance of 2 since each valid codeword differs in at least 2 bit positions. This means that it will not detect 2-bit errors since the resulting (corrupted) bit pattern will be a different but valid codeword. It will, however, detect all single-bit errors since, if a single bit in a codeword is corrupted, an invalid codeword will result.

In general, the error detecting and error correcting properties of a coding scheme are both related to its Hamming distance. It can be shown that to detect for n errors, a coding scheme with a Hamming distance of $n + 1$ must be used, whilst to correct for n errors a code with a Hamming distance of $2n + 1$ must be used.

The simplest error correcting coding scheme is the Hamming single-bit code. Such a code will not only detect when a single-bit error is present in a received codeword but also the position of the error. The corrected codeword is then derived by inverting the identified erroneous bit. As an example, consider a Hamming code to detect and correct for single-bit errors assuming each codeword contains a 7-bit data field – an ASCII character for example.

Such a coding scheme will require four check bits since, with this scheme, the check bits occupy all bit positions which are powers of 2. As an example, the bit positions of the data value 1001101 are:

```
Bit Position 11 10 9  8  7  6  5  4  3  2  1
              1  0  0  X  1  1  0  X  1  X  X
```

The four bit positions marked with X are used for the check bits which are derived as follows. The 4-bit binary numbers corresponding to those bit positions which have a binary 1 are added together using modulo 2 arithmetic and the four check bits are then the 4-bit sum:

```
11 = 1 0 1 1
 7 = 0 1 1 1
 6 = 0 1 1 0
 3 = 0 0 1 1
   ─────────
     1 0 0 1 = Modulo 2 sum.
   ─────────
```

The transmitted codeword is thus:

```
Bit Position 11 10 9  8  7  6  5  4  3  2  1
              1  0  0  1  1  1  0  0  1  0  1
```

Similarly, at the receiver, the 4-bit binary numbers corresponding to those bit positions which have a binary 1 – including the check bits – are again added together and, if no errors have occurred, the modulo 2 sum should be zero:

```
11 = 1 0 1 1
 8 = 1 0 0 0
 7 = 0 1 1 1
 6 = 0 1 1 0
 3 = 0 0 1 1
 1 = 0 0 0 1
   ─────────
     0 0 0 0 = Modulo 2 sum.
   ─────────
```

Now consider a single-bit error; say bit 11 is corrupted from 1 to 0. The new modulo 2 sum would now be:

```
8 = 1 0 0 0
7 = 0 1 1 1
6 = 0 1 1 0
3 = 0 0 1 1
1 = 0 0 0 1
    ─────────
    1 0 1 1  = Modulo 2 sum.
    ─────────
```

Firstly, the sum is non-zero, which indicates an error, and secondly the modulo 2 sum – equivalent to decimal 11 – indicates that bit 11 is the erroneous bit. The latter would therefore be inverted to obtain the corrected codeword and hence data bits.

It can also be shown that if two-bit errors occur, the modulo 2 sum will be non-zero – thus indicating an error – but the positions of the errors cannot be determined from the sum. The Hamming single-bit code can thus correct for single-bit errors and detect two-bit errors but other multiple-bit errors will not be detected.

As has been mentioned in Chapter 2, the main types of error in many data communication networks are error bursts rather than, say, isolated single- or double-bit errors. Hence, although the above coding scheme in its basic form would appear to be inappropriate for use with such networks, a simple technique is often used to extend the application of such a scheme. Consider, for example, a requirement to transmit a block of data comprising a string of, say, eight ASCII characters over a simplex channel which has a high probability of an error burst (of, say, 7 bits) occurring.

The approach would be for the controlling device to first convert each ASCII character into its 11-bit codeword form, thus resulting in a block of eight 11-bit codewords. Then, instead of transmitting each codeword separately, the controlling device transmits the contents of the block of codewords a column at a time. Thus the eight, say, most significant bits would be transmitted first, then the eight next most significant bits and so on, finishing with the eight least significant bits. The controlling device at the receiver then performs the reverse operation reassembling the transmitted block in memory prior to performing the detection and, if necessary, correction operation on each codeword.

The effect of this approach is firstly that a standard USRT device can be used as the transmission interface circuit and secondly, and more importantly, that if an error burst of up to 7 bits does occur it will affect only a single bit in each codeword rather than a string of bits in one or two codewords. This means that assuming just a single error burst in the 88 bits transmitted, the receiver can determine a correct copy of the transmitted block of characters.

The above is just a simple example of an error correcting code. There are in fact many more sophisticated codes which have been devised and the interested reader should refer to the list of references at the end of the book for further sources.

Appendix B **Data Encryption and the DES**

In many applications, the data which are stored within a computer, and hence the messages which are being transmitted over a computer communication network, are of a highly confidential nature; details of a person's bank account and transactions involving it provide just one example. In cases like this it is usual for the computer to perform some form of coding operation both on the data which are stored within its memory and also on each message prior to its transmission through a network so that, if the data are accidentally or deliberately intercepted, the received data will be incomprehensible to the recipient. This assumes, of course, that both the sender and intended recipient know the type of coding operation being used and also, ideally, that their code is unique.

Such coding operations are known as *encryption* (or *encipherment*) and the corresponding decoding operation *decryption* (or *decipherment*). The message data prior to being encrypted is known as *plaintext* and the message data after encryption the *ciphertext*. Normally, as will be seen, the encryption and decryption processes used are the same for all message transfers across a network and a *key*, known only by each pair of correspondents and featuring in both the encryption and decryption processes, is then used to make each message transfer between a particular pair of correspondents unique.

The most widely used encryption method is that defined by the US National Bureau of Standards. It is known simply as the *Data Encryption Standard* or *DES*. As an introduction to the subject of data encryption, therefore, this appendix gives a brief description of the DES algorithm. Fuller descriptions of DES are, of course, readily available and a reference to one of these is given at the end of the book.

The DES algorithm is a *block cipher* which means that it works on fixed-sized blocks of data. Each complete message is first split (segmented) into blocks of plaintext each comprising 64 bits. A (hopefully) unique 56-bit key is then used to encrypt each block of plaintext into a 64-bit block of ciphertext and it is this that is subsequently transmitted through the network. The receiver then uses the same key to perform the inverse (decryption) operation on each 64-bit data block it receives and, in turn, reassembles them into complete messages.

The larger the number of bits used for the key the more likely the key selected by the two correspondents is to be unique. Also, the larger the key the more difficult it is for someone to determine the key which is being used by two correspondents. The use of a 56-bit key in the DES means that there are in the order of 10^{17} possible keys to choose from and hence DES is regarded as providing sufficient security for most commercial applications.

The DES is a *product cipher* which means that it is a combination of a number of different transposition and substitution operations. Essentially, a *transposition operation* takes a fixed block of bits and transposes the bits into a different order. A *substitution operation*, however, substitutes the complete set of bits by a different set of bits, the new set determined by performing some processing operation on the old set.

A diagrammatic representation of the DES algorithm is shown in Fig. B.1. The 56-bit key selected by the two correspondents is first used to derive 16 different subkeys each of 48 bits and it is these that are used in the subsequent substitution operations. The algorithm comprises 19 distinct steps. The first step is a simple transposition of the 64-bit block of plaintext using a fixed transposition rule. The resulting 64 bits of transposed text then go through 16 identical iterations of substitution processing except that at each iteration a different subkey is used in the substitution operation. The most significant 32 bits of the 64-bit output of the last iteration are then exchanged with the least significant 32 bits. Finally, the same transposition as was performed at step 1 is repeated to produce the 64-bit block of ciphertext which is transmitted. The DES algorithm is so designed that the received block is deciphered by the receiver, performing the same steps as are used for encryption but in the reverse order.

The 16 subkeys which are used at each substitution step are produced as follows. First a fixed transposition is performed on the 56-bit key. The resulting transposed key is then split into two separate 28-bit halves. The two halves are then rotated left independently and the combined 56 bits are then transposed once again. Each subkey comprises 48 bits and these are chosen according to a set selection process on the final 56 bits of transposed data. The other subkeys are produced in a similar way except that the number of rotations performed is determined by the number of the subkey.

The processing performed at each of the 16 intermediate steps in the encryption process is relatively complex since it is this that forms the effectiveness of the DES algorithm. The processing performed is shown in outline in part (b) of the figure. The 64-bit output from the previous iteration is first split into two 32-bit halves. The least significant half then forms the most significant 32-bit half of the output. The least significant 32-bit output, however, is derived by performing a sequence of transposition and substitution operations on the most significant input half, the precise operations being a function of the subkey for this stage.

This mode of working of DES is known as *Electronic Code Book* or *ECB* since each block of ciphertext is independent of any other block. This means that each block of ciphertext has a unique matching block of plaintext and hence the analogy with entries in a code book. Because of this, the ECB mode is mostly used for the coding of data prior to its being stored on, say, a disc system within the computer memory, and an alternative mode known as

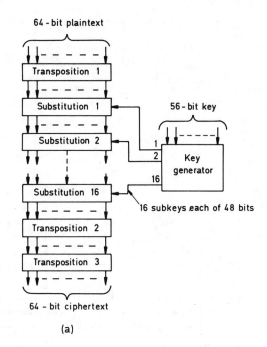

64 - bit plaintext

64 - bit ciphertext

(a)

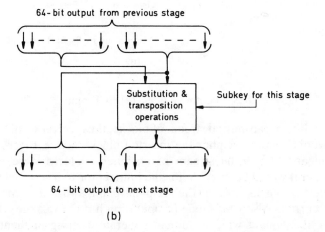

64 - bit output from previous stage

64 - bit output to next stage

(b)

Fig. B.1 The DES algorithm: (a) overall operation; (b) substitution processing

chaining is preferable for data communication purposes. The ECB mode of working is shown in diagrammatic form in part (a) of Fig. B.2.

B.1 CHAINING

Although the ECB mode of operation of DES gives good protection against errors or changes which may occur in a single block of enciphered text, since each block is treated separately, if an additional correctly enciphered block is

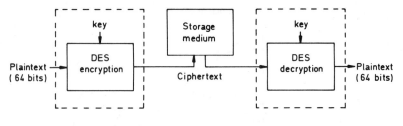

(a)

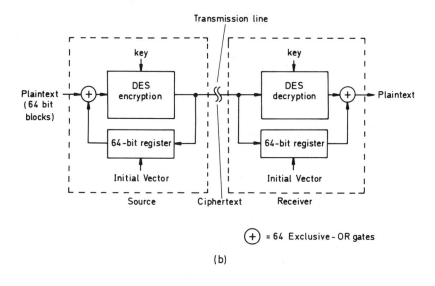

(b)

Fig. B.2 DES operating modes: (a) ECB mode; (b) CBC mode

inserted into a transmitted stream of blocks, the receiver would not detect this as it would simply decipher the inserted block and treat it as a valid block. This means that if the stream of enciphered blocks were intercepted by someone, it would be possible for the interceptor to insert, delete or alter the sequence of blocks without the recipient being aware that any modifications had occurred. Also, this mode of operation has the weakness that repetitive blocks of plaintext will, of course, generate a string of identical blocks of ciphertext. This can be of great benefit to someone trying to break the code (key) being used by two correspondents, and hence an alternative mode of operation is to use the notion of *chaining*. This mode of operation of DES is known as *Chain Block Cipher* or simply *CBC*.

Although the chaining mode uses the same block encryption method as above, each 64-bit block of plaintext is first Exclusive-ORed with the enciphered output of the previous block before it is enciphered. This is shown in diagrammatic form in part (b) of Fig. B.2. The first 64-bit block of plaintext is Exclusive-ORed with a 64-bit random number called the *Initial Vector* after which subsequent blocks operate in a chained sequence as shown. In this way, since the output of a block is a function both of the block contents and the output of the previous block, any alterations to the transmitted sequence will be detected by the receiver. Also, identical blocks of plaintext will yield different blocks of ciphertext, and hence this is the mode of operation which is normally used for data communication purposes.

B.2 PUBLIC KEYS

Both of the above methods rely, of course, on the same key being used for the dual purpose of encryption and decryption. An obvious disadvantage of this is that some form of key notification must be used prior to the transfer of any encrypted data between two correspondents. This is perfectly acceptable providing the key does not change very often but, in some instances, this is not the case and it is common practice to change the key being used on a daily, if not more frequent, basis. In instances like these an alternative mode of operation based on the use of a public rather than a private key is often used.

The principle of a public key system is that, instead of both the sender and receiver using the same (private) keys, any potential recipient of a message first generates a matched pair of keys: one which is known as its *public key* (since it is made available to any system that may wish to communicate with it) and the other known as its *private key* since this is known only by itself. The two keys are generated in such a way that they have the properties firstly that it is not possible to derive the private key from the public key, and secondly any data which are enciphered using a receiver's public key can be deciphered by the receiver using only its own matching private key.

To send a message using this method of encryption, the sender first uses the public key of the intended recipient to encipher the message – normally this is retained in a *key library* – and the message is then sent. The message is then deciphered by the intended recipient using its own matching private key and, of course, the message will be incomprehensible to any other recipient. The principle of operation of the public key method is shown in part (a) of Fig. B.3.

B.3 MESSAGE AUTHENTICATION

Another important and related issue to data encryption is concerned with *message authentication*. Essentially, the above methods are concerned only with ensuring the reliable transfer of message data between two correspondents. In addition to this, however, there is also a requirement in some applications to provide some means of authenticating or verifying that each message that is received from a particular source was in fact sent by that source and not another system impersonating it. For example, with a public key method, since it is possible for any system to initiate the sending of a message to any other system simply by using the intended receiver's public

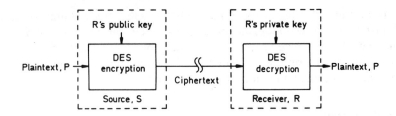

(a)

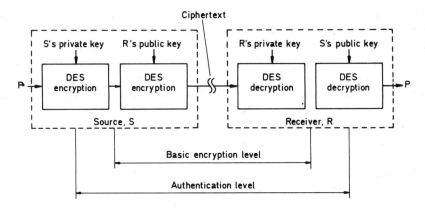

(b)

Fig. B.3 Public key systems: (a) without authentication; (b) with authentication

key, it is necessary to have some means of authenticating the identity of the sender of a message.

To meet this requirement, public key systems of the type described earlier provide this capability. Essentially, the two keys – public and private – used in this method have the dual property that not only is a receiver able to decipher all messages it receives (which have been encrypted with its own public key) using its own private key, but also that if a message is encrypted by a sender using the *sender's* private key, any receiver can decipher that message using the sender's public key.

A schematic diagram showing how this property may be exploited to achieve message authentication is shown in part (b) of Fig. B.3. The encryption and decryption operations are performed at two levels. The inner level of encryption and decryption is the same as that which has been described earlier. At the outer level, however, the sender uses its own private key to encrypt the original (plaintext) message. Thus if the receiver is able to decrypt this message using that sender's public key, this is treated as proof that that sender did in fact initiate the sending of the message.

As was mentioned at the beginning, this appendix is intended simply to introduce the reader to the fascinating subject of cryptography and the more interested reader is referred to the reference section at the end of the book for further reading. As the uses of computer communication networks expand, however, so the various topics which have been introduced in this appendix will become increasingly important.

Glossary of Terms and Abbreviations

AM
A modulation technique used to allow data to be transmitted across an analogue network such as a switched telephone network. The amplitude of a single (carrier) frequency is varied (modulated) between two levels – one for binary 0 and the other for binary 1.

ANSI
An abbreviation for the American National Standards Institute which is one of the bodies in the United States responsible for formulating standards.

ASCII
An abbreviation for American Standards Committee for Information Interchange, and in normal usage is used to refer to the character code defined by this committee for the interchange of information between two communicating devices. As an example, the ASCII character set is in widespread use for the transfer of information between a computer and a peripheral device such as a visual display unit or a printer.

ASYNCHRONOUS TRANSMISSION
Strictly this implies the receiver clock is not synchronised to the transmitted clock when data are being transmitted between two devices connected by a transmission line. More generally, it is used to indicate that data are being transmitted as individual characters. Each character is preceded by a start signal and terminated by one or more stop signals which are used by the receiver for synchronisation purposes.

AUTOMATIC REPEAT REQUEST (ARQ)
A technique used for error control over a transmission line; if errors in a transmitted message are detected by the receiving device, it requests the sending device to retransmit the message together with any other messages that may have been affected.

BANDWIDTH
The difference between the highest and lowest sinusoidal frequency signals that can be transmitted across a transmission line or through a network. It is measured in Hertz (Hz) and also defines the maximum information-carrying capacity of the line or network.

BASEBAND
Is used to indicate a particular operating mode of a transmission line: each binary digit (bit) in a message is converted into one of two voltage (sometimes current) levels – one for binary 1 and the other for binary 0 – and these are applied directly to the line. The

line signal thus varies with time between these two voltage levels as the data are transmitted.

BAUD
The number of line signal variations per second. Also used to indicate the rate at which data are transmitted on a line, although this is strictly correct only when each bit is represented by a single signal level on the transmision line and hence the bit rate and the line signal rate are both the same.

BIT STUFFING (ZERO BIT INSERTION)
A technique used to allow pure binary data to be transmitted on a synchronous transmission line. Each message block (frame) is encapsulated between two flags which are special bit sequences. Then, if the message data contains a possibly similar sequence, an additional (zero) bit is inserted into the data stream by the sender which is subsequently removed by the receiving device. The transmission method is then said to be data transparent.

BROADBAND
Is used to indicate a particular mode of operation of a coaxial cable. A single coaxial cable can be used to simultaneously transmit a number of separate data streams by assigning each a portion of the total available bandwidth. Data are transmitted by modulating a single frequency signal from the selected frequency band and the data are then received by demodulating the received signal.

BUS
A network topology in widespread use for the interconnection of communities of digital devices (computers etc.) which are distributed over a localised area such as a factory or block of offices. The transmission medium is normally a single coaxial cable to which all the devices are attached. Each transmission thus propagates the length of the medium and is therefore received by all other devices connected to the medium.

CATV
An abbreviation for Community Antenna Television. It is used in the context of local area data netwoks since the principles and network components used in CATV networks can also be used to produce a flexible underlying data transmission facility over a local area. CATV networks operate using the broadband mode of working.

CCITT
An abbreviation for Consultative Committee of the International Telegraph and Telephone. It is an international organisation which formulates standards for interfacing digital devices to the different types of data communications equipment and networks.

CIRCUIT SWITCHING
The mode of operation of a telephone network and also some of the newer digital data networks. A communications path is first established through the network between the source (calling) and destination (called) terminals and this is then used exclusively for the duration of the call or transaction. Both terminals must operate at the same information transfer rate.

COAXIAL CABLE
A type of transmission medium consisting of a centre conductor and a concentric outer conductor. Used when high data transfer rates – greater than 1 Mbps – are required.

CRC
An abbreviation for Cyclic Redundancy Check. It is used for the detection of errors when data are being transmitted. A CRC is a numeric value which is computed from the bits in the message to be transmitted. It is appended to the tail of the message prior to transmission and the receiver then detects the presence of errors in the received message by recomputing a new CRC.

CSMA/CD
An abbreviation for carrier sense, multiple access with collision detection. It is a method used to control access to a shared transmission medium such as a coaxial cable bus to which a number of stations are connected. A station wishing to transmit a message first senses (listens to) the medium and transmits the message only if the medium is quiet – no carrier present. Then, as the message is being transmitted, the station monitors the actual signal on the transmission medium and, if this is different from the signal being transmitted, a collision is said to have occurred and been detected. The station then ceases transmission and retries again later.

DATA CIRCUIT-TERMINATING EQUIPMENT (DCE)
The name given to the equipment provided by the network authority (provider) for the attachment of user devices to the network. It takes on different forms for different network types.

DATA TERMINAL EQUIPMENT (DTE)
A generic name for any user device connected to a data network. It thus includes such devices as visual display units, computers, office workstations etc.

DATAGRAM
A type of service offered on a packet-switched data network (*see also* Virtual Call). A datagram is a self-contained packet of information which is sent through the network with minimum protocol overheads.

EBCDIC
An abbreviation for Extended Binary Coded Decimal Interchange Code. It is the name of the character set used on all IBM computers.

FRAME
The unit of information transferred across a data link. Typically, there are control frames for link management and information frames for the transfer of message data.

FREQUENCY DIVISION MULTIPLEXING (FDM)
A technique used to derive a number of separate data channels from a single transmission medium such as a coaxial cable. Each data channel is assigned a portion of the total available bandwidth.

FREQUENCY SHIFT KEYING (FSK)
A modulation technique used to convert binary data into an analogue form comprising

two sinusoidal frequencies. It is widely used in modems to allow data to be transmitted across a (analogue) switched telephone network.

GATEWAY
A device that allows data to be passed from one network to another. Typically, the two networks operate with different protocols and hence the gateway performs the necessary protocol conversion functions.

HDLC
An abbreviation for High-level Data Link Control. It is an internationally agreed standard protocol defined to control the exchange of data across either a point-to-point data link or a multi-drop data link.

HOST
Normally a computer belonging to a user which contains (hosts) the communications hardware and software necessary to connect the computer to a data communications network.

IA5
An abbreviation for International Alphabet Number 5. It is the standard character code defined by the CCITT and recommended by ISO. It is almost identical to the ASCII code.

IEEE 802
A committee of the American Institution of Electrical and Electronic Engineers set up to produce standards for local area data networks.

ISO
An abbreviation for International Standards Organisation. This is an international organisation which formulates standards activities.

LOCAL AREA NETWORK (LAN)
A data communications network used to interconnect a community of digital devices which are distributed over a localised area of up to, say, ten square kilometres. The devices may be office workstations, mini and microcomputers, intelligent instrumentation equipment etc.

MANCHESTER ENCODING
A scheme used to encode clocking (timing) information into a binary data stream prior to transmission. The resulting encoded signal has a transition (positive or negative) in the middle of each bit-cell period with the effect that the clocking information (required to receive the signal) is readily extracted from the received signal.

MEDIUM ACCESS CONTROL (MAC)
Many local area networks utilise a single common transmission medium – a bus or ring, for example – to which all the interconnected devices are attached. A procedure must be followed by each device, therefore, to ensure that transmissions occur in an orderly and fair way. In general, this is known as the medium access control procedure. Two examples are CSMA/CD and (Control) Token.

MODEM

The name given to the device that converts a binary (digital) data stream into an analogue (continuously varying) form prior to transmission of the data across an analogue network (MODulator) and reconverts the received signal back into its binary form on reception (DEModulator). Since each access port to the network normally requires a full-duplex (two-way simultaneous) capability, the device must perform both the MODulation and DEModulation functions, hence the single name MODEM is used. As an example, a modem is normally required in order to transmit data across a telephone network.

MULTIPLEXER

A device used to enable a number of lower bit-rate devices – normally situated in the same location – to share a single higher bit-rate transmission line. The data-carrying capacity of the latter must be in excess of the combined bit rates of the low bit-rate devices.

NOISE

The term given to the extraneous electrical signals which may be picked up in a transmission line. Typically, it may be caused by neighbouring electrical apparatus. If the noise signal is large compared with the data-carrying signal, the latter may be corrupted and result in transmission errors.

NRZ, NRZI

Two similar (and related) schemes for encoding a binary data stream. The first has the property that a signal transition occurs whenever a binary 1 is present in the data stream and the second whenever a binary 0 is present. The latter is utilised with certain clocking (timing) schemes.

OPTICAL FIBRE

A type of transmission medium over which data are transmitted in the form of light waves or pulses. It is characterised by its potentially high bandwidth – and hence data-carrying capacity – and also its high immunity to interference from other electrical sources.

PACKET SWITCHING

A mode of operation of a data communications network. Each message to be transmitted through the network is first divided into a number of smaller, self-contained message units known as packets. Each packet contains addressing information and, as each packet is received at an intermediate node (exchange) within the network, it is first stored and, depending on the addressing information contained within it, forwarded along an appropriate link to the next node and so on. Packets belonging to the same message are then reassembled at the destination. This mode of operation ensures long messages do not degrade the response time of the network and also the source and destination devices may operate at different data rates.

PARITY

A mechanism used for the detection of transmission errors when single characters are being transmitted. A single binary digit, which is known as the parity bit and whose value (1 or 0) is determined by the total number of binary 1s in the character, is transmitted with the character and the receiver can thus determine the presence of single-bit errors by comparing the received parity bit with the (recomputed) value it should be.

PHASE SHIFT KEYING (PSK)
A modulation technique used to convert binary data into an analogue form comprising a single sinusoidal frequency signal whose phase varies according to the data being transmitted.

PIGGYBACK
A technique used to return acknowledgment information across a duplex (two-way simultaneous) data link without the use of special (acknowledgment) messages. The acknowledgment information relating to the flow of messages in one direction is embedded (piggybacked) into a normal data-carrying message flowing in the reverse direction.

PROTOCOL
A set of rules which have been formulated to control the exchange of data between two communicating parties.

PSDN
An abbreviation for public switched data network; that is, a communications network which has been set up and is controlled by a public telecommunications authority for the exchange of data.

PSTN
An abbreviation for the normal public switched telephone network.

PTT
An abbreviation for Postal, Telegraph and Telephone. It is the administration authority that controls all the postal and public telecommunications networks and services in a country.

RING
A network topology in widespread use for the interconnection of communities of digital devices (computers etc.) which are distributed over a localised area such as a factory or block of offices. Each device is connected to its nearest neighbour until all the devices are connected in the form of a closed loop or ring. Data are transmitted in one direction only and, as each message circulates around the ring, it is read by each device connected in the ring. After circulating around the ring, the source device removes the message from the ring.

RS-232C, RS-422, RS-423
Standards laid down by the American Electrical Industries Association for interfacing a digital device to a PTT supplied modem. RS-232C is also used as an interface standard for connecting a peripheral device such as a visual display unit or a printer to a computer.

SLOTTED RING
A type of local area (data) network. All the devices are connected in the form of a (physical) ring and an additional device known as a Monitor is then used to ensure that the ring contains a fixed number of message slots (binary digits) which circulate around

the ring in one direction only. A device then sends a message by placing it in an empty slot as it passes. This is then read by all other devices on the ring and subsequently removed by the originating device.

STATISTICAL MULTIPLEXER (STAT MUX)
A device used to enable a number of lower bit-rate devices – normally situated in the same location – to share a single, higher bit-rate, transmission line. The devices normally have human operators and hence data are transmitted on the shared line on a statistical basis rather than, as is the case with a basic multiplexer, on a preallocated basis. It thus endeavours to exploit the fact that each device operates at a much lower mean rate than its maximum rate.

SYNCHRONOUS TRANSMISSION
A technique used to transmit data between two devices connected by a transmission line. The data are normally transmitted in the form of blocks each comprising a string of binary digits. With synchronous transmision the transmitter and receiver clocks are in synchronism and a number of techniques are used to ensure this.

TOKEN BUS
A type of local area (data) network. Access to the shared transmission medium – implemented in the form of a Bus to which all the communicating devices are connected – is controlled by a single control (permission) token. Only the current owner of the token is allowed to transmit a message on the medium. All the devices wishing to transmit messages are connected in the form of a logical ring and, after a device receives the token and transmits any waiting messages, it passes the token on to the next device on the ring.

TOKEN RING
A type of local area (data) network. All the devices are connected in the form of a (physical) ring and messages are transmitted by allowing them to circulate around the ring. A device can only transmit a message on the ring when it is in possession of a control (permission) token. There is a single token which is passed from one device to another around the ring.

TRANSMISSION MEDIUM
The communications path which links two communicating devices. Some examples are twisted-pair wire, coaxial cable, optical fibre cable, and a microwave (radio) beam.

TWISTED-PAIR
A type of transmission medium consisting of two insulated wires which are twisted together to improve its immunity to interference from other (stray) electrical signals which may otherwise corrupt the signal being transmitted.

VIRTUAL CALL (CIRCUIT)
A type of service offered on a packet-switched data network (*see also* Datagram). Using this service, prior to sending any packets of information relating to a particular call (message transfer), a virtual circuit is established through the network from source to destination. All information carrying packets relating to this call then follow the same route and the network ensures that the packets are delivered in the same order they were entered.

V.24, V.35
Standards layed down by the CCITT for interfacing a digital device to a PTT supplied modem. V.24 is also used as an interface standard for connecting a peripheral device such as a visual display unit or a printer to a computer.

X.25
An internationally agreed standard protocol which has been defined for the interface of a data terminal device such as a computer to a packet-switched data network.

X.3, X.28, X.29
A set of internationally agreed standard protocols which have been defined to allow a character oriented device such as a visual display terminal to be connected to a packet-switched data network.

ZERO BIT INSERTION
See Bit Stuffing.

References and Bibliography

Arthurs, E. et al. (1982), *IEEE Project 802 Local Area Network Standards*, Traffic Handling Characteristics Committee Report, IEEE.

Bleazard, G. B. (1982), *Handbook of Data Communications*, NCC Publications, Manchester, England.

CCITT (1981), *Character Terminal Access to Public Packet-Switched Data Networks*, X.3, X.28, X.29 (Triple X).

Davies, D. W., Barber, D. L. A., Price, W. C. and Solmonides, C. M. (1979), *Computer Networks and their Protocols*, New York, NY: Wiley.

Difie, W. and Hellman, M. (1976), *IEEE Transactions on Information Theory*, New Directions in Cryptography, IT-**22**(6).

IEEE (1983), *Local Area Network – CSMA/CD Access Method*, IEEE 802.3.

IEEE (1983), *Local Area Network – Token Bus Access Method*, IEEE 802.4.

IEEE (1983), *Local Area Network – Token Ring Access Method*, IEEE 802.5.

IEEE (1983), *Local Area Network – Logical Link Control Procedures*, IEEE 802.2.

Intel Corporation (1978), *The Intel 8251A/S2657 Programmable Communication Interface*.

Intel Corporation (1978), *Using the 8273 SDLC/HDLC Protocol Controller*, Application Note.

ISO (1977), *HDLC – Classes of Procedure*, ISO TC97/SC6/N1501.

ISO (1981), *Network Service using X.25 and X.21*, ISO TC97/SC5/N2743.

ISO (1983), *Transport Service/Protocol*, ISO DP8072/3.

ISO (1983), *Session Service/Protocol*, ISO DP8326/7, ISO/TC97.

Joint Network Team (1983), *Local Area Network – Slotted (Cambridge) Ring Technology*, CR 82.

National Bureau of Standards (1977), *Data Encryption Standard*, FIPS publication 46.

Peterson, W. W. (1961), *Error Correcting Codes*, Cambridge, Mass: MIT Press.

US National Bureau of Standards (1983), *Specification of a Transport Protocol for Computer Communications*, Vol. 1: Overview and Services.
266

ISO material can be obtained from:

International Telecommunications Union,
Place des Nations,
1211 Geneva,
Switzerland.

IEEE material can be obtained from:

IEEE Press,
345 East 47th Street,
New York, NY10017,
USA.

Index